THE GROWTH OF RELIGIOUS DIVERSITY

BRITAIN FROM 1945

VOLUME II
ISSUES

EDITED BY
GERALD PARSONS

IN ASSOCIATION WITH
THE OPEN UNIVERSITY

The Open
University

Copyright © The Open University 1994
First published 1994
by Routledge
11 New Fetter Lane, London EC4P 4EE

in association with The Open University

Simultaneously published in the USA and Canada
by Routledge
29 West 35th Street, New York, NY 10001

A catalogue record for this book is available from the British Library.

ISBN 0 415 08328 1

Edited, designed and typeset by The Open University.
Printed and bound in the United Kingdom by the Alden Press, Oxford.

CONTENTS

PREFACE

This book is the second part of a two-volume set on the history of religion in Britain between 1945 and the early 1990s. It is published by Routledge in association with the Open University. All of the essays in both volumes were written with the needs of Open University undergraduate students primarily in mind. But the authors also hope that the essays in both volumes will be of interest and value to many other readers with an interest in the place of religion within British society in the period since the end of the Second World War.

The authors wish to acknowledge the essential contribution made to the production of both volumes by a number of other members of Open University staff: Jenny Cook (course manager), Jane Wood and Kate Clements (editors), Tony Coulson (librarian), Pam Higgins (designer), and Lyn Camborne-Paynter and Cheryl-Anne O'Toole (secretaries).

The authors also wish to thank Professor John Kent of the University of Bristol for his careful and constructive comments on first drafts of their essays. Each of the authors has benefited from Professor Kent's criticism and observations: needless to say, any inaccuracies or questionable judgements that remain are the responsibility of the authors alone.

The authors of the essays in the two volumes are:
Gerald Parsons (Lecturer in Religious Studies, The Open University)
John Wolffe (Lecturer in Religious Studies, The Open University)
Terence Thomas (Staff Tutor in Religious Studies, The Open University)
David Englander (Senior Lecturer in European Humanities, The Open University)
George Chryssides (Senior Lecturer in Religious Studies, University of Wolverhampton)
Kim Knott (Senior Lecturer in Theology and Religious Studies, University of Leeds)

INTRODUCTION: DECIDING HOW FAR YOU CAN GO

by Gerald Parsons

Multifaith petition to Downing Street for peace in Yugoslavia, 26 August 1992. Left to right: Mohamed Chahid Raza (Secretary to Imams and Mosques in the UK), Rabbi Hugo Gryn (West London Synagogue, Chair of Inter-faith Network for UK), Bishop Victor Guazzelli (Roman Catholic Bishop of East London), Ajit Singh (Interfaith Relations for the Namdhari Sangat UK), Michael Feeney (refugee officer for the Roman Catholic Diocese of Westminster), Revd Jonathan Lloyd (Anglican Diocese of Southwark Board of Social Responsibility). Photo: Carlos Reyes-Manzo, Andes Press Agency.

In his novel *How Far Can You Go?* David Lodge presents a witty and amusing, but also deeply serious and at times profoundly moving, portrait of a group of English middle-class Roman Catholics as they move from the restrained stability of their student days in the early 1950s, through the turbulent excitement of the 1960s, and into the complexities and ambiguities of the mid 1970s. Along the way, the various characters are confronted with the dissolution of the distinctive, disciplined and precisely defined Catholic subculture of their youth and early adulthood in which their Catholic duties, beliefs and obligations were clearly and meticulously set down. In its place there emerges a very different Catholicism: less distinctive and much closer to the mainstream of both religious and cultural life in modern Britain; no longer disciplined and precisely defined in its beliefs and obligations but, rather, amorphous, ambiguous and pluralistic in nature. Thus Lodge's novel is also a portrait of an entire religious community and tradition in transition (Lodge, 1980a; 1980b, pp.187–8).

As they live through this transformation in their church, the various characters in the novel find first the desire, then the increasing possibility, and finally the necessity to 'choose for themselves' in matters of religion, of personal morality and of lifestyle. Inevitably, because one of the most profound – and most profoundly unresolved – controversies within Roman Catholicism during this period (and since) concerned the church's teaching on sexuality and contraception, questions of sexual morality and practice are central to the narrative of the novel and to the choices which the characters make. How far they can go in the expression of their sexuality becomes intimately and inextricably bound up with how far they can go in questioning, challenging, dissenting from, or remaining loyal to, the teachings of their church.

But the novel is by no means simply or even predominantly about Catholics and sex. On the contrary, as a key passage in the text makes clear, the central question posed by the novel is not simply 'how far can you go in sexual morality and practice?', but rather, 'how far can you go in questioning and dismantling your religious tradition and belief without throwing out something vital?' (Lodge, 1980a, p.143). And the answer the novel offers is ambiguous. The characters end up at various distances from the Catholicism of their youth and student days. Some remain highly committed Catholics, albeit now variously committed to the very different versions of the pluralistic Catholicism of the mid 1970s. Others stand at a distance from the church, some of them in more or less creative tension with the new Catholicism, questioning even its more liberal parameters; some of them nostalgic for at least a few of the old certainties. Others are now barely Catholic at all – and a few have ceased to believe in even a residual Catholicism. Even the priest and chaplain of their student days has played out a long theological version of 'how far can you go' and ended up outside the priesthood, married, and no more than 'a kind of Catholic' (Lodge, 1980a, ch.7).

In raising such questions, *How Far Can You Go?* is far more than merely a 'Catholic novel'. The issues the novel raises concerning the relationship between religious authority and religious questioning, the tensions between individual conscience and communal beliefs and practices, and the consequences of dismantling a distinctive religious subculture, are pertinent to other religious traditions and communities as well. The relevance of Lodge's narrative to other Christian churches in Britain during the period since the 1950s has been recognized a number of times (Ecclestone, 1985, p.47; Houlden, 1989, p.268; Parsons, 1992), not least in the companion to this volume. Thus, in these other Christian churches and denominations, the decades after 1945, and especially those from the 1960s onwards, also brought an increasingly intense series of debates over how far you could (or should) go in theological, liturgical or moral experiment and reform, or in ecumenical relationships, or political action and commitment. In addition, however, the novel and the underlying questions that it raises are highly relevant to other religious traditions present in Britain since 1945, and also to a variety of more general questions about the place and status of religion in recent British life and society. Indeed, the explicit theme of this introduction is that the question 'how far can you go?' constitutes, in varying ways and specific formulations, the implicit and underlying theme of all the essays in this volume.

This is most obviously the case in essay 7, in which in examining some of the relationships between religion and changing attitudes to sexual morality the author uses *How Far Can You Go?* as a key text in analysing this theme. Implicitly, however, the theme of how far you can go also lies at or near the heart of the other essays in this volume. Characteristically, though not exclusively, and with varying degrees of directness, the essays focus on questions of how far religious groups or communities can go in adjusting or (re)asserting their allegiances and beliefs in the particular context of recent British life and society. In particular, the essays explore the adjustments and reassertions which have taken place within the overall context of a shift from a society which, in 1945, might still be described relatively unproblematically as 'Christian', to a society in the early 1990s which was unmistakably – if also ambiguously – religiously plural.

Such questions of adjustment or reassertion arise most obviously in relation to particular religious traditions – and not only for those religious traditions that constitute, in a British context, 'minority religions', but also for the historically predominant Christian traditions of Britain. Thus, the author of essay 1 examines the various stages that may be discerned in the responses of Christians and of the churches in Britain to the steady growth in religious pluralism in Britain in the decades since the Second World War. Significantly, he not only notes the relatively slow start made by the churches and individual Christians in recognizing this new dimension to British religious life, but also emphasizes the variety and diversity of the responses that did eventually emerge. For the Christian tradition in Britain, no less than for other religious groups, the challenge of responding to an increasing religious pluralism included both attempts to adjust traditional Christian doctrines and also reassertions of conventional Christian claims. The encounter between Christianity and other religions within Britain thus included continuing and renewed emphasis upon 'witness and evangelization' as well as 'inter-faith dialogue' and explorations of 'multi-faith worship'.

The accuracy and importance of this emphasis upon the variety of Christian responses to the increased religious pluralism of modern Britain – and the tension between adjustment and reassertion of traditional Christian claims which resulted – is well illustrated by the ongoing debate within the Church of England concerning multi-faith worship. Thus, on the one hand, there are those within the Church of England who vehemently oppose multi-faith worship on the grounds that it compromises the Christian duty to proclaim the gospel in terms that unambiguously assert the uniqueness and finality of Christ. On the other hand, there are other members of the Church of England who enthusiastically support such ventures, seeing them as an important contribution to a positive understanding and response to the *de facto* religious pluralism of contemporary British life; and there is a further group – probably by far the largest – who would occupy a middle position somewhere between these two poles.[1]

The second essay in this volume illustrates no less strikingly the pressing issues raised for a variety of religious traditions by their position, in a British context, as minority religious groups. Such groups, it is pointed out, are confronted by profound questions concerning what is fundamental to the religious tradition in question – and therefore non-negotiable, whatever the cost in terms of alienation from the mainstream of society as a whole, or opposition from the majority – and what is inessential or peripheral, and therefore open to adjustment, adaptation, or even being discarded altogether. The essay suggests three broad alternatives available to a minority religious tradition and its adherents: 'apostasy', involving the

---

[1] The opponents of multi-faith worship are particularly associated with the 'Open Letter Group' and the organization 'Action for Biblical Witness to Our Nation', for both of which see the introductory essay by Christopher Lewis in *Many Mansions* (Cohn-Sherbok, 1992), a collection of essays that illustrates graphically the sheer complexity of the ongoing debates over interfaith dialogue and its implications. For the response to the issue of multi-faith worship of an official Church of England Consultative Group, see *Multi-Faith Worship? Questions and suggestions from the Inter-Faith Consultative Group* (General Synod Board of Mission, 1992).

abandonment of the very heart of the religious tradition in question; 'accommodation', involving the adjustment and adaptation of a religion, discarding the peripheral, retaining the essential, and expressing it in new terms; and 'renewed vigour', involving the reiteration and reassertion of the religion in question in full, traditional terms.

The dividing line between these responses, it is acknowledged, is by no means clear or fixed. Nor, moreover, is it suggested that the three options of 'apostasy', 'accommodation' and 'renewed vigour' are the only way of defining the alternatives available to religious minorities in Britain.[2] What is clear, however, is the sheer inevitability of having to confront the underlying issue. Whatever response is offered in any particular case, the need to respond to the challenges and dilemmas of 'minority' religious status within a society and culture that is historically 'Christian' – and is now arguably dominated by an imprecise combination of Christian and secular presuppositions – is in itself inescapable.

As recent studies of the changing character – in a British context – of the religious traditions of communities of South Asian origin have shown, the factors involved in the interaction between these traditions and the predominant religious and cultural traditions of recent and contemporary Britain are immensely complex. A proper understanding of the interactions involved will require awareness not only of the particular religious tradition, but also of particular social, cultural and religious backgrounds in the Indian subcontinent; of the ongoing religious life of the subcontinent and its potential impact upon those who have migrated but retain family, cultural and religious links with their former home[3] ; of the history and context(s) of initial migration; of the reactions, both initial and subsequent, of British society to the presence of new religious groups and communities; and of the corresponding reactions and responses of the newly domiciled groups to the demands, dilemmas, challenges and opportunities of their new context (Knott, 1991 and 1992b).

Similarly, it is essential to recognize that the various minority religious traditions have not been (and will not in the future be) simply passive and reactive in their relationship with British society and culture. On the contrary, the various minority religious traditions in recent and contemporary Britain are themselves dynamic and possess varied

---

[2]   Thus, for example, in Volume I, essay 3, the alternative strategies available to Muslims in recent and contemporary Britain are defined as 'assimilation', 'isolation', 'integration' and 'redefinition'.

[3]   Thus, for example, ongoing relationships between Sikhs, Hindus and Muslims in India can exert a significant influence upon Sikh, Hindu and Muslim self-perceptions and senses of 'identity' in Britain as well. A particular example of such influence is the impact upon Sikh consciousness in Britain of the storming of the Golden Temple in Amritsar in 1984 – for a brief discussion of which see essay 5 in Volume I.

resources for the encounter with the British context – not least in supplying important symbols and senses of identity for young people who might otherwise have found their inherited religious and cultural traditions and identities steadily eroded (Knott, 1992a, pp.12–14 and 1992b, p.5). Nor was it only religions of South Asian origin that displayed such potential in responding to the British context – both Judaism, with its much longer presence in Britain, and the distinctive religious experience of Britain's Afro-Caribbean community, displayed similar vitality.[4]

The fact remains, however, that an engagement with the demands and dilemmas posed by the British context was (and is) inevitable. Such engagement occurs most obviously at 'official' levels – as leaders of religious communities and representative organizations seek to formulate policies to promote and protect their communities' interests in a whole range of areas, including education, the right to observe dietary and other customs, the provision of appropriate facilities for worship and the observance of rites of passage. But it occurs also less obviously – but perhaps equally or even more significantly – in 'unofficial' contexts: in playgrounds, shops and clinics, and on street corners (Knott, 1992c, p.98).[5]

Such engagements and encounters will, inescapably, entail change for those involved – at both official and unofficial levels and in the lives of both communities and individuals. The responses may be in the direction of adaptation, adjustment, assimilation or accommodation; or they may be in the direction of reassertion, renewed vigour, restated distinctiveness or resistance. But whichever the direction of the response, there will have been change; for even the fiercest of reassertions of distinctive and traditional identity will have been given new dimensions precisely by virtue of the new context and challenge which has produced the 'return' to tradition. Moreover, for the community or individual that reasserts or 'returns to' tradition, the very act of 'reasserting' or 'returning' in response to life in Britain constitutes a change from their previous position – change, after all, may be in a conservative direction, as well as a liberal one. And behind such processes of change – whether conservative or liberal – there lies the common underlying question: 'how far can you go?' Thus the

---

[4] For accounts of the diversity of responses within these and other particular religious traditions in Britain since 1945, see the essays in Volume I.

[5] It is also likely that many of the 'unofficial' engagements will tend to prove distinctly subversive of 'official' attempts to impose clear and rigid distinctions and boundaries – a point neatly illustrated by the case of a fourteen-year-old Valmiki girl in Coventry, who expressed the fact that her parents came from families which followed, respectively, distinctively Hindu and Sikh traditions by saying simply, 'My Dad's Hindu. My Mum's side are Sikhs' – a disarmingly accurate personal statement of identity which might well frustrate and irritate those concerned to define and draw distinctions with undue precision (Nesbitt, 1991, p.9).

'conservative' who reasserts distinctiveness is, in reality, answering Lodge's question by signalling that you cannot go *that* far, or indeed, that things have gone too far already, so that something vital has, already, been lost. Conversely, the 'liberal' is engaged in an ongoing process of calculation and assessment of how far she or he can still go in adjustment and reinterpretation, but without compromising on 'essentials' or endangering the 'integrity' of the religious tradition concerned.

It was not only minority religious traditions, however, that faced variations on the theme of 'how far you can go' in either the adjustment and modification or the maintenance and reassertion of a distinctive religious identity and the association of this with a particular cultural or national community. Indeed, it is possible to read the third essay in this volume, on the relationships between religion, the state and a whole variety of recent and contemporary British identities, as an implicit commentary on precisely this theme.

As the author of essay 3 demonstrates clearly, in the period from 1945 to the early 1990s, the relationships between a variety of particular Christian traditions and denominations and equally varied concepts of English, Scottish, Welsh and Northern Irish identities were matters of concern and controversy. How far did the Church of England still represent something important about English religious and cultural 'identity'? And if it did still represent something significant in this respect, how far was it morally and politically acceptable in an increasingly religiously plural society that it should retain an established status and at least nominal privileges and salience? Or again, how far were 'Scottishness' and Presbyterianism intimately related? And what did claims that they *were* intimately related imply about the large number of Scottish Catholics? Or for that matter about the smaller numbers of Scottish Anglicans, Methodists, Baptists, Quakers, Jews, Muslims, agnostics, atheists and various other groups?

Similarly, how far was there a historical relationship between the Christian religion and concepts of Welsh identity, culture and nationality? And again, if there was a historic relationship between them, how far did this present profound moral and political implications in the increasingly pluralistic context of the late twentieth century? And in Northern Ireland, meanwhile, the continuing potency of long and deeply held associations between particular traditions of Christian belief and particular cultural and political communities contributed all too painfully to the continuing tragedy of sectarian violence. Nowhere in Britain in the late twentieth century were the various versions of 'how far can you go?' – how far in compromise, how far in determined distinctiveness – more desperately pressing in their implications or more passionately debated than in Northern Ireland.

Such questions were openly debated within the Christian community. Indeed, after the rearrangement of the organizational structures for ecumenical relationships among the British churches in the late 1980s, one of the early publications of the newly constituted Council of Churches for Britain and Ireland was a collection of essays on the theme 'Belonging to Britain'. Subtitled 'perspectives on a plural society', the authors of the essays explored critically many of the questions identified in the preceding paragraph and related their discussion to issues of race and community in recent and contemporary Britain (Hooker and Sargant, 1991). Yet even this very publication and its origins embodied, in a minor but significant way, the ambiguities of this whole area of debate. The general tone of the volume was questioning and critical of received associations between religious and national identities in Britain: although not rejecting such associations out of hand, the authors urged caution in their expression and awareness of their potential dangers. And yet the volume itself was one of the first products of a reconstituted ecumenical body which self-consciously replaced the former single British Council of Churches by four councils for, respectively, England, Ireland, Scotland and Wales, linked in turn to an overarching Council for Britain and Ireland. The paradox of an ecumenical structure – exploring how far the churches could go in overcoming historical divisions – divided according to 'national' boundaries is suggestive. Although not to be pressed too far, it provides an effective reminder of the enduring ambiguities in the relationships between Christian and national identities within late twentieth-century Britain.

Nor was this the only ambiguity to be found in late twentieth-century discussions of the relationship between Christian and national identities in Britain. Thus, for example, as shown in essay 3, in Wales the Anglican Church, after disestablishment and thus constitutional separation from the Church of England, became increasingly a self-consciously Welsh institution. Indeed, it has been argued that, as Welsh Nonconformity has declined, the Anglican Church in Wales, with its continuing commitment to a nationwide parochial structure, has become in recent decades the church with the broadest national status and range of pastoral ministry in Wales (Price, 1989). In England, meanwhile – where the Church of England remained established – while a significant (and perhaps increasing) number of the Church of England's own clergy appeared to favour the severing of the remaining links with the state, defenders of the Church of England's continued establishment in the early 1990s included, notably, a leading Roman Catholic church historian, Adrian Hastings (1991) and the Chief Rabbi, Jonathan Sacks (1991, pp.68, 97–8).

Significantly, however, such defences of the continued value of the established status of the Church of England tended to depend, crucially, upon the appeal to establishment as a witness to the continued importance and value of religion in general in British society, not the specific virtues or claims of the Church of England – and also upon the assumption that the Church of England would not take on a role or assert its privileges in a manner that was prejudicial to other religious groups. How far you could go in defending establishment was thus clearly and closely related to how far the continuing establishment was willing *not* to go in asserting special privileges or priorities over others. It was establishment as symbol, rather than establishment as substance that was thus defended – and even this, for some commentators, was going too far and represented an unhealthy constraint upon the development of a genuinely and wholesomely pluralist society (Smart, 1989).

It was, then, a broad (one might also say 'weak') and rather 'cultural' concept of Anglicanism that was at stake in such defences of continued establishment. But that, in itself, posed further questions about how far such a broadly conceived Christian establishment was sustainable in a society which – according to some observers – showed increasing signs of losing touch with its inherited legacy of Christian belief, culture and assumptions. Thus commentators on religion in both England and Scotland discerned an increasing decay in the general awareness of Christian beliefs and in knowledge of the Bible, of hymns and of the 'classic' literary and musical texts of Christianity in Britain. By the 1980s and 1990s, it seemed, the effects of liturgical revision, the decline of Sunday schools, changing patterns of religious education, and a host of other similar developments had already gone too far for a hitherto taken-for-granted familiarity with a whole variety of Christian concepts, texts and phrases to be still sustainable (Brown, 1987, p.255; Osmond, 1993).

Even if this were so, was there a morally and politically viable alternative? For any reassertion of the Christian identity (or, rather, identities) of Britain presented a variety of other issues and difficulties. As both essays 4 and 7 demonstrate, there were potentially sharp controversies about how far various Christian groups were entitled to go in seeking to influence government policies and legislation in relation to both social and economic issues and questions of personal – and especially sexual – morality. How far were the churches and church leaders entitled to go in criticizing particular government social and economic policies, or in defending the principles and provisions of the welfare state? And how far were morally conservative Christians entitled to go in seeking to (re)impose on society in general their particular perception of a proper relationship between the law of the land and a variety of areas and aspects of personal and sexual morality? Meanwhile, any reassertion of the specifically Christian identity of Britain – whether 'liberally' or 'conservatively' conceived in theological terms – also raised acute questions concerning the position and status of other religious groups and traditions. This was made inescapably clear by the heated and prolonged debates over education – and in particular the relationship of religion to education and the appropriate form of provision for specifically religious education – which were an important feature of religious and political discussion during the 1980s and early 1990s, especially in relation to the 1988 Education Reform Act. As demonstrated in essay 5, attempts to emphasize the historical and contemporary predominance of Christianity in Britain, even while explicitly acknowledging the presence and importance of other religions, promoted a debate which was as fierce as it was enduring.

Moreover, the issues raised by the debate over religion and education were in turn part of a much wider debate about the extent to which – and the ways in which – the distinctive religious customs and values of minority groups in British society were to be respected, defended or protected. Significantly, both of the essays in this volume that address the relationships between religion and politics directly, identify this as an area of debate that became increasingly important in the latter decades of the period under review, and especially from the 1980s onwards. Whether about education; the right to slaughter animals for meat according to religious requirements; the right to wear the symbols of one's religion; the right to observe daily, weekly or life-cycle rituals in the religiously appointed manner; the right to observe traditional customs concerning marriage and relationships between the sexes; or the right to protest and seek redress against perceived insult to one's religion – beneath and within all these particular issues there was an underlying continuity of concern over how far the state could (and should) go in accommodating the separate and distinctive customs of the various minority religious traditions of recent and contemporary Britain.

The discussion of these issues, moreover, was also intimately bound up with wider discussions and debates over race, racism, the claims of 'multi-culturalism', and the rights of racial as well as religious minorities. Thus, for example, in response to the Rushdie affair, the Commission for Racial Equality organized an important series of seminars on the relationship between the law and concepts of 'blasphemy' and 'free speech' in a 'multi-faith society', and on the possible meanings and implications of 'pluralism' or a 'plural society' (Commission for Racial Equality, 1990a, b, and c). Similarly, in the wake of the 1988 Education Reform Act, the Commission published a review and discussion of the issues raised by the debate over the case for extending to Muslim schools the 'voluntary maintained' status already enjoyed by some Church of England, Roman Catholic and Jewish schools (Commission for Racial Equality, 1990d). Or again, examination of the articles that appeared during the 1980s and early 1990s in the journal *New Community* (which was sponsored by the Commission for Racial Equality) reveals a steadily increasing recognition of the relevance of religious themes and issues in the discussion of race relations in recent and contemporary Britain – an interaction also reflected in the pages of one of the standard histories of race relations in Britain in the post-Second World War era (Hiro, 1991).

However, recognition of such interaction itself prompts two further questions: namely, how far is it possible to discuss questions of race, racism and ethnic minority identities in Britain without attention to religious issues? And conversely, how far can you go in equating the two issues? That the two are intimately and importantly linked is clear. What is perhaps less clear in much discussion of such issues is that the relationship is extremely complex. Thus, on the one hand, it has been pointed out that in discussions of the relationship between race, ethnicity and religion it is often – mistakenly – assumed that religion is a relatively passive, 'given' factor in the construction and maintenance of ethnic identities. Yet to assume this is to neglect the potentially active, dynamic role that religion may play in defining and articulating a given ethnic community's identity and deepest concerns (Knott, 1992a, especially pp.11–14; see also Knott, 1986). Arguably, then, it may be said that discussion of race, race relations and ethnic minority identities in Britain cannot meaningfully go very far at all without a proper regard for the subtle, complex and potentially creative role of religion in such matters.

On the other hand, however, it has also been argued forcefully that in much recent discussion of race, religion and the identities and rights of ethnic minority communities, there has been a potentially dangerous tendency towards the 'racialization of religion'. In particular, it has been argued, many discussions of 'multi-culturalism' have collapsed ideas of culture into matters of religion – a trend much increased in the wake of the Rushdie affair. In the process, it is urged, stereotypical images and conceptions of ethnic minority communities and their religions have, paradoxically, been perpetuated; the restrictive agendas of particular groups and (usually male) leaders within those communities have been facilitated; and the rights of dissenting groups – and especially women – within the ethnic and religious communities concerned have been correspondingly neglected and ignored (Sahgal and Yuval-Davis, 1990 and 1992; Yuval-Davis, 1992; see also Knott, 1992c, pp.96–7).

The particular case of the experience of women within such communities thus presents a compelling caution against going too far in imposing a spurious uniformity upon the religious traditions of minority communities – or indeed taking at face value the claims to 'orthodoxy' or 'normativeness' of particular groups or leaders within such communities. Indeed, as shown in essay 6, the rich variety of women's religious experiences and practices in recent and contemporary Britain demonstrates graphically the danger inherent in taking any merely formal or institutional statement of the nature and norms of a given religion as definitive. Thus, in the last four and a half decades, women in a wide variety of religious traditions and communities in Britain have explored and developed an increasingly diverse range of religious forms and practices, both within and across 'official' religious boundaries. And in examining such developments the author of essay 6 also poses the further question: how far can you go in identifying distinctively female religious insights, experiences and perceptions?

Religion, then, in the closing decades of the twentieth century, continued to pose a variety of difficult, pressing and intriguing questions for British society. Nor were these simply the particular and peculiar concern of a variety of actively religious minorities within late twentieth-century Britain, a minority interest of little relevance to a generally secular and secularized majority. On the contrary, quite apart from the question of just how far late twentieth-century Britain was or was not in fact a secular society, many of the religious issues which forced themselves onto the agenda of public and political debate in the 1980s and early 1990s carried with them profound implications for British society as a whole. Thus, for example, where (as demonstrated in essays 4, 5 and 7) religious groups sought to enter more effectively into the political process, and influence public policy and legislation on education, broadcasting, attitudes to the family, abortion, and a whole range of issues related to sexual morality, they presented an important challenge to the broadly privatizing and secularizing trend which predominated in British social life and legislation at least from the 1960s onwards. They also posed the question: 'how far should society go in reversing such trends?'[6]

It was the Rushdie affair, however, that stood as the most compelling and potent symbol of the resurgence and continuing relevance of questions about the claims and status of religion in late twentieth-century Britain. This was so not only because it raised so many complex and demanding questions about the rights of religious minorities and the relationships between race, ethnicity and religion, but also because of the particular concept and issue that lay at the heart of the matter. The allegation against Rushdie was one of blasphemy: a quintessentially and fundamentally religious accusation.

Until the late 1970s, the law on blasphemy was commonly thought to be – in practice – a dead letter: an obsolete leftover from a previous era. Then, in 1977, Mary Whitehouse brought it back to life with a successful

---

[6] For the view that the emergence in the 1980s and early 1990s of an increasingly assertive and well-organized network of Christian groups committed to political lobbying was appropriately interpreted as an attempt to reverse secularizing and liberalizing trends, see, for example, Thompson, 1992, passim, but especially p.85; Tracey and Morrison, 1979, chs 1, 9 and 10; and Weeks, 1989, pp.277–82 and 292–8; as well as essays 4 and 7 in this volume.

prosecution of the publishers of the magazine *Gay News*.[7] Blasphemy, then, remained a potentially 'live' offence in late twentieth-century Britain. As pointed out in essays 2 and 3, the *Gay News* prosecution and conviction in turn prompted a debate on whether the law on blasphemy should be abolished or extended to include religions other than Christianity. That debate, however, proved inconclusive and reform – of any kind – was therefore left unattempted. But the Rushdie affair brought the issue of blasphemy back again into British life and debate and, additionally, sharpened the controversy by extending the range of issues involved: by 1989 the Rushdie affair had moved beyond blasphemy alone to include issues of race, racism and ethnic minority rights; questions of free speech and censorship; and the limits of legitimate protest in response to perceived religious offence.[8]

The ensuing debate was as complicated as it was heated, but the underlying issue in many of the different questions raised was the one with which we have already become so familiar. How far could Rushdie legitimately go in his literary critique of Islam? How far could the Muslim community go in legitimate protest against the book in question? How far could other religious believers, from other traditions, go in supporting them? How far could the state go in meeting Muslim grievances in this matter? How far could you go in maintaining that Britain was a genuinely plural society if these grievances were not met (or at least treated with a similar seriousness and potential for redress as had applied in the *Gay News* case a decade or so earlier)?

Conversely, just how far could Muslim action go? And how far could sympathizers with Muslim outrage go in their support of such protest, without causing equal – though opposite – offence to those in Britain who believed the issue of free speech, and the avoidance of censorship on

---

[7]   For an analysis of the origins, aims and conduct of the *Gay News* prosecution, see Tracey and Morrison, 1979, pp.3–17. For the place of this case and its importance within the broader pattern of debates over personal and sexual morality in Britain in the period since the Second World War, see Weeks, 1989, chs 14–15 and, more briefly, essay 7 in this volume.

[8]   It was also significant that, in both the *Gay News* prosecution and the Rushdie affair, the allegations of blasphemy were directly associated with writing – in one case a poem, in the other a novel – of a sexually explicit nature, an association that also occurred in the campaign mounted by some evangelical Christians to prevent the screening of Martin Scorsese's film version of the novel, *The Last Temptation of Christ*. Thus, as Sara Maitland has observed in a discussion of the relationship between artistic creativity and blasphemy (prompted by the controversy over *The Satanic Verses*), recent attempts to use the blasphemy laws as a means of censorship have centred on 'areas of sexual fear'. There is, she suggests, a widespread neurotic sensitivity about sex, as a result of which, 'writing that raises questions about and explores the connection between sex and religion touches raw nerves' (Maitland, 1990, p.124).

religious grounds, to be the primary issues at stake? Or again, how far could critics of the Muslim reaction go in supporting Rushdie without themselves being guilty of offence to Islam? And if Rushdie were to be regarded as having gone too far, then how far could any writer – whether poet, novelist, academic, critic or journalist – go in criticizing particular religious beliefs and traditions without being accused of 'blasphemy' or giving offence to the religious community in question? How far, indeed, were religious opinions and sensibilities entitled to claim protection from criticism or offence at all? How far could you go – supposing you wished to at all – in defining, legally, what constituted criticism or portrayal of a religion in an offensive and unacceptable manner? Indeed, it has been observed that to think seriously about the latter question was to begin to realize how fundamentally unworkable any extension of the blasphemy laws was likely to be. Such reflection was apt to suggest that, once begun, a process of seeking to prohibit publications which caused offence to the religious convictions of others would quickly cease to be a matter of 'how far can you go?' and become instead a problem of 'where on earth – or beyond it – do you stop?' (Easterman, 1992, pp.89–140).

Where, then, do such reflections leave us? And where do they leave the essays in this volume? The essays tend, on the whole, to identify questions rather than to provide answers. They suggest the complexity and the importance of a variety of religious issues within recent and contemporary Britain. They are thus intended as contributions to a continuing debate, attempts to clarify what is at stake and to encourage recognition of the fact that the issues involved are difficult and demanding, not simple or easy to resolve. And they suggest, in particular, that a unifying theme within most, if not all, of the diverse questions and issues addressed is the underlying and enduring dilemma, 'how far can you go?' More specifically, they ask how far any of us can go in any particular direction without throwing out something vital to the preservation of a viable balance in British society between the interests of a variety of particular religious groups, the interests of dissenting groups and individuals within them, the concerns of those who stand outside and claim the right to criticize all religions, and the well-being, coherence and creative co-existence of the community of communities that is Britain at the end of the twentieth century.

Bibliography

BROWN, C. (1987) *The Social History of Religion in Scotland since 1730*, Methuen, London.

COHN-SHERBOK, D. (ed.) (1992) *Many Mansions: interfaith and religious intolerance*, Bellew, London.

COMMISSION FOR RACIAL EQUALITY (1990a) *Law, Blasphemy and the Multi-Faith Society: report of a seminar organised by the Commission for Racial Equality and the Inter-Faith Network of the United Kingdom*, Commission for Racial Equality and The Inter-Faith Network for the United Kingdom, London.

(1990b) *Free Speech: report of a seminar organised by the Commission for Racial Equality and the Policy Studies Institute*, Commission for Racial Equality, London.

(1990c) *Britain: a plural society. Report of a seminar organised by the Commission for Racial Equality and The Runnymede Trust*, Commission for Racial Equality, London.

(1990d) *Schools of Faith: religious schools in a multicultural society*, Commission for Racial Equality, London.

EASTERMAN, D. (1992) *New Jerusalems: reflections on Islam, Fundamentalism and the Rushdie Affair*, Grafton, London.

ECCLESTONE, G. (1985) 'Church influence on public policy', *The Modern Churchman*, new series 28, pp.36–47.

GENERAL SYNOD BOARD OF MISSION (1992) *Multi-Faith Worship? Questions and suggestions from the Inter-Faith Consultative Group*, Church House Publishing, London.

HASTINGS, A. (1991) *Church and State: the English experience*, Exeter University Press, Exeter.

HIRO, D. (1991) *Black British White British: a history of race relations in Britain*, Grafton Books, London.

HOOKER, R. and SARGANT, J. (eds) (1991) *Belonging to Britain: Christian perspectives on a plural society*, Council of Churches for Britain and Ireland, London.

HOULDEN, J. (1989) 'The limits of theological freedom', *Theology*, 92, pp.268–76.

KNOTT, K. (1986) 'Religion and identity and the study of ethnic minority religions in Britain', *Community Religions Project Research Papers*, new series 3, University of Leeds, Leeds.

(1991) 'Bound to change? The religions of South Asians in Britain' in Vertovec, S. (ed.) *Oxford University Papers on India, volume 2*, Oxford University Press, Oxford.

(1992a) 'The role of religious studies in understanding ethnic experience', *Community Religions Project Research Papers*, new series 7, University of Leeds, Leeds.

(1992b) 'The changing character of the religions of the ethnic minorities of Asian origin in Britain: final report of a Leverhulme Project', *Community Religions Project Research Papers*, new series 11, University of Leeds, Leeds.

(1992c) 'Points of view: transforming inter-faith relations' in Willmer, H. (ed.) *20/20 Visions: the futures of Christianity in Britain*, SPCK, London.

LODGE, D. (1980a) *How Far Can You Go?*, Martin Secker and Warburg, London.

(1980b) 'The church and cultural life' in Cumming, J. and Burns, P. (eds) *The Church Now*, Gill and Macmillan, Dublin.

MAITLAND, S. (1990) 'Blasphemy and creativity' in Cohn-Sherbok, D. (ed.) *The Salman Rushdie Controversy in Interreligious Perspective*, Edwin Mellen Press, Lampeter.

NESBITT, E. (1991) *My Dad's Hindu, my Mum's side are Sikhs: issues in religious identity*, National Foundation for Arts Education, Warwick.

OSMOND, R. (1993) *Changing Perspectives: Christian culture and morals in England today*, Darton, Longman and Todd, London.

PARSONS, G. (1992) 'Paradigm or period piece? David Lodge's *How Far Can You Go?* in perspective', *Journal of Literature and Theology*, 6, pp.171–90.

PRICE, W. (1989) 'Church and society in Wales since disestablishment' in Badham, P. (ed.) *Church, State and Society in Modern Britain*, Edwin Mellen Press, Lampeter.

SACKS, J. (1991) *The Persistence of Faith: religion, morality and society in a secular age*, Weidenfeld and Nicolson, London.

SAHGAL, G. and YUVAL-DAVIS, N. (1990) 'Refusing Holy Orders', *Marxism Today*, March, pp.30–5.

(1992) 'Introduction: fundamentalism, multi-culturalism and women in Britain' in Sahgal, G. and Yuval-Davis, N. (eds) *Refusing Holy Orders: women and fundamentalism in Britain*, Virago, London.

SMART, N. (1989) 'Church, party and state' in Badham, P. (ed.) *Church, State and Society in Modern Britain*, Edwin Mellen Press, Lampeter.

THOMPSON, W. (1992) 'Britain's moral majority' in Wilson, B. (ed.) *Religion: contemporary issues*, Bellew Publishing, London.

TRACEY, M. and MORRISON, D. (1979) *Whitehouse*, Macmillan, London.

WEEKS, J. (1989) *Sex, Politics and Society: the regulation of sexuality since 1800*, Longman, London.

YUVAL-DAVIS, N. (1992) 'Fundamentalism, multi-culturalism and women in Britain' in Donald, J. and Rattansi, A. (eds) *'Race', Culture and Difference*, Sage Publications, London.

1

HOW MANY WAYS TO GOD? CHRISTIANS AND RELIGIOUS PLURALISM

by John Wolffe

Interfaith celebrations at Westminster Cathedral Hall, 28 October 1990. Left to right: Mr J.S. Bhambra, Cardinal Basil Hume, Sir Sigmund Sternberg. Photo: Carlos Reyes-Manzo, Andes Press Agency.

From Greenland's icy mountains,
From India's coral strand
Where Afric's sunny fountains
Roll down the golden sand,
From many an ancient river,
From many a palmy plain,
They call us to deliver
Their land from error's chain.

Can we, whose souls are lighted
With wisdom from on high,
Can we to men benighted
The lamp of life deny?
Salvation! oh, salvation!
The joyful sound proclaim,
Till each remotest nation
Has learn'd Messiah's name.

(Hymns Ancient and Modern, 1909 edn, p.663)

These verses were written in the early nineteenth century by Reginald Heber, subsequently Bishop of Calcutta, and opened the 'Missions' section in *Hymns Ancient and Modern*, still used widely in the Church of England in the later twentieth century. This particular hymn, however, tended to fall from favour in more recent anthologies and it can be inferred that Christians in our period were reacting to it in a variety of ways. Some could share wholeheartedly in the spirit of Heber and the missionary movement, convinced that adherence to their own creed was essential for salvation and that the full-blooded proclamation of the Christian gospel to adherents of other religions remained as vital and challenging a task as ever. Others might find a nostalgic attraction in Heber's words as reaffirming traditional certainties, but at other times were increasingly perplexed that not only was there little sign of 'each remotest nation' learning 'Messiah's name', but also that a growing number of people in Britain itself were adherents of different creeds. Others again came to see Heber's sentiments as those of a vanished age of religious dogmatism and imperial arrogance, embarrassing and even offensive in the multi-religious society of post-war Britain.

The purpose of this essay is to explore this range of responses to other religions on a variety of different fronts. Firstly, we shall examine the historical development of Christian thought regarding other faiths and the relationship of these to the theological self-understanding of Christianity. Secondly, there will be a discussion of the various practical measures taken by Christians, including both traditional mission and various forms of dialogue and co-operation. Finally, and more briefly, we shall survey the wider public reaction to other religions, among both the adherents of the churches and those outside them.

1 Ideas and attitudes

It is worth dwelling a little more on the perceptions which lay behind Heber's hymn. There was a clear polarization of 'truth' and 'error', with the beliefs of Innuits, the Hindu, Muslim and Sikh creeds of India and the primal religions of Africa, all bracketed together by the negative definition of being not Christianity. Moreover other religions were perceived as exotic and remote, and the appropriate manner of engagement with them was considered to be an explicitly missionary one, both in the original sense of the word (from the Latin *mittere*, to send), and also in the conviction that the objective had to be the full conversion of their adherents to Christianity. This endeavour was not felt to be offensive to the adherents of other faiths, who were portrayed by Heber as themselves calling for deliverance, because it offered them their only prospect of salvation. Their acceptance of Christ would mean joy and spiritual security in the present life and eternal resurrection with him in the hereafter. In a frequently cited analogy of missionary rhetoric it was no kindness to a man whose house was on fire to refuse to wake him up; equally those in peril of hell fire would (literally) be eternally grateful to those who rescued them from it. Furthermore the 'idolatry' of which other religions were guilty was an offence to the majesty of God, which must be vigorously confronted by the Christian.

These perceptions reflected the conservative theology of those who spearheaded the British missionary movement in the Victorian period. During the second half of the nineteenth century, however, alternative approaches were gaining some ground. Liberal Anglicans such as Frederick Denison Maurice and Rowland Williams acknowledged positive qualities in other religions, while still judging them to be distorted and partial revelations that needed to be completed by acceptance of the Christian Gospel. The combination, however, would open new spiritual possibilities, as anticipated by Brooke Foss Westcott, Bishop of Durham, in 1901:

> 'The races of the East we can hardly doubt will in their season lay open fresh depths in the Gospel which we are unfitted to discover ... [in] our own India, through which lies the entrance to all the missions of the East.'
>
> (Quoted in Maw, 1990, p.162)

This approach, which was focused particularly on Hinduism as the dominant creed of India, became known as fulfilment theology, from the sense that other religions would meet their own deepest aspirations in acceptance of a modified but still consistent Christianity. This view was widely accepted by missionaries in India by the time of the World Missionary Conference at Edinburgh in 1910 and received its most influential statement in John Nicol Farquhar's book, *The Crown of Hinduism* (1913). As the title implied, Farquhar argued that Christ is the culmination of the spiritual searchings of the Hindu (Langley, 1982, p.132; Maw, 1990, p.325; Sharpe, 1977, pp.24–32; Thomas, 1988, pp.288–94). Meanwhile Max Müller and Monier Monier-Williams pioneered the comparative study of religion. Müller translated numerous *Sacred Books of the East* thus introducing the texts of other religions to an English-speaking readership. He came to see all religions, including Christianity, as springing from 'the sacred soil of the human heart'. Monier-Williams on the other hand, although profoundly sympathetic to Hinduism, still held firmly to the primacy of Christianity (Thomas, 1988, pp.294–7).

During the first half of the twentieth century, the idea that other religions had positive value as a preparation for Christianity was very influential, particularly in Protestant missionary circles, especially after the horror of the First World War had further weakened presumptions to total moral and spiritual superiority. There was also a growing interest in mystical experience, which provided an important potential area of contact (Sharpe, 1977, pp.45–6, 76–81). However at the same time other theologians were reasserting the view that the revelation of God in Jesus Christ was absolutely unique and, accordingly, that all religious activity in which this was not explicitly acknowledged was at best 'misdirected' and subject to divine judgement. The starkest statement of this position was implicit in the work of the great Swiss neo-orthodox theologian Karl Barth, but the argument was developed by the Dutchman Hendrik Kraemer (1888–1965) in *The Christian Message in a Non-Christian World*, written for the international missionary conference at Tambaram in India in 1938. Kraemer held that 'God has revealed *the* Way and *the* Life and *the* Truth in Jesus Christ and wills this to be known through all the world.' The religions of people who did not submit to Christ were ultimately human constructions of self-justification. However Kraemer was concerned to separate this theological affirmation from claims to Christian *cultural* superiority, which he strongly opposed (D'Costa, 1986, pp.52–60).

During the two decades after the Second World War the primary context for discussion in Britain of the relationship of other faiths to Christianity continued to be that of overseas mission. An important exception to this was the attitude to the long-standing Jewish community in Britain, now overshadowed by appalled recollection of the Nazi holocaust (Neill, 1961, p.21; *The Times*, 25 June 1946). In general, however, until the 1960s the issues seemed of little relevance to the situation of the churches at home. When the Modern Churchmen's Conference discussed 'Christianity, A Faith for the World' in 1958, the presence of adherents of other religions in Britain was acknowledged, but as something of an afterthought in a discussion in which it was presupposed that encounter would continue predominantly to take place outside Europe (Smith, 1958, pp.83–4).

Accordingly during the first half of the period almost the only British writings on the subject came from missionary strategists, notably Max Warren (1904–77), General Secretary of the Church Missionary Society from 1942 to 1963 and Bishop Stephen Neill (1900–84). Both had been raised amid the full flood of Edwardian missionary and imperial optimism, but reached positions of leadership at a period when the British empire was in retreat politically and other religions were resurgent, notably in the Indian subcontinent and in the Middle East. Their response to this situation was, following Kraemer, the vigorous reaffirmation of the uniqueness and centrality of Christ as the incarnate Son of God and the crucial starting point for all judgements of other religions. However this was coupled with an awareness of how Christian missions in the past had often been linked with western cultural imperialism and hence that the new political situation offered a 'great new opportunity' for authentic Christian witness (Neill, 1961, pp.205–32; Warren, 1963, p.10). Moreover other religions, despite their limitations, still had to be met with respect:

> ...we may forget that God was here before our arrival. We have ... to ask what is the authentic religious content in the experience of the Muslim, Hindu, the Buddhist, or whoever he may be. We may, if we have asked humbly and respectfully, still reach the conclusion that our brothers have started from a false premiss and reached a faulty conclusion. But we must not arrive at our judgment from outside their religious situation. We have to try to sit where they sit, to enter sympathetically into the pains and griefs and joys of their history and see how those pains and griefs and joys have determined the premisses of their argument. We have, in a word, to be 'present' with them.
>
> (Warren, 1963, pp.10–11)

This approach, which became known as 'Christian presence', did not, unlike the fulfilment theology of the early decades of the century, imply that other religions were essentially a preparation for Christianity. By contrast it reflected an appreciation of the genuine differences between different systems of belief and a refusal to patronize and distort them by imposing external Christian categories.

While Protestant missions were thus reassessing their attitudes in the post-imperial era, the Second Vatican Council between 1962 and 1965 saw a corresponding development in the Roman Catholic position. The traditional axiom of *extra ecclesiam nulla salus*, there is 'no salvation outside the Church', did not always in practice mean an entirely negative evaluation of other religions, but at no time had it been officially qualified (D'Costa, 1990, pp.130–47). The Council affirmed that 'Christ is the light of all nations', and that the Church had the task of 'bringing all men to full union with Christ'.

However it also published a 'Declaration on the Relationship of the Church to Non-Christian Religions' (*Nostra Aetate*) which had developed out of Pope John XXIII's original desire for a statement regarding the Jews. This dwelt on the essential unity of humankind and took a positive view of the religious strivings of non-Christian peoples. The Declaration continued:

> The Catholic church rejects nothing which is true and holy in these religions. She looks with sincere respect upon those ways of conduct and of life, those rules and teachings which, though differing in many particulars from what she holds and sets forth, nevertheless often reflect a ray of that Truth which enlightens all men.

> (Abbott, 1967, p.662)

Catholics were urged to take part in dialogue and to collaborate with adherents of other faiths when common ground could be found. Particular attention was given to relations with the Jews and to their common heritage with Christians in the Covenant originally given to Abraham (Abbott, 1967, pp.14–15, 656–71). In 1964 a 'Secretariat for non-Christians' was set up with the objective of promoting understanding with adherents of other religions (Sharpe, 1977, p.125).

For a fuller exploration of the theological position represented in the Vatican II Declaration, one may turn to the writings of the German Jesuit Karl Rahner (1904–84). Like Kraemer, who had been so influential in forming the outlook of Protestant theologians, Rahner made absolute claims for his own creed, but differed from Kraemer in basing his position on 'Christianity' as well as on 'Christ'. 'Christianity', he wrote, 'understands itself as the absolute religion, intended for all men, which cannot recognize any other religion besides itself as of equal right' (quoted in D'Costa, 1986, p.84). This standpoint reflected the traditional Catholic emphasis on the visible Church. Non-Christians, however, could still gain a revelation of Christianity through their own religion 'mediated through the specific form of [their] social and historical life' (quoted in D'Costa, 1986, p.85) and hence could be regarded as an 'anonymous Christian'. Mission, though, remained vital as the means by which this hidden attitude of the heart would be translated into objective social reality in adherence to the Church (D'Costa, 1986, pp.80–9). A more liberal Catholic viewpoint was developed by the Swiss theologian Hans Küng, who held that a human being could attain salvation through non-Christian religions 'until such time as he is confronted in an existential way with the revelation of Jesus Christ' (Hick, 1973, pp.128–9; Küng, 1976, pp.89–116).

Hence much of the theological equipment with which British Christians could respond to the presence of other religions in their midst from the 1960s had been developed in response to wider pressures outside the country. On the Catholic side, views of other faiths were part of the authoritative redefinition of the nature and the place of the Church in the modern world that was carried out by Vatican II. For Protestants they stemmed from the changing situation of overseas missions. The implications of such positions for the Church at home had yet to be worked through.

There were, especially among Protestants, a wide range of shades of opinion. The view that other religions were wholly false, mere delusions, products of human sin or of demonic influence, still had its followers (Hunter, 1985, pp.18–19; Newbigin, 1977, pp.256–7). These were likely to be adherents of a theology influenced by Calvinism, in which the objection that a loving God would hardly consign the majority of humankind to eternal perdition would be met by the axiom of God's absolute sovereignty and inscrutable purposes (Hick, 1980, p.4). Mainstream evangelicals, too, adhered firmly to the view that encounter with Christ was a prerequisite for salvation, but saw this rather as an inspiration to vigorous and uncompromising mission (Hick, 1980, p.49). The essence of this position was reaffirmed in 1974 at Lausanne in Switzerland at the International Congress on World Evangelization, convened at the instigation of the American evangelist Billy Graham. The 'Lausanne Covenant', largely drafted by the leading Anglican evangelical, John Stott, stressed the uniqueness of Christ as the 'only mediator between God and man'. Meanwhile, however, other evangelicals were qualifying the practical application of this conviction by arguing that God could somehow reveal Christ, even if not in this life, to non-Christians (Knitter, 1985, pp.78–9; Langley, 1982, p.143). Thus Sir Norman Anderson, a prominent evangelical layman, wrote in 1970:

> ...I believe that if in this world a man has really, as a result of the prompting and enabling of the Holy Spirit, thrown himself on the mercy of God ... he will have been 'justified' ... What will happen to him beyond the grave can best be described as an adoring recognition of his Saviour and comprehension of what he owes to him.
>
> (Anderson, 1970, p.106)

At the same time, however, Anderson also reaffirmed the urgency of the missionary task, as a response to Jesus's explicit command, and a means of giving present experience and assurance to the hidden believer (Anderson, 1970, pp.105–7).

Other Protestant writers adhered firmly to the uniqueness and centrality of Christ. Lesslie Newbigin (b.1909), then bishop in Madras, argued in the late 1960s that the Christian Gospel was the key to the understanding of human history and that the necessity for conversion remained. However this did not imply any finality for the 'changing and developing corpus of belief, practice and association' which constituted contemporary Christianity (Newbigin, 1969, pp.65, 73). In a similar state of mind, Stephen Neill called for 'the deepest humility' in the Christian's approach to other faiths:

> He must endeavour to meet them at their highest, and not cheaply to score points off them by comparing the best he knows with their weaknesses, weaknesses such as are present in the Christian scheme as it is lived out by very imperfect Christians.
>
> (Neill, 1961, p.18)

In more liberal hands the distinction between Christ and Christianity could imply a radical readiness to learn from other faiths. Thus in 1968 David Jenkins (b.1925), later Bishop of Durham, emphasized that 'Christians are entirely exclusive and absolute about Jesus Christ' and 'anything in other faiths which contradicts or goes against Jesus on the Christian view is wrong and must be opposed'. Jenkins maintained, however, that 'Jesus Christ … is not to be equated with Christianity', since the latter was still struggling to emancipate itself from bondage to imperialistic western culture. Hence,

> Loyalty to the absolute and exclusive claims of Jesus Christ, a loyalty which is shaped by the reality of Jesus Christ, requires absolute openness to all the human faiths, and a complete readiness to serve in a common exploration and in a common living.[1]
>
> (Jenkins, 1990, pp.89–98)

On the other hand it is noteworthy that, at the time, the theological radicals of the 1960s made little specific contribution to the discussion, probably because they were, in effect outflanking it by their much broader reassessment of fundamental religious concepts (Sharpe, 1977, pp.114–15). Thus, for example, John Robinson's *Truth is Two-Eyed*, which addressed questions of religious pluralism, was not published until 1979.

An important new turn to the discussion arose following the appointment in 1967 of John Hick (b.1922), a Presbyterian minister and a philosopher of religion, to the post of H.G. Wood Professor of Theology at the University of Birmingham. Hick was at the time wrestling with the problem of how to reconcile his conviction of God's universal saving activity with there being only one true religion. In Birmingham he found a city with substantial Hindu, Jewish, Muslim and Sikh minorities and, in defiance of

---

[1] Other writers, notably D'Costa (1985, 1986) and Race (1983), have classified the various views surveyed so far as either 'exclusivist', implying there is no salvation outside Christianity, or 'inclusivist', suggesting that other religions can be a means of salvation under certain conditions. These categories seem to me to mislead by implying a polarization which does not do justice to the subtleties of individual positions.

31

right-wing political extremists, he threw himself into the promotion of racial justice and the improvement of community relations. At the same time he attended the worship of other faiths and became convinced that 'essentially the same kind of thing is taking place in them as in a Christian church – namely, human beings opening their minds to a higher divine Reality' (D'Costa, 1987, pp.12–13; Hick, 1980, p.5; Hick, 1985, pp.4–11).

Hick's *God and the Universe of Faiths* (1973) was the first substantial piece of theological writing to engage directly with the issues raised by the presence of other faiths in Britain. It was written largely in ignorance of the wider historical development of Christian thought on the subject and the author's approach was shaped rather by his wider philosophical preoccupations (Hick, 1977, pp.vii–ix; Sharpe, 1977, pp.136–7). The core of his position had first publicly been enunciated in lectures at Carrs Lane Church Centre in February and March 1972. In an analogy with sixteenth-century developments in understanding of the structure of the universe, he called for a 'Copernican revolution' in theology. He regarded the principle that 'outside the church, or outside Christianity there is no salvation' as analogous to the ancient Ptolemaic view that the earth was the hub of the universe. It was inconsistent with the facts, and while it might be patched up by 'epicycles', 'supplementary theories, designed to modify the original dogma while leaving it verbally intact', it should be discarded. Rather there must be a 'realisation that it is *God* who is at the centre, and that all the religions of mankind, including our own, serve and revolve around him' (Hick, 1977, pp.xii, 120–32). All religions were valid, if they were the product of genuine revelation and tried and tested by long periods of human experience. The apparent inconsistencies were due to the manner in which each religion, including Christianity, only had a partial understanding of God. Hick quoted the words of Krishna in the Bhagavad Gita: 'Howsoever men approach me, even so do I accept them; for on all sides, whatever path they choose is mine'. He also recounted the parable of the blind men and the elephant, attributed to the Buddha: one man felt a leg and thought the animal was a great living pillar; another the trunk and thought it was a snake; and a third a tusk and said it was like a sharp ploughshare. Hick did not contemplate a syncretistic fusing together of the world's religions but rather rejoiced in their diversity, as the products of different cultures. Accordingly his view has been labelled as 'pluralism',[2] implying a theological acceptance of the prospect that all faiths would continue throughout human history as parallel 'ways through time to eternity' (Hick, 1977, pp.133–47).

---

[2] The use of this term in a theological context needs to be distinguished from its more general usage to denote the objective social reality of a plurality of belief systems in the modern world, as in the title of this essay.

Hick appreciated that his 'Copernican revolution' was in tension with central traditional Christian doctrines concerning the nature and status of Jesus Christ as uniquely God incarnate. Accordingly the formulation of a radically revised christology was an essential part of his argument. Hick claimed that the belief that Jesus was both fully God and fully man was philosophically indefensible, and that in any case Jesus had made no such claim for himself. The doctrine of the incarnation rather emerged in the Church in the succeeding decades and centuries and was not fully defined until the third and fourth centuries. This did not mean that the concept of incarnation should be discarded, but, in Hick's view, it was not literally true and should be accepted rather as 'an effective mythic expression of the appropriate attitude to' Jesus (Hick, 1977, pp.148–79). This dimension of Hick's thought was more fully developed in 1977, in association with six other radical theologians, in a volume of essays entitled *The Myth of God Incarnate* (Hick, 1985, pp.11–15).

Hick's arguments provoked considerable debate, but it is significant that, among ordinary church people at least, it was *The Myth of God Incarnate* rather than *God and the Universe of Faiths* which provoked the greater controversy. The theological issues seemed pressing only when fundamental doctrines were explicitly questioned. There were calls for the writers to resign their orders and some queried whether their position could still validly be regarded as Christian (Hastings, 1986, pp.650–1, Hick, 1985, p.12). Others, however, rallied to Hick's defence, arguing that his position was the most, or perhaps even the only, coherent stance for a Christian theologian who wished honestly to come to terms with religious diversity and the implications of recent biblical scholarship and philosophical enquiry (Hunter, 1985; Knitter, 1985; Race, 1983).

Meanwhile more conservative writers were re-examining their positions and restating them. John Stott saw no need for revision:

> We do not ... deny that there are elements of truth in non-Christian systems, vestiges of the general revelation of God in nature. What we do vehemently deny is that these are sufficient for salvation and (more vehemently still) that Christian faith and non-Christian faith are alternative and equally valid roads to God.
>
> (Stott, 1975, p.69)

In 1975 Max Warren, however, expressed his readiness to accept a 'Copernican revolution', but with the crucial proviso that for him not an abstract 'God' but 'an historical person Jesus in whom God is to be recognised as uniquely revealed' must be at the centre of the universe of faiths. This nevertheless implied a readiness to reassess some traditional Christian modes of thinking and discover Christ in other faiths (Dillistone, 1980, pp.202–3, 239–42; Warren, 1975). In 1977 the centrality of Jesus Christ was also firmly reiterated by Bishop Lesslie Newbigin, now returned from India and, like Hick himself, holding an academic post in Birmingham. It was interesting that two major protagonists in the debate were thus writing from a personal experience of a multi-religious situation in Britain, but reaching divergent theological conclusions, an indication that much still depended on the presuppositions that were being brought to bear. Newbigin acknowledged that the Church was not 'the exclusive possessor of salvation' and recognized 'all the ethical and religious achievements which so richly adorn the cultures of mankind'. However all these, and institutional Christianity itself, would find their ultimate fulfilment in a self-emptying at the Cross of Christ which represents 'a historic deed, in which God exposed himself in a total vulnerability to all man's purposes, and in this meeting exposed mankind as the beloved of God'. Christians must be uncompromisingly obedient in their witness to Christ, but this in itself implied a readiness to place at risk their own prior understanding of Christianity (Newbigin, 1977; 1985, pp.243–4). When, in 1984, Sir Norman Anderson republished his analysis of the issues from a conservative evangelical standpoint, he made extensive use of Newbigin's work in developing his own critique of Hick. More explicitly than in 1970 he distanced himself from the view that 'all those who have never heard the gospel are inevitably lost' (Anderson, 1984, p.175 and *passim*). An important Roman Catholic contribution to the debate subsequently came from Gavin D'Costa, who pointed out that the God at the centre of Hick's universe of faiths was all-loving and therefore essentially Christian in conception. Accordingly 'it would seem that Hick's Copernican revolution is just another, but rather confused, Ptolemaic epicycle' (D'Costa, 1984, p.329). In setting out his own position D'Costa turned rather to the work of Karl Rahner, which, he argued, provided an intellectually coherent basis for acknowledging that God was active in and through other religions while preserving a conviction of the distinctiveness and uniqueness of the divine revelation in Jesus Christ (D'Costa, 1984, 1986, 1987).

During the 1980s the debate continued in books and theological journals. By 1990 the spectrum of opinion, closely related to underlying convictions about Christian theology, could be characterized as a broad centre with two somewhat embattled wings. The majority, including numerous Roman Catholics and evangelicals as well as moderate liberals, felt no need to reject orthodox Christian belief in the divinity of Christ and the supreme importance of the divine revelation given in Jesus of Nazareth. They were able to work out various formulas for reconciling these convictions with an evaluation of other religions that was positive in varying degrees. These ranged from, at the conservative end, Anderson's image of 'a patchwork quilt, with brighter and darker components' (Anderson, 1984, p.172), to the readiness of some to see other faiths as providing profound insights that traditional Christianity lacked. On the one wing, meanwhile, were the convinced pluralists calling for radical theological re-orientation, but seen by their opponents as either inconsistent or no longer recognizably Christian.[3] On the other wing were the more rigorous evangelicals, who insisted not only on the primacy of Christ but also on explicit acceptance of conversion and assent to a specific doctrinal framework, and for whom other religions were wholly negative human structures or even demonic creations (Anderson, 1984, pp.170–1; Cole et al., 1990, pp.52–7).

In the next section of this essay we shall consider some of the practical measures taken by Christians in responding to other faiths. In concluding this discussion of the more theological dimensions of the subject, however, we can note how the patterns of change in this respect related to the wider development of the mainstream Christian churches as surveyed in essay 1 in Volume I. We have seen a further illustration of a shift from traditionalism through a time of fundamental questioning to, in the 1980s, a period of enormous variety of opinion in which restated versions of traditional positions seemed to be gaining some ground. The difference from the general pattern lay in the manner in which, while the 1960s saw important changes, it was not until the 1970s that the most radical possibilities were fully explored. British Christianity was, in general, slower to respond to the presence of other faiths than to the impact of intellectual scepticism and a morally liberalizing society and culture.

2 Encounter, dialogue and mission

The three words chosen here to introduce this section point to the immense variety of forms of contact that took place between Christianity and other religions in Britain during the 1970s and 1980s. 'Encounter' is the most all-encompassing and neutral term that has been used to refer to this process. It takes place whenever human beings of different religions come into meaningful contact, at home, at work, in local communities and in politics, as well as in specifically religious activities. There is a sense in which all the essays in these two volumes are concerned with encounter, with the manifold interactions between world religions, the organized churches, and the legacy of cultural Christianity in national life. The reader of Volume

---

[3] In an important recent book Keith Ward argues that the heart of Christianity can be maintained within a framework of what he calls 'convergent pluralism' whereby existing religious traditions 'converge on a more adequate understanding of the ultimate goal' (Ward, 1991, p.176).

I will be aware of many of the complex movements that have been operative, and the observer can further reflect on the almost infinite variety of permutations that result when strong religious convictions are refracted through the prisms of personality, background, events and circumstances. One woman living among Muslims and Jains formed very warm personal relations with them and told her vicar that 'A good Christian shouldn't be bigoted' (GS, 8, 1970, pp.543–4); another, taken on a visit to a local mosque, disregarded instructions to dress appropriately and then complained loudly that she would not have a 'filthy Pakistani blanket' over her legs (Wingate, 1988, p.66).[4] Moreover theological standpoints were often in tension with practical experience: missionaries employed to convert adherents of other religions came to form deep respect for their culture; liberals struggled to square their belief in the validity of all religions with their perception that other faiths were at times manifestly illiberal.

Despite the enormous variety of the encounters that did take place it must be emphasized that other religions and their adherents impinged little if at all on the lives of the majority of Christians during our period. For suburban, small-town and rural congregations the non-Christian inhabitants of Small Heath, Manningham and the Gorbals were as remote as those of Bengal, Zululand and Arabia had been to their great-grandparents. Indeed they were perhaps even more remote, because the support and fund-raising apparatus of missionary societies fostered an awareness of other faiths overseas, which initially was lacking in relation to their presence in Britain.

Not only was encounter concentrated geographically and socially, but it was also limited chronologically largely to the last fifteen years of the period under review here. There had certainly been some important initiatives in inter-faith relations at an earlier date, notably the foundation of the World Congress of Faiths (WCF) by Sir Francis Younghusband in 1936, and the Council of Christians and Jews (CCJ) in 1942 (Langley, 1982, pp.134–5). During the war Archbishop Temple had spoken out strongly against Nazi persecution in defence of the Jews; and his successor, Archbishop Fisher, was an active supporter of CCJ (Braybrooke, 1991, pp.13–23). In 1946 he appealed for support for a body which had been set up

> with the express purpose of combating religious and racial enmity, especially by the promoting of good will between the two communities and fostering active co-operation between them in public service.
>
> (The Times, 25 June 1946)

---

[4] It must in fairness be noted that the woman who expressed this sentiment later voiced a much warmer opinion of a Muslim.

There was a consciousness in the immediate post-war years of the need to promote religious co-operation in the cause of world peace and justice, which was articulated in a resolution passed by the WCF in 1946:

> Lasting peace and progressive order cannot be established on earth until a spirit of fellowship quickens in human souls, and mankind conceives that all spring from the same divine source. No exterior means, international agreements, sanctions, or atomic bombs can safeguard permanent stability in human relations ... This congress appeals to all representatives of religious opinion to consider practical measures needed to make the voice of religion heard throughout the world.
>
> (*The Times*, 23 September 1946)

At the same period comparative religion was being studied seriously at an academic level: when in 1953 *The Times* published an article in which the activity of the University of Durham in the field was emphasized, loyal alumni of London, Manchester and Aberdeen universities wrote to the editor to draw attention to the comparable achievements of their own institutions (*The Times*, 21, 31 January; 3, 6 February, 1953).

However it must be stressed that while this early activity engaged the support and enthusiasm of individual Christians, and even at archiepiscopal level, the responses of the churches as such continued until the 1970s to be dominated by the traditional missionary outlook. The cautious attitude of ecclesiastical authority to co-operation was illustrated in the mid 1950s when Roman Catholic members of the Council of Christians and Jews withdrew on instructions from the Vatican, which was fearful of producing 'religious indifferentism'. The Catholics rejoined in 1961 (Braybrooke, 1991, pp.33, 38).

The limited allusions to people of other religions in the debates of the Church Assembly[5] during the quarter century after 1945 serve as an indication of the attitudes of one major denomination and its hesitant attempts to respond to the situation. In 1946 there was discussion of seamen and students who came to the country from overseas who were seen as presenting a mission field on the church's doorstep. One speaker warned against over-enthusiastic hospitality: for some of the newcomers, he believed, polygamy was 'perfectly natural' and herein lay dangers for Christian young people if social mixing were to be encouraged (*CA*, 26, 1946, p.203). He need hardly have worried about undue zeal however, because a decade later the Assembly was still discussing in desultory fashion how the Church was to respond to overseas students. A small

---

[5] The deliberative assembly of the Church of England, which was replaced in 1970 by the General Synod.

hostel had been set up, but by 1958 it was threatened with closure (*CA*, 38, 1958, p.82).

The 1960s saw a somewhat increased sense of urgency, but little re-examination of underlying assumptions. In 1962 the Assembly acknowledged a 'pastoral and evangelistic responsibility towards immigrants into this country', but a Coventry clergyman spoke of the practical difficulties he had experienced in seeking to make contact with Gujeratis in his parish and warned that 'the passing of pious resolutions' would achieve nothing (*CA*, 42, 1962, pp.761–3). In 1967 there was the first explicit discussion of relations with adherents of other religions in England: concern was expressed by two Evangelical speakers about dismissive comments in a recent publication concerning Christian evangelistic intentions towards Muslims. Raymond Johnston considered the task of the Church to be 'to convert all men, whatever their colour, to our faith' (*CA*, 47, 1967, p.677), while Sir Norman Anderson argued from his personal experience with Muslim students at London University that good-neighbourliness and evangelism were not mutually exclusive (*CA*, 47,1967, pp.678–9). The Bishop of Durham (Ian Ramsey) saw this as a basis for a wider vision. An 'evangelism' that indoctrinated people was hardly Christian, but

> If we struggle with the Muslim community and those problems associated with it, we may be pointing to another concept of evangelism which may come close to Professor Anderson's concept of good neighbourliness and, theologically speaking, we may find further study of concepts and vast areas of theology which have been conveniently forgotten.
>
> (*CA*, 47, 1967, pp.680–1)

Such sentiments, however tentative, were still in advance of their time. In 1974 Clifford Longley, the religious affairs correspondent of *The Times*, observed that the Muslim, Sikh and Hindu presence in Britain had as yet scarcely had any impact on the life of the Christian churches. Significantly, when relations with other faiths were examined at all this was usually merely as an offshoot of Christian concerns for community and race relations rather than in any sustained engagement with the specifically religious issues at stake (*The Times*, 11 February 1974). (This had indeed been the case in the Church Assembly discussion in 1967 which had formed a brief interlude in an extensive debate on race relations arising from a report by the Church's Board for Social Responsibility.)

There were, however, signs of changing attitudes, although at first these were largely external to Britain. The Vatican's Secretariat for Non-Christians during the late 1960s and early 1970s fostered contact between the Papacy and other religions and also published a range of guides, which improved Catholics' understanding even if they did not revise predetermined positions. In 1971 the World Council of Churches (WCC) set up a sub-unit on Dialogue Between Men [sic] of Living Faiths and Ideologies. This promoted various consultations but the report produced at the WCC Assembly in Nairobi in 1975 was an anti-climax which somehow contrived to be both indecisive and controversial, and subsequent activities were curtailed by financial problems (Braybrooke, 1980, pp.91–108).

Back in Britain, Longley, in his 1974 *Times* article, had mentioned a pamphlet just published by the Catholic Commission for Racial Justice in which it was stated that

> The obvious line of division in this country ... is not between Christians and believers in other faiths, it is between people with a religion and people with none.
>
> (The Times, 11 February 1974)

Christians, the writer thought, were prone to rationalize latent racialism by reference to religion. On the last day of 1974 the General Secretary of the British Council of Churches (BCC) described British society as 'permanently characterized by a multiplicity of religious creeds'. This led John Stokes, Conservative MP for Halesowen, to accuse the BCC of neglecting its 'duty' to 'preserve our Christian heritage', but the Bishop of Guildford (David Brown) retorted that 'those who seek most truly to be Christ's disciples often have a deep and lasting respect for the faiths of other men' (*The Times*, 6, 10 January 1975).

Such pronouncements by church leaders reflected a wider climate of debate and self-examination which had its theological counterpart, as we have seen, in the controversies fuelled by John Hick's views. The mid 1970s were also a significant watershed in institutional activity. In 1975 the Archbishops' Consultants on Inter-Faith Relations were set up in the Church of England. In 1978 the BCC established a Committee for Relations with People of Other Faiths (CRPOF), which quickly spawned consultative groups on theological issues, legal and parliamentary matters and religious education.

During the next decade most major denominations (the Church of England, the Roman Catholic Church, the Methodist Church, the United Reformed Church, the Scottish Episcopal Church, and the Quakers) set up official committees to liaise with the CRPOF and promote their own activities. Among Baptists there was the informally organized Joppa Group. The Church of Scotland set up a Committee for relations with Israel and with People of Other Faiths in 1983, which, as its title implied, specialized in Christian–Jewish relations (Reports to the General Assembly, 1983, pp.316–7; 1984, pp.404–7). An interdenominational Churches Agency for Inter-Faith Relations in Scotland was in existence by

1992.[6] There was also Christian participation in the Inter-Faith Network, set up in March 1987 to promote dialogue and understanding, and provide a central point of information and advice on inter-faith relations (Inter-Faith Network for the UK, 1991).

When in 1977, shortly after the publication of *The Myth of God Incarnate*, the General Synod of the Church of England discussed the BCC report on 'The New Black Presence', it was clear that outlooks had changed significantly during the previous decade. Certainly responses to other faiths still tended to be seen as a branch of race relations, as reflected in the wording of the original motion before the Synod. However there was a significant intervention from the Bishop of Winchester, John Taylor, formerly General Secretary of the Church Missionary Society, who had some years before been the author of *The Primal Vision*, regarded as a milestone in Christian understanding of other religions. He stressed the importance of recognizing the reality of religious differences and proposed a corresponding amendment. The motion as passed constituted the first official acknowledgement by the Church of England that the country was 'a society which comprises different racial, cultural and religious groups' and asserted that this enriched 'national and personal life'. It was left to a convert from Hinduism to restate missionary priorities, turning on its head the increasingly fashionable assumption that evangelism among adherents of other religions was a threat to their identity:

> I am 5 ft-nothing and a black man. That made me feel inadequate in myself, but when I found Jesus I found my true identity ... What a dignity we have in Jesus! That is what we can give to the black people who think they are nothing.
>
> (*GS*, 8, 1977, pp.516, 527–47)

From around 1980 the prevailing climate was one in which for most church leaders 'inter-faith relations' became a sphere of activity and concern in its own right, no longer seen as merely a spin-off from evangelism on the one hand or race relations on the other. This did not, however, mean an acceptance of pluralist theology: in 1980 the General Synod reaffirmed the 'unique character of the incarnation', and, significantly, the Interfaith Consultative Group was still in 1990 part of the Church of England's Board for Mission and [Christian] Unity (BMU). Nevertheless the official emphasis was now on 'dialogue' rather than 'mission'. In 1984 a BMU report implied that meaningful dialogue required Christians to modify the exclusive claims made for Christ. Although this was contested by Evangelicals who remained convinced of the validity and importance of

---

[6] I am indebted to CRPOF, the Revd Dr Derek Tidball and the Revd Maxwell Craig for supplying information summarized in this paragraph.

mission, they nevertheless implicitly moved to a position in which conversion was a long-term rather than immediate objective (Evangelical Alliance, 1983, pp.32–4; Sugden, 1985). This practical development of respect for other religions, qualified by an anxiety not to compromise the core of Christian conviction, corresponded to the broad mainstream theological consensus described above.

The period between 1975 and 1990 saw a crescendo of concern and activity: committees and conferences debated; publications proliferated (CRPOF, 1991). At a local level, numerous inter-faith groups were formed, while churches and missionary organizations appointed workers specifically to operate among adherents of other religions. There is no space here to describe the full range or complexity of this endeavour, but it should be noted that in various ways it engaged the energies of representatives of all the major traditional denominational groups and strands of theological opinion. In 1991 the CRPOF included representatives of the Church of England, the Church of Scotland, the Roman Catholic Church in England and Wales, the United Reformed Church, the Methodist Church, the Scottish Episcopal Church, the Quakers, the Presbyterian Church of Wales and the Baptist Union (CRPOF, 1991, pp.8–9, 30). However the real distinction was between the relatively small numbers of activists – church leaders, academics, and those whose life and work brought them into regular contact with other faiths – and an apathetic majority among church congregations whose consciousness of the issues remained low. Accordingly any account of Christian initiatives in relations with other religions during the latter part of our period can convey only a partial picture, and one in which it is much easier to examine general approaches than to evaluate their detailed impact.

We have noted above that inter-faith interests had often emerged in the context of Christian concern over race relations. The relationship between the two sets of issues continued to be a close one. Many saw practical involvement with the political and social concerns of minority communities as both a Christian responsibility in itself and a good starting point for more specifically religious activities. Thus Christians were urged not only to take a firm stand against right-wing political extremism, but also to seek to understand and facilitate the wishes of other faith communities in relation to matters such as health-care and education. There was also a value in general good-neighbourliness, which could be expressed in making church halls (but not normally buildings actually used for Christian worship) available for use by non-Christian groups, and accepting graciously the sale of redundant churches to become gurdwaras, mosques or temples (Lamb, 1985; Sheppard, 1983, p.85; Sookhdeo, 1979, pp.106–12, 120–2). Significantly, such approaches were in the 1980s often advocated by those of more conservative theological standpoints, for whom explicitly religious co-operation raised particular difficulties. Thus the Bishop of Liverpool (David Sheppard) wrote:

> ... if the Christian Church has no further need for a particular building, it is a proper response to the needs of a minority community, to make it available to them. To offer such practical help as we are able, to treat other religions with respect and to enter into friendly dialogue is not to abandon the belief of Christians in the uniqueness of Jesus Christ. It reflects our common humanity and our common experience of the love of God.
>
> (Sheppard, 1983, p.85)

The foundations of dialogue in everyday contact were also stressed by the CRPOF, when it published guidelines in 1981 (CRPOF, 1981). Following the World Council of Churches, the committee set out four principles:

> Dialogue begins when people meet each other;
> Dialogue depends upon mutual understanding and mutual trust;
> Dialogue makes it possible to share in service to the community;
> Dialogue becomes the medium of authentic witness.

The CRPOF booklet implied that 'all religions are entitled to equal respect and dignity', and it had not been produced without significant reservations by the more conservative members of the committee (*The Times*, 15 June 1981, p.14). When, however, the guidelines were updated in 1991 these four principles were confidently restated and were held to have 'stood the test of increasing experience'. They had indeed been officially accepted by the Church of England in 1981, the Methodist Church in 1982, the United Reformed Church in 1983 and the Scottish Episcopal Church in 1988 (CRPOF, 1991, pp.ix, 8). While some, from both pluralist and missionary perspectives, might feel that they said too little, they did provide a satisfactory basis for the activity of the majority.

The practice of dialogue as presented by the CRPOF could indeed be squared with a wide spectrum of theological positions. At the liberal end there was a tendency to regard almost all belief as negotiable in the cause of deeper understanding; at the conservative end an implicit assumption that dialogue was only justifiable in preparing the ground for conversion. The liberals were criticized for minimizing Christian distinctiveness; the conservatives for not really being serious about dialogue. In between were those who sought to maintain the distinctiveness of Christian belief, but did not see this as inconsistent with respect for the integrity and at least partial validity of the beliefs of others. It did not follow that more liberal assumptions necessarily made for more effective dialogue: in a lecture in 1977 John Taylor had cogently argued that 'intractable convictions' should not be levelled down, because paradoxically, 'the experience of having a conviction that by definition precludes the other person's belief' was one of the most significant things many Christians held in common with adherents of other faiths (Taylor, 1980 p.226). Partners in dialogue, particularly Muslims, indeed often found it easier to understand and respect clear-cut statements of the Christian position, and the minimizing of genuine differences could confuse the issue (CRPOF, 1981, p.12; *The Times*, 31 March 1980, p.18). For example, the Westminster Inter-Faith Programme, under the auspices of the Roman Catholic Church, enjoyed considerable, if localized, vitality during the 1980s. The teaching of the Second Vatican Council on other religions was now becoming more widely known and gave a degree of authority to such activity which was hard to achieve in other less centralized denominations.[7] There were indications by the 1990s that the hitherto cautious Baptists also had a distinctive and valuable contribution to make (Weller, 1990).

Examples from Glasgow, Birmingham and London will illustrate the achievements, difficulties and potentialities of inter-faith dialogue. The Glasgow Sharing of Faiths movement was a pioneering initiative which dated from the early 1970s and stemmed from the vision of Stella Reekie, a church worker whose flat became the meeting place for a group of Christians, Baha'is, Hindus, Jews, Muslims and Sikhs. Each of the six religious groups took it in turns to lead the monthly meetings, exploring a general theme in their own way. The atmosphere was one which encouraged friendship and community. The group also made considerable efforts to promote public knowledge of all the faiths involved, notably through annual presentations and a tape-slide programme. Activities continued to flourish in the mid 1980s, although creeping institutionalization reduced potential for innovation and spontaneity. In the meantime reservations had been expressed by other Christians, who voiced disappointment that no conversions had resulted from it and were worried about its alleged syncretism. The matter was discussed in 1983 by the Church of Scotland Presbytery of Glasgow which, in effect, refused to endorse the movement (Hunter, 1985, pp.87–9, 124–5).

The group in Birmingham also developed in 1983 from the vision of one person: Andrew Wingate, an Anglican clergyman and lecturer at Queen's College in the city. In other respects it differed significantly from the movement in Glasgow: its discussions were bilateral, only between Christians and Muslims, rather than multilateral; and its organization was much more informal and inconspicuous. Wingate's published diary of the encounter shows how he side-stepped an initial tendency to aridity in discussion by establishing meaningful friendships with Muslims at an

---

[7] I am most grateful to Miss Celia Blackden and Brother Daniel Faïvre for giving me information about recent Roman Catholic inter-faith activity.

early stage. As trust grew there was an increasing readiness to move beyond stereotyped official positions and both sides in the dialogue found themselves disagreeing among themselves as well as with adherents of the other religion. There was no attempt to deny the very real differences that existed between Islam and Christianity, but the individuals involved found it possible to develop great personal respect for each other, and even, on carefully considered terms, to join together in prayer. There was also a readiness to offer more general moral support to each other when illness and personal crises affected members of the group; when Handsworth erupted in flames in the riots of September 1985; and when Muslims supported the campaign for the release of the Russian Christian poet Irina Ratushinskaya (Wingate, 1988).

A series of meetings in St John's Wood, London, in 1980 and 1981 involved larger numbers and was based on the local parish church, the Regent's Park Mosque and the synagogue opposite Lord's Cricket Ground. Several hundred people from all three faiths gathered in each place of worship in turn to explore their respective perspectives on issues such as prayer, war, and the status of women. The achievements claimed for the meetings by a Jewish writer were modest, but not insignificant:

> It would be naïve to suggest that social contact ... in an affluent London suburb is a harbinger of world peace, but ... it is reassuring that the followers of three proud religions ... could come together and amicably discuss controversial topics. To that extent our meetings have been worthwhile. They have given us a platform on which to build towards a little more tolerance and understanding in today's multi-racial and multi-religioned Britain.
>
> (*The Times*, 24 January 1981)

Christian dialogue with other religions thus took widely varying forms; it could be bilateral, trilateral, and multilateral; take place in large public meetings, in private informal conversations, in run-down inner-city areas or in prosperous suburbs; and have an agenda that was heavily theological or practical and down-to-earth. Whatever the context Christian participants often found themselves considerably influenced by the experience.[8] At the very least they acquired a deeper understanding of other faiths and the relationships between them. For some the need to explain their own beliefs to others improved self-understanding, and the encounter could even stimulate a re-examination of their own spirituality and theology (*The Times*, 24 January 1981; Wingate, 1988).

---

[8] This was of course also true of non-Christian participants, on whom see essay 2 in this volume.

A controversial development associated with such dialogue was inter-faith services. The first event of this kind had been held back in 1942 by the World Congress of Faiths in memory of its founder Sir Francis Younghusband. There had been such a service at the time of the coronation in 1953 and it was then decided by the WCF to hold one annually. In 1966 a similar service was introduced as part of the Commonwealth Day celebrations with civil and ecclesiastical sanction implied by the fact that it was attended by the Queen and held in St Martin-in-the-Fields. The proceedings consisted of a series of affirmations of faith illustrated from the sacred books of various religions. It, too, became a regular event and later moved to Westminster Abbey (Braybrooke, 1980, pp.34–6; The Times, 7 June 1966, p.11).[9] Such services appear initially to have been uncontroversial – probably being seen as isolated occurrences in a Commonwealth rather than British context – but as they became more frequent and widespread during the 1970s and 1980s the concern of some Christians grew. For those who felt that adherents of the different religions did not worship the same God, services of this kind were either farcical or syncretistic. Omission of reference to Christ in order not to offend the sensibilities of participants of other faiths was also felt to constitute unacceptable concession (Braybrooke, 1980, p.35; Cole, 1990, pp.52–7). In response to such criticism participants denied that they were being disloyal to Christ and defended the naturalness of common worship when close relationships had developed. However they accepted the need for careful planning in order to avoid unacceptable compromise of the convictions of any of the participants. One option was for those present who did not feel able to identify with the worship of another faith to regard themselves as observers rather than participants. Even some evangelicals were prepared to envisage that under carefully defined and controlled circumstances it could be appropriate for people of different faiths to pray together and be present at each other's worship (CRPOF, 1991, p.16; Evangelical Alliance, 1983, pp.35–7; Hunter, 1985, p.149; Wingate, 1988, pp.41–3).[10]

Although the debate on inter-faith worship tended to centre on special services it was clear by the 1980s that the arguments had much wider ramifications. What kind of religious observance was to be offered in

[9] See also Volume I , essay 8, for discussion of the representation, or rather the lack of it, of other religions in state ceremonial.

[10] The publication in December 1991 of an 'Open Letter to the Leadership of the Church of England' signed by over 2,000 clergy, including Anglo-Catholics as well as Evangelicals, indicated however that considerable unease remained. The Open Letter called for the prevention of 'gatherings for interfaith worship and prayer in the Church of England'. On the other hand, the signatories stressed that they desired 'to love and respect people of other faiths' and to 'respect their rights and freedoms' (The Church Times, 6 December 1991).

assemblies at schools which drew their pupils from a variety of faiths? How were marriages between adherents of two different religions to be celebrated? Accordingly the hitherto rather isolated world of enthusiasts for dialogue began to be a focus for questions crucial for the general development of Britain as a multi-religious society.[11] If there was little sign that a consensus was emerging, there was at least a growing consciousness of the issues.

In the meantime the resurgence of evangelicalism in the 1970s and 1980s ensured that a missionary attitude to other religions did not disappear and, indeed, perhaps became more prominent in the late 1980s and early 1990s. Thus in 1983 the Evangelical Alliance regarded it as axiomatic that the Christian had a 'duty ... to share the good news about Jesus with his neighbour, be he Hindu, Muslim, atheist, agnostic or simply indifferent to religion altogether' (Evangelical Alliance, 1983, p.32). Accordingly workers were employed by local churches and by organizations such as the London City Mission and the Scripture Union to engage in evangelism among minority religious groups. Such salaried agents initially tended to reflect a traditional view of other faiths as an alien environment into which missionaries were sent with the financial, moral and spiritual support of their home church. The principle was the same, whether the mission field was Rochdale or Papua New Guinea.

By the end of the period, however, while the evangelistic imperative continued, there was a rethinking of the nature of the missionary task in Britain. Now that, for city-dwellers at least, adherents of other religions were likely to be encountered regularly as neighbours, friends and workmates, the responsibility of proclaiming Christ to them, by lifestyle as well as words, was one that devolved upon every believer (Sookhdeo, 1991, p.86). The role of the full-time worker became more that of a bridge-head, facilitator and educator. Literature began to be published with a view to informing churchgoers about other faiths, and agencies began to offer training. For example Carey College in Doncaster was set up in 1985 'to serve church groups, Christian fellowships, missionary societies and those in training for full-time service, by providing a course of study to help them in their witness to Muslims' (Carey College prospectus). Such efforts were concentrated particularly on Muslims, as the largest minority religious group and the one whose own missionary endeavours tended most deeply to impinge on Christian consciousness.

At the same time there was increasing sensitivity to the religious, cultural and social circumstances of minority groups. There were certainly still those who held the view that the Christian should be content with the straightforward proclamation of the gospel and should leave results to

---

[11] See also essays 2 and 5.

providence and the conviction of the Holy Spirit. However it was widely agreed that Christians needed to understand other faiths in order to be able to communicate their own message. Moreover there needed to be an awareness of cultural differences and a consciousness of the emotional and material price that might have to be paid by converts to Christianity. Thus the London City Mission sought to recruit missionaries from the cultures that they were visiting, and its General Secretary affirmed that

> The Mission is unashamedly evangelistic in its concern but also concerned to improve the material conditions in which people are found. The manner of evangelism is, however, consistent with respect for the integrity and sincerity of men and women of other faiths or none or no other attitude would be tolerated.
>
> (Letter from Revd D.M. Whyte to the author, 10 April 1992, quoted with permission)

Some evangelicals were prepared to go further, to explore the distinction between culture and religion in both themselves and potential converts; to look for new ways of presenting Christianity that were not culturally specific; and to advocate a church of the future which would give space to a wide variety of custom and social conduct (Musk, 1989; Sookhdeo, 1991). Hence practical experience of mission as well as of dialogue was beginning to stir a re-examination of traditional Christian assumptions.[12]

As the 1990s dawned and were declared by church leaders to be a 'Decade of Evangelism', secular commentators as well as representatives of other religions questioned the legitimacy of the endeavour, regarding it as threatening and intolerant. Among Muslims, fears that 'dialogue' might in reality be a back door to evangelism were reawakened (Dhalla, 1991). There was indeed a difficult balance for Christians to strike between genuine respect and understanding for their Muslim, Hindu, Sikh and other neighbours and the maintenance of the integrity of their witness to their own faith. The issues were now being explored with increasing depth and sensitivity (Forward, 1989; Hooker and Lamb, 1986). In 1991 George Carey addressed the following words to those of other faiths during his enthronement sermon as Archbishop of Canterbury:

> The faith that I have in Christ and his good news is so important that I am compelled – necessity is laid upon me – to share it with all people. But I trust I can listen to your story and respect

---

[12] This trend was reinforced by a dawning awareness of the presence of significant numbers of Asian Christians in Britain. These represented a disturbing anomaly for those who perceived Christianity as white or Afro-Caribbean, and religion as co-extensive with culture. For evangelicals, however, their presence helped to legitimate evangelistic endeavour. See also above, p.40.

your integrity, even though having listened I may still want to present to you, as to all, the claims of my Lord.

(CRPOF, 1991, p.17)

In this clear affirmation of his own faith linked with personal good will towards those who did not share it, the Archbishop had probably come close to summing up the mood of most Christians at that time.[13] It was a state of mind which reflected the fact that the British churches were still at an early stage of their direct encounter with other religions. It remained to be seen whether the awakenings of the 1970s and the frantic explorations of the 1980s were to provide clear pointers towards the new millennium.

3 Beyond the churches

In formulating their responses to other religions the Christian churches, as in so many areas of their activities during the later twentieth century, generated large quantities of paper and discussion and it is inevitable that material of this nature has formed the primary basis for the analysis carried out in this essay. In concluding, however, it is essential for us to widen our field of vision, to move beyond the ideas and activities of theologians and churchpeople and explore briefly the more general impact of other religions on the Christian legacy in British society and culture.

The churches were indeed doing little to maintain contact with their public in this matter. In the 1960s, while John Hick was still only mildly unorthodox and the Church Assembly appeared to think that inter-faith relations were simply a matter of brewing coffee for 'overseas' students, young people were already seeking spiritual fulfilment in eastern religions. In 1980 a speaker in the General Synod pointed out the challenge this presented for the Church:

> They go to India in search rather than to the parish church – to the transcendental meditation, to the Divine Light, to Hari Khrishna, to the Moonies, to find enlightenment and joy. If only we were equipped and obviously ready to offer instruction in meditation and prayer, some of them, I believe, would turn to us. They know or see or hear men of Islam praying several times a

[13] In March 1992 Carey developed his position, in declining to become Patron of the Church's Ministry among the Jews. He affirmed his commitment to evangelism, but acknowledged another commitment 'to do all in my power to encourage trust and friendship between the different faith communities in our land' (*The Church Times*, 13 March 1992).

day, and of Zen and Buddhist meditation. How good it would be if they knew these things were possible and available in the Church of England.

(GS, 11, 1980, p.816)

There were indications by 1990 that the churches were beginning to meet some of these needs through an enhanced interest in Christian meditation, retreats, spiritual self-discovery, and the like. The ecstatic tendencies of the charismatic movement could also be interpreted in a similar light. Nevertheless the impression remained that there was a significant grass-roots constituency which had little patience with the underlying conservatism of official Christianity.

For some this searching for spiritual satisfaction found its goal in conversion to another major faith, most frequently Islam or Buddhism. These two religions are, apart from Christianity itself, the ones which possess the most developed sense of themselves as universally significant for humankind and hence consciously endeavour to gain converts. Islam proved attractive to some from a Christian background because of the stark simplicity of its core theological beliefs, its disciplined spirituality and its moral clarity. Conversion could be a reaction to certain negative experiences and perceptions of Christianity (Wingate, 1988, pp.9–10).

Buddhism has been notably successful in establishing a presence in Britain without the advantage of the large-scale immigration which created the Hindu, Muslim and Sikh communities in their late twentieth-century forms. It had a strong appeal to native Britons. Indeed the absence of more than a small number of immigrant adherents may have been a positive advantage to British Buddhists in freeing them from the latent racialism and cultural distance that have constrained responses to other faiths. There is no viable method of enumerating converts to Buddhism (or Islam), but the scale of activity indicates that they must number many thousands. Seventy Buddhist groups were formed between 1969 and 1985; in 1983 over twelve thousand people went on Buddhist retreats; in 1982 the Friends of the Western Buddhist Order claimed an overall membership of over a hundred thousand, even though many of these were probably only very loosely affiliated. Monastic centres, the heart of Buddhist practice, were set up in the countryside, from Chithurst in Sussex to Lockerbie in Dumfriesshire, and attracted many visitors. Buddhism had an appeal to those who sought a world-denying asceticism, but also was able to offer a this-worldly religion which affirmed material objectives and had a significant attraction for the prosperous educated young who had become disenchanted with Christianity (Green, 1989; Knott, 1988, pp.144–5; The Times Saturday Review, 8 February 1992).

There were other less direct routes towards accommodation with other religions. As was shown in essay 7 in Volume I, the New Religious

Movements, which during the 1970s enjoyed considerable prominence, albeit limited numerical success, were in some cases substantially indebted to Buddhism, Hinduism or Islam. There was also a growth in the popularity of the techniques of transcendental meditation and yoga, both deriving from aspects of Eastern spirituality. In the 1980s these trends lost some momentum, but the decade saw the rapid development of that loose association of groups, therapies and theologies labelled as the 'New Age' movement. Here, too, there was evidence of the assimilation of religious ideas from a variety of traditional sources. The Green movement too, in its search for ecologically sound spiritualities, showed a considerable theological eclecticism (Cole, 1990). Assorted religious ideas were diffused into popular consciousness; belief in reincarnation, very much an eastern rather than western concept, gained ground; while schoolchildren, in practice at the spearhead of inter-religious encounter, found themselves celebrating the festivals of diverse creeds.

In considering the implications of such developments, which are of considerable significance for the future of religion in Britain in the 1990s and beyond, one moves well beyond the particular themes examined in this essay. However this broader context brings into clearer relief the complexity of the dilemmas facing the organized churches which have been our primary focus here. As the processes of theological reassessment, personal encounter, organized dialogue and missionary endeavour gradually gained pace, there was an impression that events and cultural processes were moving ahead much faster. There were signs that popular religious consciousness was coming to represent not so much a universe but a supermarket of faiths and ideologies.

This analysis raises the perennial counter-factual question of 'But what else could Christians have done?' There are no obvious answers to this, except to underline the points made above about the slow pace of activity of any kind in the 1960s and early 1970s, which certainly weakened the credibility of the position of the churches in a multi-religious society. Other responses to this rhetorical question will tend to revert quickly to theological presuppositions, in pointing either to the missed opportunities for evangelism, or the failure to countenance a radical reconstruction of belief. For the student of religion, however, the developments of the 1970s and the 1980s raised the ironic speculation that there was now emerging a new kind of confrontation between a changing but still essentially traditional official Christianity, and a popular religiosity gaining renewed vigour from just that kind of indiscriminate syncretism which all parties in the churches found a rare unity in rejecting.

Bibliography

The following abbreviations have been used in the text:

CA   Church Assembly [of the Church of England], *Report of Proceedings*, 1945–70.

GS   General Synod [of the Church of England], *Report of Proceedings*, 1970– .

ABBOTT, W.M. (1967) *The Documents of Vatican II*, Geoffrey Chapman, London.

ANDERSON, N. (1970) *Christianity and Comparative Religion*, Inter-Varsity Press, London, republished as:

(1984) *Christianity and World Religions: the challenge of pluralism*, Inter-Varsity Press, Leicester.

BRAYBROOKE, M. (1980) *Inter-Faith Organizations, 1893–1979: an historical directory*, The Edwin Mellen Press, New York.

(1991) *Children of One God: a history of the Council of Christians and Jews*, London, Valentine Mitchell.

COLE, M. et al. (1990) *What is the New Age?* Hodder and Stoughton, London.

COMMITTEE FOR RELATIONS WITH PEOPLE OF OTHER FAITHS (1981) *Relations with People of Other Faiths: guidelines on dialogue*, British Council of Churches, London, republished as:

(1991) *In Good Faith: the four principles of interfaith dialogue: a brief guide for the churches*, Council of Churches for Britain and Ireland, London.

D'COSTA, G. (1984) 'John Hick's Copernican Revolution: ten years after', *New Blackfriars*, 65, pp.323–31.

(1985) 'Bibliography: Christian attitudes towards other religions', *The Modern Churchman*, 17, pp.37–44.

(1986) *Theology and Religious Pluralism: the challenge of other religions*, Basil Blackwell, Oxford.

(1987) *John Hick's Theology of Religions: a critical evaluation*, University Press of America, Lanham.

(1990) '"Extra ecclesiam nulla salus" revisited' in Hamnett, I. (ed.).

DHALLA, M. (1991) 'Motivated by "dialogue"', *The Muslim News*, 20 December 1991.

DILLISTONE, F.W. (1980) *Into All the World: a biography of Max Warren*, Hodder and Stoughton, London.

EVANGELICAL ALLIANCE (1983) *Christianity and Other Faiths: an evangelical contribution to our multi-faith society*, Paternoster, Exeter.

FORWARD, M. (ed.) (1989) *God of All faith: discerning God's presence in a multi-faith society*, The Methodist Church Home Mission Division, London.

GREEN, D. (1989) 'Buddhism in Britain: "Skilful Means" or Selling Out?', in Badham, P. (ed.) *Religion, State and Society in Modern Britain*, Edwin Mellen Press, Lampeter.

HAMNETT, I. (ed.) (1990) *Religious Pluralism and Unbelief*, Routledge, London.

HASTINGS, A. (1986) *A History of English Christianity 1920–1985*, Collins, London.

HICK, J. (1977) *God and the Universe of Faiths*, Collins, Glasgow (first published 1973, Macmillan, London).

(1980) *God Has Many Names: Britain's new religious pluralism*, Macmillan, London.

(1985) *Problems of Religious Pluralism*, Macmillan, London.

HOOKER, R. and LAMB, C. (1986) *Love the Stranger: ministry in multi-faith areas*, SPCK, London.

HUNTER, A.G. (1985) *Christianity and Other Faiths in Britain*, SCM, London.

Hymns Ancient and Modern for Use in the Services of the Church (1909 historical edn), William Clowes, London.

INTER-FAITH NETWORK FOR THE UK (1991) *Statement of Inter-Religious Relations in Britain*, IFN, London.

JENKINS, D.E. (1990) *Still Living with Questions*, SCM, London.

KNITTER, P.F. (1985) *No Other Name? a critical survey of Christian attitudes toward the world religions*, SCM, London.

KNOTT, K. (1988) 'Other Major Religious Traditions', in Thomas, T. (ed.) *The British: their religious beliefs and practices 1800–1986*, Routledge, London.

KÜNG, H. (1976) *On being a Christian*, Collins, London.

LAMB, C. (1985) *Belief in a Mixed Society*, Lion, Tring.

LANGLEY, M.S. (1982) 'The Challenge of the Religions', in Davies, R. (ed.) *The Testing of the Churches 1932–1982*, Epworth, London.

MAW, M. (1990) *Visions of India: fulfilment theology, the Aryan Race Theory and the work of British Protestant missionaries in Victorian India*, Verlag Peter Lang, Frankfurt am Main.

MUSK, B.A. (1989) *The Unseen Face of Islam: sharing the gospel with ordinary Muslims*, MARC, Eastbourne.

NEILL, S. (1961) *Christian Faith and Other Faiths: the Christian dialogue with other religions*, Oxford University Press, London.

NEWBIGIN, L. (1969) *The Finality of Christ*, SCM, London.

(1977) 'The Basis, Purpose and Manner of Inter-faith Dialogue', *Scottish Journal of Theology*, 30, pp.253–70.

(1985) *Unfinished Agenda: an autobiography*, SPCK, London.

RACE, A. (1983) *Christians and Religious Pluralism: patterns in the Christian theology of religions*, SCM, London.

SHARPE, E.J. (1977) *Faith Meets Faith: some Christian attitudes to Hinduism in the nineteenth and twentieth centuries*, SCM, London.

SHEPPARD, D. (1983) *Bias to the Poor*, Hodder and Stoughton, London.

SMITH, D.H. (1958) 'A Critique of Foreign Missions', *The Modern Churchman*, vol. II, no. 2, pp.74–84.

SOOKHDEO, P. (ed.) (1979) *Jesus Christ the only Way: Christian Responsibility in a Multicultural Society*, Paternoster Press, Exeter.

(ed.) (1991) *Sharing the Good News: the gospel and your Asian neighbours*, Scripture Union, London.

STOTT, J. (1975) *Christian Mission in the Modern World*, Falcon, London.

SUGDEN, C. (1985) *Christ's Exclusive Claims and Inter-Faith Dialogue*, Grove Books, Bramcote.

TAYLOR, J.V. (1980) 'The Theological Basis of Interfaith Dialogue', in Hick, J. and Hebblethwaite, B. (eds) *Christianity and other Religions*, Collins, Glasgow.

THOMAS, T. (1988) 'The Impact of Other Religions', in Parsons, G. (ed.) *Religion in Victorian Britain, Volume II: Controversies*, pp.280–98, Manchester University Press, Manchester.

WARD, K. (1991) *A Vision to Pursue: beyond the crisis in Christianity*, SCM, London.

WARREN, M.A.C. (1963) General Introduction to 'The Christian Presence' series, in Taylor, J.V. (ed.) *The Primal Vision*, SCM, London.

(1975) 'The uniqueness of Christ', *The Modern Churchman*, 18, pp.55–66.

WELLER, P. (1990) 'Freedom and Witness in a Multi-Religious Society: a Baptist perspective,' *Baptist Quarterly*, 33, pp.252–64, 302–15.

WINGATE, A. (1988) *Encounter in the Spirit: Muslim–Christian dialogue in practice*, World Council of Churches, Geneva.

2

BRITAIN'S CHANGING FAITHS: ADAPTATION IN A NEW ENVIRONMENT

by George Chryssides

A Sikh being booked for not wearing a crash helmet on arrival at court in Bedford, 15 August 1973. Photo: Syndication International/Hulton Deutsch.

'How shall we sing the Lord's song in a strange land?' asked the psalmist when the Israelites were exiled in Babylon (Psalm 137). At first appearance there may not seem to be any obvious problem of continuing to practise the religion of one's choice in an alien environment. Yet when a religion migrates from one culture to another, quite radical changes often occur. Anyone who is at all familiar with Buddhism, for example, cannot fail to observe that when Buddhism moved to countries such as Tibet, China and Japan, it assumed a form that was radically different from the traditional Theravada Buddhism which had been practised in countries such as Sri Lanka, Myanmar (formerly Burma) and Thailand. Did the first Tibetan Buddhists fail to notice the plethora of deities, esoteric rituals and supernatural beings which were introduced into Buddhism's world view? Have the Nichiren Shoshu Buddhists who emerged in Japan and spread their message worldwide failed to notice that their version of Buddhism appears to encourage the satisfaction of material desires rather than their elimination?

Surprising as it may seem, such radical departures are probably largely unnoticed by the host community. One might compare the phenomenon of religious adaptation with what often happens when a work of art is copied or forged. The copy may look identical to the generation in whose time it was copied, but with hindsight copying is more readily detected. This is because a generation has its own sets of conventions and expectations, to which it is so close and so attached that much of the time it is not even apparent what these conventions and presuppositions actually are. A similar phenomenon occurs when religious migration takes place: the new host culture often does not recognize that it is superimposing its own ways of seeing the world on the incoming religion. Those who are being asked to embrace the new immigrant religion for the first time may be unfamiliar with that religion and not understand even its fundamental teaching. And it is often unclear whether an indigenous practice is compatible with the incoming religion, whether it is fully religious or partly cultural or, indeed, whether it might be possible to follow the old and new religious paths simultaneously.

Some changes may occur out of sheer necessity when a host culture does not provide an easy means for the immigrant religion to enact its practices. One obvious example in the early years of immigration to Britain was the virtual absence of sacred buildings for Hindus, Buddhists, Muslims and Sikhs to practise their devotional activities. How acceptable was it for followers of these religious traditions to use Christian premises, or to set aside an area in someone's home for congregational worship? Another example is health care: what should happen when, say, a Muslim is admitted to hospital and finds that the prescribed facilities for washing are unavailable, or that a male doctor attempts to examine a Muslim woman? In situations like these, any religion is faced with the problem of distinguishing between what is fundamental to that faith, and hence non-negotiable, and what is peripheral and can legitimately be discarded when cultural conditions are inconducive.

There are at least three main areas in which members of immigrant religions are faced with problems of adaptation. First there is the situation in which adherents of incoming faiths have to depend on the indigenous population who, in Britain, are generally either Christian or else belong to what John Wolffe calls the 'silent majority' (see Volume I, essay 8), whose beliefs may or may not merit the title 'religious', but whose lifestyle is generally shaped by a Christian heritage. Examples of ways in which members of incoming faiths may have to rely on the indigenous population include medical treatment and counselling, as well as for help in renting and buying premises, and obtaining relevant planning permission.

The second problem of adaptation concerns the prescribed religious requirements and rites of passage, which are discussed in some detail in Volume I, essays 3, 4 and 5. While certain details of ritual activities may be negotiable (such as the precise times of Islamic prayer), by no means all aspects of religious ceremonies can be omitted or adapted, and hence it is not surprising that difficulties have arisen, particularly where a British law – which in all probability did not envisage infringements of citizens' religious freedom – conflicts with religious practices. One example of this relates to the Muslim custom of burying bodies without coffins – a practice that is normally illegal in Britain, and for which Muslims in Bradford have successfully fought for permission.

The third main problem immigrant religions face is discrimination. There are situations where the physical appearance of religious immigrants makes their allegiance obvious. Colour may be a possible, although by no means a reliable, indicator that a man or woman comes from a Hindu, Muslim or Sikh background, and this in itself has proved to be a contributory factor to religious as well as racial prejudice. However, in addition to colour, certain religious groups – most notably Sikhs, but also many Muslims – are readily identifiable by their dress. As discussed in Volume I, this can sometimes raise the question of whether Sikhs or Muslims should remove the symbols of their religious identity (such as the turban in the case of the Sikhs) in order to avoid possible discrimination, for example, when seeking employment, for although it is illegal for an employer to discriminate against a candidate on the grounds of ethnic group, religious discrimination is not illegal.

Three possible outcomes for an immigrant religion in an alien environment can be identified. The first is *apostasy*: faced with a competing culture and ideology, practitioners of an incoming faith may simply decide to abandon it and 'do as the Romans do'. The second outcome is that the incoming faith can adapt, retaining whatever it regards as essential, but abandoning the peripheral trappings and taking on board elements from the prevailing culture, thus finding a slightly new form of expression. Scholars often call this process *accommodation*. The third possible outcome is that an immigrant religion can insist on retaining its fully distinctive identity, perhaps even exaggerating it, making it plain that it will stand firm amid any opposition from a potentially alien environment. I have called this response *renewed vigour.*

The dividing line between these three responses is, of course, somewhat nebulous. Few, if any, members of a religion would claim to follow it perfectly, and hence what counts as apostasy for one person may be accommodation for another. Yet it is important to recognize a difference between the aspirant who occasionally yields to temptation and regrets it, and someone who deliberately renounces his or her former faith. One Sikh who was recently converted to Christianity by the controversial evangelist Morris Cerullo was asked to remove his turban and the khalsa symbols, and did so in the midst of the auditorium – a case of apostasy *par excellence.* By contrast, the Hindu who acknowledges that Jesus Christ is yet another *avatar* of Vishnu provides an example of accommodation. The Sikh who removes his turban in order to improve his chances of employment may or may not be an apostate: much depends on whether he continues to practise his faith in other respects, how he justifies his action (if he can), and – most importantly – how his action is regarded by the rest of the Sikh community.

In the following discussion I propose to consider, first, attitudes of the dominant religion – Christianity – to immigrant faiths, and the extent to which it enabled other faiths to find a physical foothold in Britain. Secondly, I shall focus on the social and political institutions in Britain that have necessitated a reaction from non-indigenous religious groups. Thirdly, I shall highlight the phenomenon of western conversion to 'non-Christian' faiths, giving special attention to Buddhism and to new religious movements. Finally, I shall focus on two (as yet) unresolved problems in British religious pluralism: education and blasphemy.

1 Maintaining public worship

The obvious initial hurdle for an immigrant faith community is to ensure that public worship is able to continue in its new environment. Since Sunday has been the traditional British public holiday, most incoming religions have made the decision to use Sunday for public worship, even though for Hindus, Buddhists and Sikhs there was no specific day of the week in which congregational worship was obligatory. However, in Islam we find renewed vigour rather than adaptation: in all mosques the tradition of observing the Friday noontime prayers remains, even though employment may make it difficult for some of the faithful to attend.

Worship, however, demands a sacred place as well as a sacred time, and hence the problem of finding premises in which to conduct congregational worship. Perhaps ironically, the influx of immigrants in the 1960s and 1970s coincided with the decline of organized Christianity. Churches which were once thriving were losing members and around the country churches were merging or even closing. The opportunities for other faiths were obvious: could they buy obsolete church premises, or could they rent parts of them to help eke out depleting church funds?

The 'sacred space' that was needed by Britain's newly domiciled faiths was therefore dependent to a significant degree on the attitudes of the Christian churches. In a survey commissioned by the British Council of Churches (1973), Ann Holmes surveyed five mainstream denominations (Church of England, Baptist, Congregationalist,[1] Methodist and Roman Catholic) in multi-ethnic, multi-faith Bradford, Derby and Lambeth, about their attitudes to alternative uses of church premises. This survey spanned possible secular uses of church premises (for social and political events) as well as issues of letting and selling premises to religious communities other than mainstream Christian ones. On the whole, Holmes' findings indicated a reasonably positive attitude to the letting of church halls to other faith communities. Holmes enquired how happy individual congregations would be about letting church halls for various hypothetical functions. In the following summary of her findings, I have not given details of the breakdown by denomination, but there do not appear to have been significant variations.[2]

---

[1] Much of the data were researched prior to the Presbyterian–Congregationalist union of 1972 – hence the reference to Congregationalist in this context.

[2] I have translated Holmes' data into percentages for ease of comparison. Holmes presents the data in raw form.

	Christian Aid funded meetings on local play facilities	West Indian Pente-costalist youth rally	West Indian youth disco	Greek Orthodox instruc-tion	Sikh social gathering	Hindu marriage ceremony	Muslim religious festival	Com-munist Party meeting	National Front meeting	Seventh Day Adventist worship on eve of Passover
Very happy	60.9	31.2	28.3	27.6	27.0	19.4	14.4	9.8	7.3	1.7
Happy	27.7	33.6	31.7	36.2	26.2	24.2	24.2	14.8	8.9	9.4
Fairly happy	5.5	24.0	11.7	18.1	19.0	18.5	18.4	13.1	9.7	16.2
Unhappy	2.3	5.6	16.7	8.6	15.1	15.3	15.2	13.1	27.4	33.3
Very unhappy	1.6	5.6	11.7	9.5	12.7	22.6	28.0	31.1	46.8	39.3

Asked how they would view the sale of redundant church premises variously for housing, community centres, commercial firms, local authorities, other Christian denominations, and other faith communities, responses were as follows.

	Housing	Community centre	Local authority	Commercial firm	Other Christian denomination	Other faith community
Very happy	41.9	38.2	19.2	11.6	29.9	15.0
Happy	33.9	35.0	25.8	21.5	41.9	26.7
Fairly happy	16.1	20.3	23.2	24.0	17.9	20.0
Unhappy	4.0	3.3	21.7	26.4	5.1	20.8
Very unhappy	4.0	3.3	10.0	16.6	5.1	17.5

Despite the divergence of opinion among mainstream Christians on the issues of renting and selling, there was sufficient support for the idea to enable members of other faiths to make use of church buildings for their own devotional activities.

Lending out the sanctuary area of a church was a greater problem. Holmes did not collect statistical data on this topic because many churches cannot lend out sanctuary areas: in most cases Trust Deeds have designated sanctuaries for Christian worship only. In any case, times of worship in other faith communities often coincided with those of Christians. The physical environment of churches was often unsuitable for non-Christian use too, with their prominent Christian symbols such as crosses and stained glass windows depicting biblical scenes, and – more often than not – with fixed pews instead of an open floor space, which is much more congenial to virtually all other faith communities. One Buddhist group confided to me recently that they had been allowed to use the sanctuary area of a church for meditation until the minister discovered that their practice was to remove the cross from the altar and replace it with a buddha rupa (an image of the Buddha). The minister would not allow the central image of Christianity to be displaced by the Buddha, and – conversely – the Buddhist group felt it inappropriate to meditate in front of a Christian cross.

Generally, purchasing premises has been the preferred option for religious groups, because of the autonomy this provides. When finances have permitted, certain groups have been able to construct their own purpose-built sanctuaries, such as the London Central Mosque in Regent's Park (sponsored by a number of Muslim governments to the tune of £6 million) and the elaborately designed Buddhapadipa Temple in Wimbledon which was funded by the Thai government and people. Both these buildings provide fine examples of Muslim and Buddhist architecture respectively, enhancing London's cultural diversity. However, not all new religious architecture relied on the support of foreign governments: the Birmingham and Cardiff mosques are impressive examples of local sponsorship. Other communities have had to settle for more modest projects, partly because of financial constraints, and partly because in certain areas minority religious communities are thinly spread.

Two effects of these factors can be seen. First, many minority religious communities have been obliged to buy premises from mainstream churches, and adapt them as they are obviously not purpose-built, and secondly these religious communities – and particularly the Hindus – have been prepared to be more ecumenical in the variety of *bhakti* (devotional) cults which are represented in temples in Britain. Whereas in India a Hindu sect very clearly imposes its identity on a temple, defining it as Vaishnavite, Saivite, Kali, or whatever, by contrast it is quite common to find Hindu temples in Britain representing a large variety of Hindu traditions. One example is the Bhawan Shree Geeta Hindu Temple in Birmingham, the first in the West Midlands, where Krishna and Radha form the main focus, and to whom aarti is offered daily. Yet the same temple contains images of Durga (to whom Durga Puja is offered in the evening), Ganesha (the 'elephant god' and son of Shiva), a large painting of Jalaram Baba (a modern Indian guru), and a large lingam and yoni – the symbols of Shiva.

Not all religious establishments are able to be quite as ecumenical as this Hindu community. Although the larger purpose-built mosques in Britain claim to accommodate both the Sunni and Shi'ite Muslim communities, those smaller mosques which are adapted from private residences tend to represent very specific Muslim groups. There are limits to ecumenism too: several Sikh gurdwaras attract congregations on the basis of caste (see Volume I, essay 5, pp.232–3); the Ahmadiyyah have not been accepted by mainstream Islamic communities, and are thus obliged to use their own mosque in South London. Although some Buddhist groups claim to span all traditions, westerners who have converted to Buddhism have generally converted to one very specific Buddhist tradition (such as Theravada, Tibetan, Nichiren or Zen) and prefer to follow that particular tradition rather than dilute it with others (Oliver, 1979).

Where premises were not originally designed with a faith community in mind, the results can sometimes be a compromise, and at other times interesting adaptation. A British mosque, established in a former Christian building or in a set of terraced houses, may lack the traditional minaret and layout associated with Islam. The Jain community in Leicester recently purchased a disused church building which they then redesigned as a temple, a set of shrine rooms in various Jain traditions, and a meeting hall. The Christian stained glass was removed, and replaced with stained glass pictures of scenes from the life of Mahavira. Stained glass, of course, has never been part of a traditional Jina-bhavana, which is much more likely to use lamps, mirrors and images of the various Jain *tirthankars* (enlightened beings who appear at various times in human history).

2 Immigrant religions and social institutions

As well as having to accommodate to British legal requirements, immigrant religious communities have been confronted by the social institutions of Britain. When immigrants have on occasion been accused of 'not integrating', the truth of the matter has often been that they have merely been insisting on practising their own religions faithfully. When one reflects that the centre of British life is often the parish church or the local pub, it is obvious that the former does not provide a plausible focus for those who do not subscribe to Christianity, and the latter excludes Muslims, Baha'is, and those Hindus who do not drink alcohol. Within the educational system, some Muslim pupils believe they are faced with a choice between being disloyal to Islam – for example, by participating in religious education lessons, or by taking part in music or drama – or else becoming a very noticeable minority which continues to practise its religion faithfully (Gilani, 1992, pp.14–22).

Of all the things that emphasize distinctions between individuals, dress is undoubtedly one of the most obvious. The Sikhs' problems of maintaining the wearing of the turban and the carrying of the *kirpan* (dagger), while complying with the law and securing employment was discussed in Volume I, pages 228–31. Generally speaking, there is no unanimity in attitude to traditional dress. In his study for the Bradford Race Relations Research Unit, Ramindar Singh reports (1992, p.32) that there has been a noticeable return to the wearing of the turban ('renewed vigour') and to keeping one's hair uncut, and he attributes this to several factors: permission to wear a turban granted by public organizations such as bus companies has facilitated the practice; and the periodic arrival of *sants* – holy men – from the Punjab has encouraged the more traditional Sikhs to maintain the practice, or indeed to return to it if they have been apostate.

However, some Sikhs, known as *sahejdharis*, maintain emphatically that turbans and beards do not constitute essential elements of Sikh practice (Ramindar Singh, 1992, p.32). One young Sikh to whom I recently spoke explained that, in his opinion, Guru Gobind Singh's instruction to don the five khalsa symbols was not a command that was binding on all Sikhs in every place and at every time. On the contrary, he argued, the khalsa symbols were specifically intended for use in military activities and were not intended for civil life during peacetime. Here we have an example of religious accommodation which is not simply a matter for regret, but which is legitimated by a rationale emanating from the tradition itself. Thus religious accommodation can cause supporters to reappraise their own tradition.

A similar example is that of the *burqa* (veil) worn by Muslim women. The Qur'an states that women should dress modestly, wear a veil, and suitably cover their bodies except in the presence of their immediate family (Qur'an, XXIV: 31). This bears the inevitable implication that a female Muslim patient will not readily undress to be examined by a male doctor, and that a Muslim girl or boy may not wish to use a communal shower and changing room for physical education at school. What constitutes a 'public' situation, however, can be subject to some interpretation. A veil may not be required at all in a small village in an Islamic country where almost everyone is a member of an extended family. By contrast, in Britain it is almost inevitable that we meet 'strangers' as soon as we open our front door. Hence in a society in which women are subjected to lascivious glances, sexual innuendo, and being 'chatted up', a Muslim woman may with good reason feel a greater need to hide her features than in her country of origin (Gilani, 1992, p.19). For some this entails the wearing of the veil and a maxi-skirt, while for others the *shalwar* (Asian-style trousers) provide the means of compliance (McDermott and Ahsan, 1980, p.47).

Some features of immigrant religion do not seem at first to fit in with western society. How, for example, is it possible to observe caste distinctions in Britain? One might expect that, although Hinduism has proved to be capable of being imported, the same would not be true of caste. But although many Hindus are not particularly conscious of caste, underneath the surface the caste system among British Hindus survives.

Traditionally the notion of caste in India has been tied to three concepts: occupational status, marriage and commensality (the rules governing eating between restricted kin groups) (Basham, 1959, p.245; Weightman, 1978, p.13). Although it has been shown that minor alterations in caste status are possible (for example, by arranging a particularly favourable marriage or by assuming a vegetarian diet), a change of occupation does not secure an automatic elevation in caste. Caste is determined by family tradition, not by individual career advancement; hence a *chamar* (a member of the leather-working caste) who succeeds in becoming a doctor still remains low in the caste hierarchy. Since contact with low castes is considered polluting to those who are higher up the caste ladder, Hindus in Britain who come from a relatively high-caste background can be 'polluted' by contact with those of low-caste status. The inevitable consequence is that high-caste Hindus can consider themselves polluted by food from a low-caste shopkeeper or by having their hair cut by a low-caste barber. The higher castes are therefore prone to avoid low-caste merchants, thus depriving them of their means of livelihood; and the low-caste business person may seek to conceal his or her caste status.

Considerations of caste entering in to Hindu marriages in Britain are difficult to avoid. Typically Hindu marriages are arranged by parents, most of whom are, in the early 1990s, first-generation immigrants who have a background of caste and are likely to have conservative attitudes on such matters. Although there is evidence that the second generation is less prone to arranged marriages (Ramindar Singh, 1992, p.65), family pressure is strong. An Indian student, whose marriage had recently been arranged by parents, explained to me that she did not consider 'going it alone' by finding her own marriage partner to be a viable option. Hindu marriage is more than a marriage of two individuals: it is a union of two families, and if her husband were to ill-treat her, the family would intervene on her behalf. But, if she married in western style, her family would not take her back if she left her husband. Furthermore, any mismatching of caste in an arranged British marriage would have repercussions in the Indian villages from which the respective families had come. Endogamy is an important feature in determining caste status, and hence the marriages that are arranged in Britain bear implications for each families' caste status in India.

3 Legal and political institutions

Marriage rituals have presented less serious difficulties than the problems of death and dying (see the discussion of this with relevance to Hinduism in Volume I, essay 4, pp.199–201). However, life in Britain has necessitated a number of adjustments regarding marriage (Menski, 1991). In India it is the Hindu religious ceremony that defines whether people are married rather than the action of legalizing marriage in the presence of a registrar. In the early days of their settlement in Britain, it was not possible for immigrant religions to solemnize marriages in temples, mosques or gurdwaras, since these buildings were not then formally registered as places of public worship. After registration, an official registrar needed to be present until such time as an authorized person within the temple or mosque was designated to act on his or her behalf. Although Hindus, Muslims and Sikhs are now afforded the same rights of solemnizing marriages as Christian Nonconformists, initially the simplest way of legalizing a religious marriage was to participate in two ceremonies – one in the temple or mosque, the other at the registry office. Numerous Asian immigrants, however, did not undergo the civil as well as the religious ceremony, occasionally with serious results. If the husband subsequently abandoned his wife, for example, she was left with no redress in law. Increasingly, therefore, the British legal requirements have become incorporated into the religious marriage rituals.

As far as the religious ceremony itself is concerned, Hinduism has traditionally proved to be flexible about the details. If certain ritual ingredients cannot be obtained (such as a particular type of flower), the presiding priest has prescribed an appropriate substitute. Although it has been the practice in India to make astrological calculations so that a wedding takes place on an auspicious day, some couples prefer simply to marry at a convenient time for themselves instead. (This practice, however, is not always approved of by the priest or older relatives.) There are, of course, certain aspects that are almost invariably present, such as the customary clockwise circumambulation of fire and the ritual taking of seven steps by the bridegroom and bride, but the traditional flexibility of the Hindu wedding ceremony makes it possible for the details to be negotiated between the marriage partners and the priest.

Just as marriage can be defined in terms of a religious rather than a civil or legal ceremony, the same can be true of divorce. A case recently occurred in which a Muslim woman obtained a civil divorce, valid in English law, but subsequently claimed that her husband, at the time of the divorce, did not use the required Islamic formula for divorcing her: he failed to pronounce the statutory words, 'I divorce you', three times. The husband, equally, stated that he regretted the civil divorce, claiming that he only invoked British law 'to give her a fright', and that both partners now wanted a reconciliation.

How can one settle the question of whether a divorce is valid in Islamic law in a country where the law courts can only pass judgement on matters of British law? The only way to accomplish this is to set up ad hoc *shari'ah* courts which are deemed to be competent to hear such cases, and which can provide a *fatwa* (judgement). Various Muslim bodies in Britain will provide this service: the Muslim College in London, for example, can set up an appropriate committee for such purposes. There is, however, no nationally recognized body capable of resolving such issues, or of representing and promoting the interests of the Muslim community as a whole. Organizations such as the Union of Muslim Organizations of Great Britain and Eire and the British Council of Imans and Mosques have not succeeded in performing this function, and the Muslim Parliament, inaugurated by Dr Kalim Siddiqi, has the support of only a minority of Muslims (see Volume I, essay 3, p.149).

The problem of divorce highlights a more general problem for Muslims. The Muslim religion has traditionally been inseparable from ethics, law and government. The notion of practising Islam in a country such as Britain which has separate secular social and legal institutions is, for many Muslims, a contradiction in terms (Ahmed, 1992, pp.129–32; Modood, 1992). While it may be pointed out that the Muslims' situation was no different in India, from where the majority had come, none the less it was no easy task to come to terms with a secular legal system which tolerated *The Satanic Verses*, and encouraged 'permissive' morality which was often the antithesis of what the Qur'an enjoined. Although practising Islam as a complete way of life, embracing ethics, law, politics and religion, is not possible, as most Muslims would accept, none the less Muslims have closely associated their faith with governing, and many would welcome a greater opportunity to participate more actively in politics. The election of Bradford's first Muslim Lord Mayor in 1985–86 was hailed as a triumph by Britain's Muslim community, but, apart from a few local councillors, they have had little opportunity to enter political life. It might be argued that the absence of a Muslim MP is not necessarily the result of racial or religious discrimination, but the inevitable consequence of Britain's 'first past the post' system. Although it may be argued that their modest role in local politics and non-existent role in parliament is fair within the present system, some Muslims have drawn attention to the fact that members of the Upper Chamber do not gain their positions by democratic means. A senior diocesan bishop in the Church of England enjoys an automatic right to a seat in the House of Lords; but, it has been argued, in a pluralist society recognition should be given to other religious communities who are now an integral part of British life, not least of which are the Muslims. As Dr Zaki Badawi has argued:

There is another aspect which is of immense importance, namely Muslim participation in public life and in particular in the political life of this country. The Muslim community, lacking facility in the English language and often with no experience of the electoral system of government, find the public and political life of this country difficult for them to participate in. Further, the community, with its connections with the home countries still very fresh, and continuously nourished by home visits, is still fully immersed in the politics of the home countries paying little heed to the political battle in Great Britain. It is surprising that, despite the large number of Muslim voters, there are but a handful of Muslim councillors and there is not a single member of parliament. Even more astonishing is the fact that, despite the presence of hundreds of thousands of Muslim children in schools, there are few Muslim school governors. There is no doubt that a part of the blame for this state of affairs falls upon the Muslim community itself. But it must be admitted that the hostility towards immigrants, seen by the community as a common feature of the policy of the two main political parties in Britain, must act as an inhibiting factor to full participation in political life in Britain. Protestations of friendship towards people already here do little to alter the perception by the immigrant community of its status as somewhat less than full citizenship of their new country.

(Badawi, 1981, p.20)

4 *Dhabh* and *shechita*: Jews, Muslims and animal slaughter

There are more specific ways in which British politics and law appear to work against the interests of minority religions and make it necessary for them to fight for their rights. The issue of Sikhs and crash helmets was one such issue in which the minority religion won, and their right to enjoy religious freedom was supported by many of the Christian churches.

Although many Christians were sympathetic to the Sikhs' insistence on not wearing crash helmets, support for the Muslims' presumed right to enjoy *halal* meat was markedly less great. Traditionally Jews and Muslims have insisted on killing animals for food by a method known respectively as *shechita* and *dhabh*. The process requires that animals to be slaughtered are not pre-stunned by electrocution, as is normal in Britain, but have their throats slit by means of a sharp knife so that the blood drains completely from their bodies. For Jews this is required by the Torah, which states that 'you must not eat meat that has its lifeblood still in it' (Genesis 9:4). The practice of shechita gives kosher meat, while dhabh results in halal. Those who were accustomed to slaughtering animals by pre-stunning believed that shechita and dhabh were cruel and that, notwithstanding the normal rights to religious freedom, Jews and Muslims should reconsider this practice. The Royal Society for the Prevention of Cruelty to Animals lent its weight to the debate also, calling for an end to the practice. The controversy came to a head in the mid 1980s, when the Farm Animal Welfare Council (FAWC) produced a report entitled *Report on the Welfare of Livestock when Slaughtered by Religious Methods*. The report recommended that Jews and Muslims be given a three-year period in which to phase out the practice. *The Times* agreed. In an editorial on 31 July 1985, it argued:

> Hard choices had to be made when the observances of minorities ... collide with the general protective rules of society, in this case the protection of animals ... toleration cannot be absolute ... other religious communities have learned to distinguish the inessential from the essential in their ceremonies, and the Jews and Muslims among us may be requested to do no less.

The unargued assumption in the editorial was, of course, that the Jewish and Muslim methods of slaughter were peripheral to the faith – a claim that was categorically denied by both communities, and with justification. An Orthodox Jew could hardly be expected to agree that a clear command laid down in the Torah was 'peripheral', nor could a Muslim abandon something that is plainly required in the Qur'an (II: 173; V: 3). 'Accommodation' was therefore out of the question, and renewed vigour remained the only possible response, short of apostasy. In their defence, Jews and Muslims contended that shechita and dhabh were not only required by their respective faiths, but that the practice was not actually cruel to animals, only unsightly. The Jews in particular pointed out that theirs was a tradition of kindness to animals, not cruelty: from ancient times onwards they had tried to ensure that owners gave their animals sufficient rest from work. Both Jews and Muslims argued that it was traditional British methods of slaughter that were cruel: in pre-stunning (the most common western method) animals are sometimes rendered physically immobile, although with full consciousness and sensation. The application of a sharp knife in shechita and dhabh, by contrast, ensures that no pain is felt: the wound inflicted is clean, and the loss of blood causes the animal to lose consciousness within seconds.

The hostility to shechita and dhabh united the extreme right and left political factions within Britain. The ultra-right racist element within the country used Jewish and Muslim methods of slaughter to vindicate their antipathy towards Jews and immigrants. The ultra-left campaigners, in the form of the Animal Liberation Front, targeted kosher and halal butchers as part of their animal rights campaigning.

The FAWC Report proved to be too problematic for the British government to handle. If the government had implemented its recommendations, it could have been construed as aligning itself simultaneously with right-wing and left extremists. It would also have alienated the Jewish and Muslim populations and those members of mainstream religious organizations who supported religious freedom. In the end, the government decided to ignore the FAWC Report and do nothing, since the whole subject was too emotive for any legislation to be introduced. In spite of the attempts of the RSPCA and other animal rights groups, the subject has, at least for the meantime, been put in abeyance, and Jews and Muslims continue to practise their dietary laws.

5　First-generation converts

So far I have considered the impact of Britain on those who brought their faith from overseas and endeavoured to continue practising it. However, the substantial immigration in post-war Britain meant that the message of the accompanying religions also became available to westerners. No longer were these faiths merely intellectual pursuits to be studied in textbooks.

Some religions proved more attractive to westerners than others, Buddhism proving the most popular choice apart from Christianity. Why this should be the case must be a matter of speculation, for there has been relatively little research carried out to explain patterns of conversion. Possible reasons include the fact that Buddhism appeared to get a somewhat better press than the other traditions: Christian missionaries tended to regard it as the 'second top', being the best that the human mind was capable of producing unaided by divine grace (Almond, 1988, pp.134–5). For many westerners it was the 'religion of reason': it did not seem to demand acceptance of paradoxes such as a saviour being simultaneously divine and human; it did not require any 'leaps of faith'; it did not appear to emphasize miracles; and it was a religion of self effort, thus implying, perhaps, that one's spiritual progress was in one's own hands and that one could expect to receive the just deserts for one's actions. Added to this, it had a reasonably accessible body of written literature, both in the form of primary texts and popular writings. One exceedingly popular writer was D.T. Suzuki, the Zen master whose prolific writings soon percolated through to Britain. Another very influential figure was Christmas Humphreys, the well-known QC and late President of the Buddhist Society of Great Britain, whose popular book entitled *Buddhism*, published in 1955, brought the religion very much into the public arena.

The phenomenon of first-generation converts is significant for two reasons. Firstly, as Barker has shown (1990, pp.11–12), generally the first-generation convert has a greater enthusiasm for the newly found faith than those who have been brought to embrace it through education and upbringing; western converts are therefore more likely to add increased momentum to the immigrant religion. Secondly, westerners cannot 'snap into' radically different systems of thought: they come to their new faith with western intellectual baggage, western preconceptions and, perhaps, with traces of a former religion. The religion to which they convert is therefore not a 'pure' form (if such a thing exists) but the immigrant religion overlaid with western modes of thinking.

One fairly evident way in which Buddhism became overladen with western thinking was through the persistence of Christian-dominated westerners in asking what other faiths *believed*. In reality, Christianity is the only world religion that has continually defined itself in terms of its doctrines, but it was nevertheless inevitable that westerners, whose previous religious knowledge only extended to the Christian faith, should expect other faiths to define themselves credally too. Originally, the Buddhist 'creeds' and 'catechisms' were written abroad, as an attempt to rival the Christian missionaries; however, they can readily be found today in Buddhist *viharas* (monastic residences) throughout Britain. The best known of these Buddhist 'creeds' is Colonel Henry Steel Olcott's 'Fourteen Fundamental Buddhistic Beliefs', written in 1881 in Sri Lanka to enable Buddhists to articulate their religion more clearly. Olcott also compiled two Buddhist 'catechisms', one for adults and a simpler one for children (Chryssides, 1988a, p.140).

A more recent attempt to define a Buddhist creed was made by Christmas Humphreys (1978, chs 12–13). He produced a celebrated list of twelve tenets which he believed to be common to all Buddhists, and after the Second World War travelled to many Buddhist countries, securing the agreement of Buddhists (with the exception of those in Myanmar) that these tenets were fundamental to Buddhists worldwide.

Olcott's catechism is comprehensive. Beginning with the question of how one becomes a Buddhist, it deals with the person and history of the Buddha, the *Dharma* (teaching) which envelops the Noble Truths and the Eightfold Path, and the nature of the monastic order. Some questions seem designed to 'correct' the teachings of the Christian Bible: for example, 'Is the iniquity of the parents visited on the children?' (Subhadara Bhikshu, question 120). Such a view is described as a 'superstitious assumption'.

Others seem designed to counter popular western misconceptions of Buddhism: for instance, 'Is not the spirit and essence of the doctrine pessimistic?' (question 150). In common with Christian catechisms, much of this catechism provides proof texts giving relevant references to the Pali scriptures.

The notion of a Buddhist creed and catechism may have enabled the articulation of Buddhist doctrine, but Buddhism has never been a credal religion, and although 'right view' is the first point of the Eightfold Path, this does not involve mere intellectual assent to a set of credal statements, but a deeper recognition of the unsatisfactoriness of existence (*dukkha*) and a commitment to the Eightfold Path by which dukkha can be eliminated (*Digha Nikaya*, II: 312, in Woodward, 1973, p.9). Buddhism lays more stress on practice rather than on doctrine, and one can only be expelled from a Sangha for engaging in divergent or inappropriate practices, not for entertaining beliefs which are unpopular or 'heretical' (Gombrich, 1988, p.113). It is the 'taking of Refuge' which makes one a Buddhist; acceptance of a creed has never been a formal requirement. Historically lay Buddhists have not needed to articulate matters of doctrine: to support the Sangha by providing food for the monks was perfectly sufficient to gain merit which would secure a more favourable rebirth. While intending to fortify Buddhism, then, Olcott had set it on a different path, not only in setting it up as a credal religion like Christianity, but by endowing it with institutions such as creeds and catechisms which are more characteristically Christian.

The notion of rebutting the tenets of a competing religion gives rise to an interesting phenomenon that occurs when a religion develops alongside an alien culture. I call this phenomenon 'negative definition' (Chryssides, 1988a, pp.44-5): denials of tenets belonging to the rival religion become tenets of the religion. For example, the question of the existence of God has never been a particularly important issue to traditional Buddhists, who have been much more concerned with dukkha than with concepts of deity: neither the Four Noble Truths, the Eightfold Path, the Precepts, nor the three Marks of Existence, mention God at all. However, for some western converts to Buddhism one important attraction of the religion is that it does not demand belief in a deity which they find hard to accept. Accordingly, for movements such as the Western Buddhist Order it is almost as important to deny God's existence as it is to affirm the traditional points of the Eightfold Path (Sangharakshita, 1978, p.7; Subhuti, 1983, p.178).

Buddhist hymnody is a further innovation. Traditionally, Buddhist singing has consisted of chanting (principally mantras, scriptures, and the Three Refuges). I have not personally witnessed the use of Buddhist hymns, but one Buddhist hymnary – said to be popular in Malaysia and the USA – shows considerable Christian influence. To quote one example:

> What e'er ye sow that shall ye reap,
> Such is the Law Divine,
> Think not that thou can'st e'er escape
> The Karma which is thine.
>
> (Wee, p.49)

Notice the style of the Scottish metrical psalm, the language of the King James Version of the Bible, and an almost direct quotation from the New Testament in the first line (Galatians 6:7). Other hymns, interestingly, assume the militaristic imagery of the Christian faith: the Buddha can have 'soldiers true' who 'come like knights of old' (Wee, p.38). The effect of some of these hymns is to make Gautama the Buddha into an object of devotion like Christ – an unprecedented move within Buddhism.

Until recently, western Buddhism consisted essentially of studying the teachings and meditation. This has caused at least one more recent Buddhist group to criticize the older generation of Buddhists for taking 'their Buddhism more or less as a hobby' (Subhuti, 1983, p.5). According to the Western Buddhist Order, these Buddhists' interest in Buddhism was combined with a fairly conventional western lifestyle, in which they continued to eat meat, drink alcohol and wear furs. For example, many Western Buddhist Order members find it hard to accept that Christmas Humphreys found it possible to combine his Buddhism with being the prosecuting counsel in the Ruth Ellis trial in 1955. (Ruth Ellis was the last woman in Britain to be given the death sentence for murder.)

The Western Buddhist Order seeks to ensure that acceptance of Buddhism is combined with an appropriate lifestyle. They are staunchly vegetarian and committed to the notion of 'right livelihood'. ('Right' or 'perfect livelihood' is the fifth point of the Buddhist Noble Eightfold Path.) Men and women live in single sex communities in which strict chastity is enjoined. At the same time, the Western Buddhist Order deliberately sets out to be a new form of Buddhism, adapted for the West. Just as Buddhism has traditionally changed its character when it has transported itself from one climate to another, a new form of Buddhism, they claim, is needed in western culture. Such a fully developed form of Buddhism has still to be awaited, they contend, but in the meantime some significant adaptations can be noted. Within the Western Buddhist Order there are no monks to be seen in traditional saffron, maroon or black robes. Those who wish to commit themselves to Buddhism become ordained not as monks, but as *mitrata*. (*Mitrata* is the plural of *mitra*, meaning 'friend'.) Only the founder-leader of the Order, the Venerable Sthavira Sangharakshita has undergone traditional ordination (although Sangharakshita is rarely to be seen wearing the robe).

The Western Buddhist Order believe that the alms round is inappropriate in the West, reducing the Buddhist to a beggar, and therefore they prefer to earn income through business enterprises: mitrata have therefore formed building companies, secondhand shops, vegetarian restaurants and the like, so that they can engage in 'right livelihood' in a way that is compatible with practising Buddhism. There is less emphasis on accepting Buddhist doctrines: these, they claim, have still to find a form that is acceptable both to Buddhism and to the western mind. By contrast, the meditative life is to be pursued, and much effort is channelled into organized meditation, in communities, at retreats and in open evenings to which the public are invited (Subhuti, 1983, pp.135–47).

Not only does the Order ensure that all its members eat strictly vegetarian food: it has opened several vegetarian restaurants in major cities, thus offering practical encouragement to those who are already following a vegetarian diet, as well as drawing attention to the presumed necessity of non-violence (ahimsa) to animal life. Although the Order regards strict vegetarianism as part of Buddhist ethics, vegetarianism is in fact a western adaptation of Buddhism. For the Buddhist who has adopted the traditional precepts, the prohibition on the taking of life means literally what it says: one does not kill any living being, whether it be human, animal or insect. By contrast, the sixth Judaeo–Christian commandment, 'You shall not kill', has typically been held to be compatible even with the taking of human life under certain circumstances, being essentially a prohibition on murder. Typically, westerners have thought that the more stringent demands made by Buddhists' respect for life make a case for not consuming animal meat, and hence many western Buddhists have tended to be vegetarian.

Yet vegetarianism has seldom been practised by the traditional Sangha in the East. The monk on his alms round is expected to eat whatever is given to him, whether it is vegetable or animal. There is only one constraint: if the monk sees, hears or suspects that an animal has been killed specially for him, then he must refuse (Chryssides, 1988a, p.50; Gombrich, 1988, p.101). Many western Buddhists are familiar with the ideas of American Zen Roshi Philip Kapleau, who argues that the Buddha could not have permitted meat-eating, since animals are slaughtered for whoever eats them, and that meat-eaters are indirectly responsible for the slaughter of animals, thus violating the First Precept (Kapleau, 1983, p.20). Kapleau's argument has force, but his case is conducted by means of a singularly western approach to morality.

If western Buddhism has more thorough-going respect for life than traditional eastern Buddhism, the reason lies in the different ways of thinking about morality. Western morality is 'inferential' – that is to say, it involves giving reasons, drawing out inferences, universalizing its prescriptions (for example, 'What if everyone acted like that?'). By contrast, Buddhist morality is 'absolutist'. If Buddhist monks appear to be more concerned about *when* they eat rather than *what* they eat, one looks in vain for a western-style set of logical reasons: it is sufficient that the Dharma prescribes that monks do not eat after noon and that active killing is wrong.

From a western point of view, individual meat-eating can be regarded as a vote in favour of the taking of animal life, and a western vegetarian would tend to discourage the eating of meat. But this is not a traditional Buddhist view. They take the precept 'I must not kill' literally. If other people kill, then that is their decision, which of course will affect their *karma* and their future rebirth. A member of the Sangha is not a social reformer who sets out to change such attitudes, but rather one who is pursuing a spiritual path towards enlightenment (Chryssides, 1988a, pp.43–4).

6 Britain's new religions and the 'new pluralism'

No discussion of immigrant religious communities would be complete without some reference to new religious movements. Although membership of new religious movements in Britain is now predominantly British, only a handful of them originated inside Britain, and the vast majority of them have migrated to Britain in the post 1945 era. Although many of these have ingredients taken from the major religious traditions, there are problems about classifying them straightforwardly as belonging to any single major tradition, and therefore they deserve consideration in their own right. In addition, they have generally entered Britain through a different route from the major world faiths. Whereas the major religions have come with immigrant communities, the new religions are generally brought by western converts, and tend to come from the United States.

The 1960s saw the immigration of Scientologists to Britain, a tide that was stemmed, albeit temporarily, by the ban imposed on them by the government in 1968; this was finally lifted in 1979. The Unification Church (more popularly known as 'the Moonies'), although originally derived from American Christian missionary preaching in Korea, took its distinctive shape in the Korean peninsula before coming to Britain via the United States in the early 1970s. Although ISKCON now sees its identity as thoroughly Hindu (and hence claims that it is the most ancient existing religious tradition rather than a new one), it was imported from the United States after Prabhupada persuaded some of the American youth to take up the Hare Krishna chant.

ISKCON

The new religions themselves do not necessarily migrate in their indigenous forms. Just as western Buddhism has adapted itself to the western intellect, so have various new movements which originate from a Hindu background. Kim Knott has contended that Indian immigrants have imported 'popular Hinduism' rather than its 'intellectual counterpart' (see Volume I, essay 4, p.177). Although Thomas has pointed out the difficulties entailed in the distinction between 'popular' and 'intellectual' versions of a religion, what Knott means is clear enough: immigrant Hindus in Britain are more familiar with placating local devata (minor deities) and spirits, with 'purity' and 'pollution' and with the caste system; they are less likely to be familiar with the philosophies of Shankara, Ramanuja and Madhva, or even with detailed exegesis of familiar texts such as the Bhagavad Gita. By contrast, it is easier for westerners to familiarize themselves with Hindu philosophy and Hindu scriptures, since reading them does not require the background of a Hindu world view. They are less likely to embrace practices that entail a caste system of which they have never been part, or concepts such as 'pollution' which are associated with it. ISKCON has therefore made its appeal to westerners because it emphasizes the philosophy of 'Krisha consciousness' rather than popular village practices which comprise many Hindus' lifestyle in India. In Britain, ISKCON has drawn its followers firstly from the indigenous British population, and only secondly from Indian Hindus.

If ISKCON's intellectualized version of Hinduism is a form of accommodation to the western mind, recent controversies relating to the movement have caused it to respond with renewed vigour. In 1966, former Beatle George Harrison bought a large mock Tudor mansion in Hertfordshire – Bhaktivedanta Manor – for the use of ISKCON. The manor had previously been used as a convent, and it was believed that there would not be legal difficulties in its subsequent use for religious purposes, even though the religion in question was radically different. Accordingly, in 1973 ISKCON was granted planning permission from Hartsmere Borough Council to use the manor as 'a theological college in connection with the promotion of the religion of Krishna consciousness' (*Nama Hatta*, 1991a, p.1). The word 'promotion' is significant, although no doubt the Council did not realize the full implications of the term at that time. As the reputation of Bhaktivedanta Manor grew, the wider Hindu community became aware of the quality of the worship and ceremonies offered there. No visitor to the Sunday evening aarti ceremony could fail to note that the majority of worshippers were Asian Hindus rather than European converts, and on festival days there could be as many as 20,000 visitors in one day. Inevitably this resulted in severe traffic congestion in the small village of Letchmore Heath, where the manor is situated, and residents complained about noise as well as congestion. Ironically, most of the complainants bought their properties at Letchmore Heath long after the establishment of ISKCON's headquarters there, although in law this point adds no weight to the devotees' legal position.

The residents successfully persuaded Hartsmere Borough Council that the buildings had undergone a change of use: a theological college was for the private training of students; its current use was for public worship. ISKCON devotees argued that it is impossible to have a theological college without a shrine, and religious worship is not typically carried out in private, but permits open access. ISKCON's position was challenged by Hartsmere Borough Council in late 1986, when they served an enforcement order: the building must be used for the original purpose for which planning permission had been granted, or ISKCON must defend its position in court.

ISKCON chose the latter course of action. As well as defending its position in British courts, ISKCON attempted to raise public consciousness by a number of publicity campaigns. In reply to the various criticisms, devotees produced a special newsletter which carried a leading article 'Hinduism under attack' (1987). The (unnamed) author insisted that the Temple had co-ordinated a traffic-control system with local police, the Automobile Association and Hartsmere Borough Council, and that no visitors ever parked outside the Temple grounds, which had parking space for 110 vehicles. The Council, they claimed, had checked noise levels at the Janmashtami Festival (their largest), and agreed that levels were satisfactory. They also pointed out that since Hinduism advocates *ahimsa* (non-violence), there were never any disturbances or crimes, and local police never had any cause to make arrests. To cope with the traffic problem, devotees offered to build a road at their own expense to link the manor to the main A41 highway but, even before ISKCON could purchase the land, the proposal was turned down (*Nama Hatta*, 1988, p.8).

The British court which heard their appeal in 1992 found against ISKCON, and after 1993 the only people who were to be permitted to use the shrine were students resident within the manor, and staff who were employed in essential work relating to the day-to-day running of the college (for example, cooks and gardeners). Even those devotees who lived in the village itself (of which there were several) could be denied access by the ruling. At the time of writing, ISKCON is pursuing an appeal in the European Court of Justice on the grounds that the enforcement order entails an important infringement of religious freedom.

The sheer practicality of finding an alternative site of comparable size is daunting. ISKCON reckons that any such site would have to afford at least forty acres, since it would require twenty-five priests, cows and pasture land, 200 local members, and their own school which educates some forty-five children (*Nama Hatta*, 1988, p.8; 1991a, p.1).

The Unification Church

Of all new religious groups entering Britain in the post-war period the Unification Church (the 'Moonies') has probably been the most controversial. Founded by its leader Sun Myung Moon in 1954 in Korea, the Unification Church preaches the necessity of removing the sin which entered the world through the Fall; as a result of humankind's disobedience, Jesus was unable to complete his mission, being crucified before he could marry and give birth to sinless families. After a 2,000-year period of 'restoration', Sun Myung Moon and his wife are held to be jointly the new messianic figures who have restored true parenthood and can offer the Blessing (the 'mass wedding', as the media call it) to the world (Chryssides, 1991, pp.19–45).

After evangelization in Korea and Japan, early leaders arrived in the United States in the late 1960s, and by the early 1970s Sun Myung Moon had become sufficiently well known and controversial to attract sizeable audiences at public gatherings. The early 1970s also saw the influx of Unification Church missionaries to Britain, where they established centres in many of the major cities. Scarcely had they arrived than they incurred massive unpopularity. The mainstream Christian denominations took exception to their teaching that Jesus' mission was incomplete, and that a new messiah had come to finish his task – and the Unification Church's text, *Divine Principle*, appeared to be a new scripture to supersede the Old and New Testaments (although the Unification Church was at pains to explain that it was an interpretation of scripture, not a new scripture). Their methods of evangelizing and fundraising were thought to be questionable: they frequently concealed their true identity when campaigning,[3] and rank-and-file 'Moonies' worked long hard hours at street peddling to amass the wealth of the new rich 'Moonie' empire. Allegedly they 'brainwashed' enquirers, and the 'mass wedding', much publicized in the media, incurred general disapproval, the usual criticism being that the Reverend Moon imposed his choice of marriage partner on members. When the Unification Church attempted to gain membership of the British Council of Churches, its application was flatly turned down.

It would be inappropriate to discuss here the extent to which these criticisms were justified. Suffice it to say that in 1981 the Unification Church had had enough of being constantly pilloried in public. When the *Daily Mail* published an article entitled 'The Church that splits up families' the Unification Church decided to sue. What followed was the longest libel suit ever heard in an English court; after six months the Unification Church not only lost, thus incurring costly legal fees, but the judge recommended

---

[3]The Unification Church insists that this no longer occurs, and that they regret many of their past evangelizing tactics.

78

that the Unification Church's position as a charity should be investigated to determine whether its charitable status should be permitted to continue.

Discouraged by this unfavourable outcome, more than half of the full-time Unification Church members returned to the United States in the hope of finding better fortune there. The colossal legal expenses caused the Unification Church to rationalize its bases within Britain: a large proportion of the dozen centres spread throughout the mainland and Northern Ireland were sold off, and only five principal centres remained. Thus the Unification Church contracted from an enthusiastically proselytizing body, whom most members of the public had encountered at one time or another, to a thinned-down organization with an altogether much lower profile.

The Unification Church fared better with regard to its charitable status. In December 1984 the Attorney General finally issued the summons they had been expecting. It was alleged that the Unification Church was essentially political, and hence not truly religious in character, and that it lacked the 'necessary element of public benefit' required for it to remain as a registered charity. Among the reasons given for questioning its 'public benefit' were: (1) that the Unification Church purported to be essentially Christian, but was not truly so, and its claim to be Christian was deceptive; (2) that the Unification Church confused 'recruits' and subjected them to undue pressure to join; (3) that the Unification Church was totalitarian, since the Reverend Moon exercised undue control over all aspects of members' lives; and (4) that the Unification Church's teachings and practices – especially those on family life – were contrary to the public good.

After nearly four years of preparation on both sides, however, the Attorney General dropped the matter – a decision that caused an uproar in Parliament when it was announced, and inevitable hostility among anti-cultists. Although the decision surprised many, the Attorney General explained to Parliament that:

> Whatever view may be taken of its tenets, the Unification Church must, as a matter of law, be regarded as a religion. In English law there is a strong presumption that any trust for the advancement of any religion, without distinction, is charitable unless the contrary is proved by evidence admissible in court proceedings.
>
> (*Hansard*, 3 February 1988)

This decision was not only a matter of relief to the Unification Church. If the trial had gone ahead in April 1988 as scheduled, they feared that their beliefs would have been made to stand trial as well. The prospect of a secular court conducting, in effect, a heresy trial was one that appalled not only the Unification Church, but several other religious denominations. In fact, the Unification Church, who had become acquainted with the leaders of other religious denominations over the years, was able to put their case to them and enlist their support. Among those who made representation to the Attorney General were officials from the Church of England, the Council of Christians and Jews, the Unitarian and Free Christian Churches, the Ethiopian Orthodox Church, the Arya Samaj London (a Hindu organization) and the Islamic Federation. At an Interfaith Thanksgiving celebration held at the Unification Church's national headquarters shortly after the Attorney General's decision, the British Council of Churches' Secretary to the Committee for Relations with People of Other Faiths said:

> It is ... important to stress why the case was withdrawn. It was not withdrawn as the popular press claims because of some supposed technical loophole in the law... but because there wasn't a case ... If a case had existed, with four years to prepare, the Attorney General ... would not have hesitated to proceed to trial. He didn't. No case to answer.
>
> (Bennett, 1988, p.5)

7 Two major controversies: education and blasphemy

Although immigrant religious traditions have undergone a relatively successful process of acclimatization, with the possible exception of new religious movements, it is plain that minority religions remain victims of discriminatory legislation.

One much discussed area is education. At present it is permissible for any community – religious or secular – to establish and run its own school, subject to its being able to demonstrate that it can provide a satisfactory education for its pupils. Some Hindu, Buddhist, Muslim and Sikh communities have done so. However, such schools must remain independent, and cannot be grant-assisted or state schools. By contrast, Christian denominations, such as the Roman Catholic Church and the Church of England, and also Jews, have enjoyed their own state and grant-aided schools. Setting aside the question of whether or not it is desirable for religious organizations to isolate their children within their own communities by requesting their own state schools, the immigrant religions are only seeking a right that is already enjoyed by Christians and Jews. If it is desirable that state schools should encourage different ethnic groups and religions to intermix, then the same rules should surely apply to all.

Religious education syllabuses, too, have given rise to debate. With the arrival of new citizens who did not subscribe to traditional Christianity, the question had to be addressed of whether it was still appropriate to teach the Christian Bible. The 1944 Education Act had already made provision for opting out of religious education – a provision that was invoked principally by Jews and Jehovah's Witnesses. However, opting out was a rather negative provision, and the advent of other major world religions caused some religious education specialists to contemplate major revisions to the traditional syllabus. One such revision which was rife in the 1960s was 'Personal Social and Moral Education', which brought ethical and social responsibilities into greater prominence than the specifically religious aspects of world faiths. In the 1970s and 1980s, this became viewed as somewhat limited, and various local authorities made provision for religious education to envelop the major traditions of Judaism, Hinduism, Islam and Sikhism as well as traditional Christianity. Buddhism tended, at least at first, to be left out, either because religious education specialists believed that it was a philosophy rather than a religion (on the grounds that belief in a creator God appeared to be absent) or that it was simply too difficult to be taught at school level.

Despite the plural nature of British society, Christians still formed the vast majority of religious believers in the early 1990s. Hence the 1988 Education Reform Act stipulated that agreed syllabuses should reflect the predominantly Christian character of the country. In 1993, the Education Secretary, John Patten, sought the views of church leaders with a view to using religious education to instil a sense of traditional moral values. While this certainly pleased the more evangelical wing of the Christian churches, the proposals were greeted with some dismay among many members of other faiths. Patten stated:

> I am determined to see that both the quality and the consistency of religious education is improved. We owe it to our young people to see that they have a fuller understanding of the beliefs and values that have bound communities together over many generations in our country ... Building on the 1988 requirements that agreed syllabuses for RE should reflect the mainly Christian traditions of this country, we are now taking firm action to see that LEAs that have not reviewed their syllabus – and there are far too many that haven't – do so ... I shall be writing to church leaders to seek their views on how we might assist local conferences in their vital task.
>
> In particular, I shall seek the views of the churches on whether guidance might be offered to local conferences through the use of model syllabuses. This could form a blueprint on religious education for those local bodies that wished to adopt it.
>
> (press release, 5 March 1993)

Another area of controversy that erupted in the 1980s was the issue of blasphemy. As British law currently stands, the Established Church is protected from 'obscene or violent abuse' (Webster, 1990, p.24), although until very recently it had been thought that the Blasphemy Laws were obsolete. Indeed, in 1949 Lord Denning stated:

> The reason for this law was because it was thought that a denial of Christianity was liable to shake the fabric of society, which was itself founded upon Christian religion. There is no such danger to society now and the offence of blasphemy is a dead letter.
>
> (Law Commission, 1981, p.16; quoted in Webster, 1990, p.24)

This opinion was shown to be false, however, when in July 1977 Mary Whitehouse brought a charge of blasphemy against the editor and publishers of *Gay News* for publishing a poem by James Kirkup entitled 'The Love That Dares to Speak its Name', which spoke of a Roman centurion's homosexual fantasies about the dead Jesus as he took his body down from the cross (Law Commission, 1981, pp.17–21).

The Western Buddhist Order was one of the first religious communities to express serious concern. In a booklet entitled *Buddhism and Blasphemy*, their leader Sangharakshita argued that if it is an offence to speak against the established religion, Buddhists are left in a difficult position since the very acceptance of Buddhism implies a rejection of Christianity. Indeed, for the western Buddhist, Sangharakshita believed, there was a need to reject explicitly the manifestations of conventional Christianity with its belief in an apparently authoritarian deity.

> One who was brought up under the influence of Christianity – under the oppressive and coercive influence of theological monarchism – and who as a result of that influence is tormented by irrational feelings of fear and guilt, has the right to rid himself of those feelings by openly expressing his resentment against the Power that bears the ultimate responsibility for their being instilled into him, i.e. by committing blasphemy.
>
> (Sangharakshita, 1978, p.23)

The fear for some religious groups such as the Western Buddhist Order was that they might be found guilty of blasphemy. The Unification Church expressed similar fears: might it be construed as blasphemous to claim that Sun Myung Moon is the messiah? For other communities, such as Muslims, the fear was that, unlike the Christians, they had no legal redress when their faith was insulted, as they believed had happened with the publication of *The Satanic Verses*. In its recent report, *Second Review of the*

Race Relations Act 1976, the Commission for Racial Equality endorsed the views of Buddhists and Muslims alike on the issue. It stated:

> It is now generally accepted that the law of blasphemy is unacceptable in principle as it stands. In protecting only one religion, it is discriminatory … Certainly either the law of blasphemy needs to be abolished or to be extended to protect other religions.
>
> (Commission for Racial Equality, 1992, p.78)

Regarding legislation governing religion in Britain's pluralist society, the Commission for Racial Equality made three important observations.

1 The current law of blasphemy protects only the established Christian religion.
2 There is in Britain no law of incitement to religious hatred.
3 There is no law in Britain protecting people from religious discrimination.

> (ibid, p.77)

Equality before the law is still some distance away. Although the post-war years have seen the acclimatization and development of the immigrant religions, and accommodation to western ideas and customs, many of their followers feel that there is much still to be done if Britain is to make the transition from being a 'Christian country' to a genuinely 'plural society'. In the meantime, they continue with renewed vigour to press for equality of recognition and full religious freedom.

Bibliography

AHMED, A.S. (1992) *Postmodernism and Islam*, Routledge, London.

ALMOND, P.C. (1988) *The British Discovery of Buddhism*, Cambridge University Press, Cambridge.

ANON (1987) 'Hinduism under attack', *Hare Krishna Newsletter*, no.1, March, pp.1–4.

ANON (1988) 'Save Bhaktivedanta Manor!', *Nama Hatta*, no.2, pp.8–9.

(1991a) 'Save Bhaktivedanta Manor: appeal accepted', *Nama Hatta*, January–February, pp.1–2.

(1991b) 'What happened in court? A Bhaktivedanta Manor update', *Nama Hatta*, November–December, pp.1–2, 9.

BADAWI, M.A.Z. (1981) *Islam in Britain*, Ta Ha Publishers, London.

BARKER, E. (1990) *New Religious Movements: a practical introduction*, HMSO, London.

BASHAM, A.L. (1959) 'Hinduism' in Zaehner, R.C. (ed.).

BENNETT, C. (1988) 'Victory for religious freedom', *Unification Movement Newsletter*, April, pp.1, 5.

BOWEN, D.G. (1992) *The Satanic Verses: Bradford responds*, Bradford and Ilkley Community College, Bradford.

CHRYSSIDES, G.D. (1988a) *The Path of Buddhism*, The Saint Andrew Press, Edinburgh.

(1988b) 'Buddhism goes west', *World Faiths Insight*, New Series 20, October, pp.37–45.

(1991) *The Advent of Sun Myung Moon: the origins, beliefs and practices of the Unification Church*, Macmillan, London.

COMMISSION FOR RACIAL EQUALITY (1992) *Second Review of the Race Relations Act 1976*, London.

FARM ANIMAL WELFARE COUNCIL (FAWC) (1985) *Report on the Welfare of Livestock when Slaughtered by Religious Methods*, Reference Book no.262, HMSO, London.

GILANI, F. (1992) 'It's against my religion', *Discernment*, vol.6, no.1.

GOMBRICH, R. (1988) *Theravada Buddhism*, Routledge, London.

HOLMES, A. (1973) *Church, property and people*, British Council of Churches, London.

HUMPHREYS, C. (1955) *Buddhism*, Penguin, Harmondsworth.

(1978) *Both Sides of the Circle*, Allen and Unwin, London.

KAPLEAU, P. (1983) *A Buddhist Case for Vegetarianism*, Rider, London.

KILLINGLEY, D., MENSKI, W. and FIRTH, S. (1991) *Hindu Ritual and Society*, S.Y.Killingley, Newcastle upon Tyne.

LAW COMMISSION (1981) *Offences against Religion and Public Worship*, Working Paper no.79, HMSO, London.

MCDERMOTT, M.Y. and AHSAN, M.M. (1980) *The Muslim Guide*, The Islamic Foundation, Leicester.

MENSKI, W. (1991) 'Change and continuity in Hindu marriage rituals' in Killingley, Menski and Firth (1991).

MODOOD, T. (1992) 'Minorities, faith and citizenship', *Discernment*, vol.6, no.2.

OLIVER, I.P. (1979) *Buddhism in Britain*, Rider, London.

RAMINDAR SINGH (1992) *Immigrants to Citizens: the Sikh community in Bradford*, The Race Relations Research Unit, Bradford.

SANGHARAKSHITA, V.M.S. (1978) *Buddhism and Blasphemy*, Windhorse Publications, London.

SUBHADARA BHIKSHU (rev.ed.1980) *A Buddhist Catechism*, Buddhist Publication Society, Kandy.

SUBHUTI, D. (1983) *Buddhism for Today*, Element Books, Salisbury.

WEBSTER, R. (1990) *A Brief History of Blasphemy*, Orwell Press, Suffolk.

WEE, V. (no date) *Buddhist Hymns*, Buddhist Missionary Society, Kuala Lumpur.

WEIGHTMAN, S. (1978) *Hinduism in the Village Setting*, Open University Press, Milton Keynes.

WOODWARD, F.L.(1973) *Some Sayings of the Buddha*, The Buddhist Society, London.

ZAEHNER, R.C. (ed.) (1959, 1977) *The Hutchinson Encyclopedia of Living Faiths*, Hutchinson, London.

3

'AND THERE'S ANOTHER COUNTRY...': RELIGION, THE STATE AND BRITISH IDENTITIES

by John Wolffe

Margaret Thatcher speaking at the 1988 General Assembly of the Church of Scotland, Edinburgh. Photo: Church of Scotland Press Office/Pathway Productions.

I vow to thee, my country, all earthly things above:
Entire and whole and perfect, the service of my love ...

And there's another country, I've heard of long ago –
Most dear to them that love her, most great to them that know.

These lines, written by Cecil Spring-Rice against the backdrop of the First World War and later set to Gustav Holst's stirring music, have served as one of the most enduring and emotive statements of the ambivalent relationships during the twentieth century between patriotic and religious loyalties. They were sung at the marriage of the Prince and Princess of Wales in 1981 and alluded to by the Prime Minister, Margaret Thatcher, when she addressed the General Assembly of the Church of Scotland in 1988. 'I always think', she said, 'that the whole debate about the church and the state has never yielded anything comparable in insight to that beautiful hymn'. She went on to identify herself with what she saw as a 'triumphant' and 'noble' assertion of secular patriotism, while emphasizing that spiritual loyalties to 'another country' were of an individual nature. For her, therefore, the primary function of churches and other religious groups was to provide spiritual resources for personal life rather than to be corporate social and political forces. 'Another country' was for her (as probably for Spring-Rice himself) the inner life of the soul, which would enrich and undergird, but not challenge, the secular politics of the nation (Wolffe, 1993, p.246).

For many others in Thatcher's Britain, however, the relationships between church and state, and between religious, national and community loyalties, were far from being so straightforward. It was ironic that Thatcher made this speech exploring the relationship between her politics and her religion in Edinburgh, a city regarded by many as, in a very literal and secular sense, the capital of another country. Moreover, an important role in the maintenance of the distinctiveness of Scotland had, over the centuries since the Union of 1707, been played by the very institution she was addressing. Elsewhere in the United Kingdom the link between spiritual and literal 'other countries' was also apparent: in the religious contribution to Welsh nationalism and in the Roman Catholic dimensions of the desire for a united Ireland. By the 1980s, too, it was evident that religious identities loomed large in the consciousness of minority groups who struggled to feel at home in a Britain that could not claim 'entire and whole and perfect the service of (their) love'. Even in the traditionally Christian and English sense in which Thatcher perceived it, the relationship between the churches and the state had, during the preceding two decades at least, been far from unproblematic.

The purpose of this essay is to explore the general constitutional and political framework in which relationships between organized religion and the British state developed between 1945 and 1990. Particular questions of social and economic policy, education, and personal morality will be discussed in the succeeding essays by Gerald Parsons. The concerns of the present essay will be focused by concentration on two pivotal areas of controversy: firstly, the position and role of the Church of England as an 'Established Church'[1] in connection with the political position of other religious groups; and, secondly, the role of religion in connection with national aspirations in the non-English parts of the United Kingdom, in Scotland, Wales and, above all, Northern Ireland.

1 Church, state and parliament

At first sight the continuing relative prominence of the Church of England[2] as a national institution might seem to have little foundation in its strength as a religious organization at the grass roots. A census of church attendance in 1989 indicated that of the 10 per cent of the English population present in church, only 31 per cent, or 3.1 per cent of the total population of the country, were Anglicans (Brierley, 1991, p.35). This was a smaller proportion than both the Roman Catholic Church and the combined strength of the Free Churches. On the other hand, in 1974 a survey of adults indicated that no less than 41.6 per cent of people in England identified in some way with the Church of England (Medhurst and Moyser, 1988, p.142). However, of these, only 9.9 per cent (4.1 per cent of the total population) regarded themselves as 'very much' practising. This number seems fairly consistent with the figure of 3.1 per cent attendance for 1989, bearing in mind the evidence of a 12 per cent decline in attendances between 1975 and 1989 (Brierley, 1991, p.35), and the probability that even among self-identified regular attenders, some (because of illness and so on) would be unable to attend on a given Sunday.

Nevertheless, in maintaining the Church of England's status as a national institution, the 37.5 per cent or so of the population who identified

---

[1]   This term itself engenders some confusion and controversy: the words 'Establish/ed/ment' are used in this essay (with a capital 'E') in a technical sense to characterize the formal links between the Church of England and the state. This should be clearly distinguished by the reader from reference to 'the Establishment', meaning 'the social group exercising authority or influence' – a usage that will be avoided here – and the general usage of the verb 'establish' to mean 'to set up on a permanent basis' (*OED*). The words 'disestablish/ed/ment', however, are generally understood as having a specific reference to religion and hence will be used here without capitalization or qualification.

[2]   The situation of the Church of Scotland and of the disestablished Anglican Churches in Ireland and Wales will be discussed in the next section.

with it without regularly attending were of considerable significance. This penumbra of support was substantially greater than that obtaining for other religious groups. Even if we suppose that all the remainder of the 60 to 70 per cent of the population regarding themselves as nominal Christians identified in some way with non-Anglican groups, that would still put their combined penumbra at a maximum of around 20 per cent of the population, a ratio to their active support (6.9 per cent) of 2.9:1, in comparison with the comparable Anglican figure of 9:1.[3]

This residue of public identification with the Church of England had its counterpart in the ambiguously privileged constitutional position accorded to the Established Church. This operates at the highest levels of the state, in the links between the Archbishop of Canterbury, the Crown and the royal family. Indeed, the Archbishop is technically the highest-ranking non-royal person in the country, taking precedence over the Prime Minister and the Lord Chancellor, while the Archbishop of York also outranks the Prime Minister. The two Archbishops, the Bishops of London, Durham and Winchester, and the twenty-one most senior of the other diocesan bishops have seats in the House of Lords. Such privileges are reflected in the place of bishops and Anglican clergy in regional, civic, and local life, with roles that in the twentieth century have become more honorific than influential, but nevertheless have continued. Although the Church of England does not receive any current public money for its core religious functions, it does enjoy the benefit of the considerable endowments vested in the Church Commissioners, the product of the munificence of previous generations towards the national church.[4] Furthermore, during the 1980s the prominence of the Church of England received reinforcement from the attention of the media, which was greater than that accorded to any other Christian group. This tendency was well illustrated in 1990–91 when the translation of George Carey, the hitherto little known Bishop of Bath and Wells, to Canterbury made him almost overnight a more prominent public figure than the long-serving and well-

[3] This calculation might be compared with figures presented in the Chadwick Report of 1970 which suggest proportions of 12.5 per cent nominal Nonconformists and 9.5 per cent nominal Roman Catholics in the English population. Nominal affiliation with the Church of England was put as high as 67.5 per cent, but the lower but still very substantial proportion given in the text of the present essay seems more defensible. The report also contained a trenchant critique from Valerie Pitt of the inclusion of nominal adherents in such figures (*Church and State*, 1970, pp.4, 72–4, 107–8). It is impossible to explore the issues raised in detail here, but for further discussion of the 'religions of the silent majority' see Volume I, essay 8.

[4] The Commissioners suffered major losses in the property slump of the late 1980s and early 1990s: accordingly their financial contribution in the future is likely to be significantly less than it has been in the past.

respected Roman Catholic Archbishop of Westminster, Cardinal Basil Hume. Although consultation and joint action between the churches gradually increased, the Church of England was still ex-officio in the position of leadership.

The privileges of the Church of England have been counterbalanced by certain constraints different from those applying to other religious groups. Despite changes which will be outlined below, bishops continued to be appointed by the Crown on the constitutional advice of the Prime Minister, while Parliament possessed residual powers in respect of the control of the Church of England which went beyond the right to ensure that it, like any other religious or secular corporation, conducted its affairs within the law. The sovereign continued to be 'Supreme Governor of the Church', a role with few practical implications, but considerable symbolic importance. The power of the state to influence the Church of England was viewed by some as an unacceptable constraint on spiritual independence; but by others as a fair recompense for privilege, and a means by which the millions of nominal Anglicans could maintain a voice in the affairs of 'their' church, protecting it from being taken over by a clique made up of clergy and activist laity. Thus seemingly technical constitutional discussions could open up wide questions about the nature of organized religion and its social functions (*Church and State*, 1970, pp.6–7, 68–84).

It is widely perceived that the relations between church and state are one of the most unchanging and traditional features of English life. In reality, however, during the four and a half centuries since the Reformation the constitutional situation of the Church of England, like that of the monarchy, has altered profoundly. Establishment continues in the 1990s, but it means fewer and different things now from in the 1790s, let alone the 1590s. There is no space here even to begin to outline the changes that took place between Henry VIII's break with Rome in 1533 and the end of the Second World War, but two points must be made. Firstly, between the 1820s and the 1880s there had been numerous reforms which had the effect of ending a virtual Anglican monopoly of civil office, and giving equality of legal and educational opportunity to non-Anglicans and, eventually, to non-Christians. There was also in 1868 an end to the obligation of all (through church rates) financially to support the Church of England. Secondly, during and after this period Parliament gradually became less preoccupied with matters relating to the internal regulation of the Church of England. The logic of this process was developed further in 1919, when the National Assembly of the Church of England (Church Assembly) was created as a forum for the discussion of matters which hitherto had been the sole responsibility of Parliament. This Assembly existed alongside the Convocations of Canterbury and York, the historic elected assemblies of the clergy. Nevertheless the Assembly's Measures still required parliamentary approval, and in 1927–28 the difficulties inherent in this situation were graphically illustrated when the House of Commons twice rejected a revised Prayer Book which had been previously adopted by the Church Assembly.

Hence the 1930s and 1940s were a period of some uncertainty in church/state relations. The Second World War was in some respects a distraction, but vigorous criticism by George Bell, Bishop of Chichester, of the bombing of German cities, aroused hostility in government circles. Following William Temple's death in 1944, the dislike of Winston Churchill and the King for Bell was a factor in his being passed over for translation to either Canterbury or London (Carpenter, 1991, pp.130, 217–9). The circumstances were exceptional, but they still stirred nervousness about the potential for the Prime Minister, or even the sovereign, to be influenced by political rather than spiritual considerations in making episcopal appointments.

Thus the post-war era opened in an atmosphere of some unease about future church/state relations. For example, the Archbishop of York, Cyril Garbett, confessed to 'grave heart-searching and discomfort' and, although only specifically advocating minor changes, felt that disestablishment might become necessary as a last resort (Garbett, 1950, pp.140, 141–58). In the event such fears were not borne out. Although the Church Assembly set up a commission to examine the situation, it only recommended minor changes which were not immediately implemented (Dyson, 1985, pp.292–7).

As in many other aspects of religious life, the 1950s proved to be a decade of relative calm and stability and significant changes did not begin to materialize until 1963. In that year the Ecclesiastical Jurisdiction Measure transferred ultimate jurisdiction in legal disputes over the doctrine and ritual of the Church of England from the Judicial Committee of the Privy Council to a new Court of Ecclesiastical Causes Reserved. The effect was to remove the historically problematic jurisdiction of a secular court and give the church better control over its own 'spiritual' affairs (Welsby, 1984, pp.43–4). In 1965, under the Prayer Book (Alternative Services) Measure, the Convocations and the House of Laity of the Church Assembly were given power to sanction new forms of services for an experimental period (Field, 1985, pp.57–9). In the light of the conflict in the 1920s between Parliament and the Church Assembly over the revision of the Prayer Book this measure was potentially a very significant change.

However, the most important watershed came in 1970, a year that saw two major developments. Firstly, under the Synodical Government Measure (1969), the Church Assembly and the Convocations were brought together in the General Synod of the Church of England, opened by Queen Elizabeth II in November 1970. This was a more streamlined body than its predecessors and hence, arguably, more effective and influential. Secondly, there was the publication of the report of another Church and State commission under the chairmanship of Professor Owen Chadwick (hereafter accordingly referred to as the Chadwick Report). Although three of the seventeen members of the commission called for disestablishment, the majority favoured the maintenance of ties between church and state while offering various suggestions as to how these might be reformed and loosened (*Church and State*, 1970).

Two key recommendations of the Chadwick Report were implemented within a few years. In 1974 the Worship and Doctrine Measure gave the General Synod permanent control over these matters. It was passed in the House of Commons in the face of vocal opposition from a minority of Conservative MPs, who were concerned that parliamentary control should be maintained and specifically anxious to safeguard the continued use of the Book of Common Prayer of 1662 (Welsby, 1984, pp.221–3). Secondly, in 1976 the Prime Minister (James Callaghan) agreed to delegate much of the process of choosing diocesan bishops to a Crown Appointments Commission appointed by the General Synod. This would submit two names to the Prime Minister, who had the right to choose either or neither in making his or her formal recommendation to the sovereign, but could not make an independent choice of his or her own. Although the traditional constitutional forms were thus maintained and an element of prime ministerial discretion remained, the effect was to transfer the initiative in episcopal appointments from Downing Street to the church (Welsby, 1984, pp.223–4).

Both these changes were a matter of ongoing controversy. The new procedures for the appointment of bishops worked well[5], but they were the less radical of the two alternative proposals in the Chadwick Report and did not really meet the concerns of those who objected on principle to the involvement of the Prime Minister. On the other hand, some in Parliament felt there was a danger of too much ground being given in response to the church's desire for increased independence, an attitude that led the House of Commons in 1984 to reject a measure for further reforms in the procedures for the appointment of bishops. Meanwhile there was continuing unease in Parliament about the declining use of the 1662 Prayer Book. This led in 1981 to an unsuccessful attempt to pass legislation which

[5] It is alleged that on two occasions (London in 1981 and Birmingham in 1987) the Prime Minister (Thatcher) chose the church's second preference for a bishopric (Medhurst and Moyser, 1988, p.110). However, even if this was indeed the case, she was acting wholly within the terms of the agreement made by Callaghan in 1976. Moreover, in both cases the church's allegedly preferred candidate later received another episcopal appointment. The normal smoothness with which the procedure operated, even under so strong and opinionated a premier is, on the contrary, testimony to its viability on its own terms. Continuing criticism of the situation thus ultimately reflected matters of principle rather than of practice.

would have empowered twenty parishioners to compel their incumbent to use the Book of Common Prayer rite once a month for the principal morning service (Field, 1985, pp.59–74).

Nevertheless, the fundamentals of the relationship between church and state remained robust enough to survive such parliamentary skirmishes. More than three decades after Garbett had written his apprehensive view of the future of the Establishment, a later Archbishop of York, John Habgood, published an analysis of the problem in which he concluded that 'the overall case for disestablishment, now or in the forseeable future, is not convincing'. It was true that debate on the subject became quite lively during the 1980s, partly because of perceived confrontation between the church and the Thatcher government, and partly because of the manner in which the position of the Church of England raised and illuminated broader theological and sociological questions about the appropriate role of organized religion in a 'secular' society. The issues were explored in a series of lectures by prominent churchmen and politicians at St James's, Piccadilly, in the spring of 1983 (Reeves, 1984; cf. Plant, 1985, pp.313–36). However, this did not lead to disestablishment coming on to the agenda of practical politics: the majority of both church leaders and of Parliament seemed happy – or at least not unhappy – with the status quo. They had no desire to face the distraction and conflict that would almost certainly have resulted from any serious attempt to achieve radical change (Drewry and Brock, 1970–71, p.226).

Moreover, in striking contrast to the situation in the later nineteenth century, the debate about disestablishment in the later twentieth century – such as it was – was very much an internal Anglican affair. It is true that, as the Chadwick Report recognized, the Church of England's remaining ties with the state were a potential obstacle to closer ecumenical ties with other denominations which had a strong tradition of wholly independent existence (*Church and State*, 1970, p.11). In practice, however, the Roman Catholics and the Free Churches appeared to regard it as an impertinence to press the point. Indeed, there seemed to be a readiness to accept the Establishment of the Church of England as a means to exercise a particular kind of ministry to the nation, on behalf of the wider Christian church. There were even indications that such an attitude extended to bodies of religious opinion outside Christianity, notably among Jews and Muslims. For them even the shadow of a Christian state was preferable to a wholly secular one (Murphy, 1992, p.51).

This attitude was widespread despite the failure to implement the significant recommendation of the Chadwick Report that 'leading members of other Communions, besides the bishops of the Church of England, should be invited to sit in the House of Lords' (*Church and State*, 1970, pp.45–7). It is true that some such prominent individuals were appointed to life peerages, including Lord Soper (Methodist), Lord

MacLeod of Fuinary (Church of Scotland) and, more recently, Lord Jacobovits (Jewish). However there were no moves to attach a peerage formally to offices such as the Archbishopric of Westminster, the Moderatorships of the Church of Scotland and the Free Church Federal Council, or the Chief Rabbinate. Accordingly the twenty-six Anglican bishops in the Lords remained the only official religious representatives in Parliament. There was also no reform of the constitutional anomalies that prevented Roman Catholic, Church of Scotland, and Church of England clergy from sitting in the House of Commons, while Anglican clergy in the non-established churches outside England, and Free Church ministers (for example, Reverend Ian Paisley) could do so (*Church and State*, 1970, pp.57–8).

The special status of the Church of England in comparison with other religious groups was reflected in differing approaches to political involvement. Although the bishops had numerous other commitments and were as individuals thus prevented from being continuously active in the business of the House of Lords, collectively they were able to make a significant impact. This was not confined to ecclesiastical matters but ranged widely over the issues of the day. The episcopal contribution to Lords debates was generally welcomed and regarded as useful (Drewry and Brock, 1970–71). The bishops also provided a direct route by which the General Synod and its associated bodies could seek to influence the legislative process: for example, the chairman of the Church's Board of Social Responsibility was usually a diocesan bishop who took an active part in the affairs of the House of Lords. In the Commons, on the other hand, the Church of England had no specific official representation, other than through the Second Church Estates Commissioner, whose formal brief was limited to financial and administrative matters. Accordingly, in furthering its interests and concerns in the lower house the church had to complement its official representation by lobbying (Medhurst and Moyser, 1988, pp.308–52).

Nevertheless, the continued presence of the bishops in the Lords, and a sense that the Church of England remained at least on the fringes of mainstream power structures, distinguished it from other religious organizations which were prone to see themselves more as outsiders, seeking to influence the political process through a pressure-group kind of activity. This was true of denominational leaderships such as the Roman Catholic bishops and the Methodist Conference; of interdenominational bodies like the Evangelical Alliance and Christian Action Research and Education (CARE), concerned to promote Christian moral standards in society; and of groups with particular areas of concern, for example, the Keep Sunday Special campaign of the 1980s and 1990s. Activity of this kind could on occasions prove quite effective, given the tendency for Christian commitment, or as least sympathy, to be proportionately more widespread among MPs than in society at large (see Volume I, p.312).

More diffuse Christian influences on politics can be discerned through the participation of believers in the mainstream political parties. The legacy of some traditional alignments between religious and political loyalties could certainly still be discerned, at least up to the 1970s. While the Church of England had never been exclusively 'the Conservative Party at prayer', it remained true that there were disproportionate numbers of Tory supporters among committed Anglicans (Medhurst and Moyser, 1988, p.227). The same was true of the Church of Scotland. Conversely many Roman Catholics continued a long-standing loyalty to the Labour Party. Nor was this simply a matter of class: in a survey conducted in Dundee in the 1966 General Election, 88 per cent of Roman Catholics in non-manual occupations voted Labour. This compares with 52 per cent of those without an active religious affiliation in the same socio-economic groups, and only 22 per cent of comparably situated members and adherents of the Church of Scotland (Bochel and Denver, 1970, p.213). Further research is needed, but such figures indicate that in the third quarter of the twentieth century there was probably still a significant proportion of the population for whom religious and political identities were closely intertwined. It should be borne in mind, however, that a consistent electoral preference for a particular party does not necessarily imply any active commitment to its affairs.

Identification between particular parties and denominational allegiances had never been rigid, but during the later twentieth century, among activists at least, alignments became more fluid than they had been. The traditional association between the Free Churches and the Liberal Party became increasingly difficult to discern in the face of mutual decline. For example, Baptists tended to withdraw from any distinctive political stance in the immediate post-war period and, when members of the denomination became more active again from the 1960s, they were to be found among supporters of all three main parties. Estrangement from the Liberals was hastened by David Steel's support for the 1967 Abortion Act (Bebbington, 1983, pp.81–90). Conversely, the remarkable success of the Conservative Party under Margaret Thatcher, herself from a Methodist background, probably owed something to her capacity to appeal to the Nonconformist legacy in political culture in a manner in which Liberal leaders since Lloyd George had failed to do. Meanwhile Roman Catholics, such as Chris and John Patten, David Alton and Shirley Williams, were prominent in the Conservative, Liberal, and Social Democratic parties as well as in the Labour Party. The tone of political reflection and activity among some leading Anglicans in the early 1980s led to the Church of England being tagged the 'Social Democratic Party at prayer'. When in 1987 leading members of each of the three main parties published their respective claims to Christian support, it is noteworthy that the differences stemmed from divergences of theological and philosophical understanding rather than from competing denominational allegiances (Gummer, Heffer and Beith, 1987). The trend therefore, in politics as in church life in general, was for the development of an increasingly ecumenical spirit among Christians, in which old denominational barriers came to count for much less. Informal attempts were also made to establish cross-party interdenominational alignments (Medhurst and Moyser, 1988, pp.313–4), a process that was encouraged by the formation of the Movement for Christian Democracy in 1990. This organization called for 'Christians in all parties and those who feel unable to join any of the parties, to come together and bring Christian values back into political life' (MCD publicity leaflet).

In similar fashion, the Jews, who had acquired the right to sit in Parliament in 1858, had formed institutions and connections that gave them effective political influence. Indeed, the proportion of Jewish MPs in the later twentieth century was substantially greater than their proportion in the population as a whole. In the 1945 General Election twenty-eight professing Jews were elected MPs, a number that reached a peak of forty-six in February 1974 in the face of overall decline in the Jewish population. Post-war Jewish parliamentarians have included such prominent figures as Emmanuel Shinwell, Keith Joseph and Nigel Lawson. It has been observed, however, that 'most Jewish MPs consider themselves as politicians who happen to be Jewish rather than Jewish politicians' (Alderman, 1983, pp.153, 174–5). Nevertheless this very tendency is testimony to the success of Jews in establishing themselves as part of the mainstream of political life. Margaret Thatcher gave considerable weight to the place of Jews in British life, a result in part of her ties with Jewish groups in her own Finchley constituency but also reflecting wider political realities (Alderman, 1983, pp.146–7; Wolffe, 1993, p.245).

Thus, around the core of formal ties between the Church of England and the state was a wider circle of Christian and Jewish influence, not recognized constitutionally, but politically quite significant. Other non-Christian groups, as well as Afro-Caribbean Christians, had yet to establish such informal but reliable networks of influence. Although they did not face any constitutional obstacles to election to parliament, unlike Roman Catholics and Jews in the early nineteenth century, they remained under-represented or even unrepresented. As late as the early 1990s, Muslims, the largest non-Christian religious group, were still without a MP. Moreover there was a lack of equivalents to the organized leaderships of Christian denominations, interdenominational pressure groups, or the Board of Deputies of British Jews, which could provide a focus for lobbying and other political mobilization on matters of community concern. Although there were some signs by the 1980s that such structures were beginning to emerge, bodies such as the Union of Muslim Organizations and the Afro-West Indian United Council of Churches still struggled to sustain credibility both with their own constituency and in the wider secular political arena. The consequent sense of powerlessness manifested itself in low levels of political participation among minority groups (Moyser, 1989, pp.358–72), which of course further compounded the problem. Such passivity was only broken when specific matters of community concern arose, such as Sikhs' anxiety to secure the right to wear the turban, and Muslims' outrage over *The Satanic Verses.*[6]

Our discussion hitherto has been concerned with the constitutional and political structures relating to religion, but in order to illuminate further the tensions of identity in operation we must touch on particular areas of debate. The agenda is potentially a long one: much might be said, for example, about foreign relations and nuclear weapons, as well as about the matters to be covered in subsequent essays. Constraints of space, however, force a concentration on two questions. Firstly, how did Christians, and the Church of England in particular, balance the sometimes competing loyalties of patriotism and their sense of belonging to a transnational religious community? Secondly, to what extent did the presence from the 1960s of substantial numbers of adherents to religions other than Christianity lead to a reshaping of existing perceptions of Christian British national identity?

Our first question had been a particularly acute one during the first half of the twentieth century, in the face of two world wars. Church leaders had manifested a wide range of attitudes, from the enthusiastic equation of Christianity with the national cause by the Bishop of London (Winnington-Ingram) in the First World War, to the questioning of military policy and the advocacy of friendship with German Christians by the Bishop of Chichester (Bell) in the Second. It is helpful to bear this historical perspective in mind because it indicates that controversy on this front during the post 1945 era was nothing new: indeed, in some respects the short-lived military conflicts of 1956, 1982 and 1991 did little more than evoke transient echoes of the agonizings induced by total war in 1914–18 and 1939–45. What was new, at least from the 1960s, was the change in Britain's international situation following the retreat from empire: no longer could the Anglican Communion be perceived simply as the spiritual arm of imperial interest, and its presence was, more evidently than in the past, a check on any tendency of the Church of England to

---

[6]   See also Volume I, pp.165–9, 212–13, 228–31.

identify itself with a narrow nationalism.[7] Despite, or perhaps because of, their relative rarity in the decades after 1945, military conflicts did bring sharply into focus the question of the role of the Established Church. Should it be a prophetic role, to bring under the spotlight of Christianity the actions of the secular government and not to flinch from criticism should this be necessary? Or was this to bite the hand that fed it in its very hour of need, and was the role of the church rather to minister to the maintenance of national morale by concentrating on its strictly 'spiritual' functions and contributing to the assertion of the diffuse but potent values of Englishness/Britishness?[8]

The responses of Archbishop Fisher to the Suez crisis and of Archbishop Runcie to the Falklands War both indicated a perception of their own role as that of a cautious prophet. In a memorable exchange with the Lord Chancellor (Kilmuir) in the House of Lords in 1956, Fisher sought to expose what he saw as the irresponsible and illegal nature of Britain's attack on Egypt. He later regretted the virulence of his criticism for which he had been criticized by Lord Hailsham (Carpenter, 1991, pp.402–5). In the Falklands conflict in 1982, Runcie was similarly concerned that international law should be maintained, but in this case such a view was consistent with qualified support for military action. However, the Archbishop's refusal to pander to triumphalism after victory had been gained over Argentina provoked anger among some Conservative MPs and the right-wing press, where very different perceptions of the role of the church evidently prevailed (Mantle, 1991, pp.151–2, 156–62).

One of the most significant points to be made about immigration and race relations in the context of the present discussion is that the controversies that arose only slowly came to be seen as having a religious dimension. A survey of the extensive literature on race relations published between the 1960s and the 1980s reveals very few references, other than the superficial or incidental, either to the religions of minority groups or to the activity of the Christian churches. In relation to the 1960s this corresponded quite closely to the reality. In this decade recently arrived South Asians had not yet done much to form organized religious structures, while Christians prepared to take a firm stand against racism in Britain – as opposed to southern Africa – were rare. It is true that these included the Archbishop of Canterbury, Michael Ramsey, who in 1966 was appointed chairman of the

[7]   The 'nationalism' in question was, of course, ambiguous. In strict logic, especially in Scotland, the Church of England could only represent 'English' rather than 'British' nationalism. In practice, however, the perception that the Church of England was a British institution was widely held south of the border: for example, on 8 July 1980, *The Times* leader-writer described it as 'the British national church'.

[8]   It seems to me that it is part of the essence of the outlook of those who hold such a position that the confusion between 'England' and 'Britain' remains unresolved.

National Committee for Commonwealth Immigrants – an unusual position for an archbishop to hold – and in 1968 vigorously opposed in the Lords legislation to restrict the immigration of Kenyan Asians (Chadwick, 1990, pp.165–76). On the other hand there were Christians who adopted a racist position and advocated controls on immigration, on the lines of a clergyman who called in *The Church Times* for 'a definitely Christian "Keep Britain White" campaign'(quoted by Leech, 1985, p.208). It is also noteworthy that Enoch Powell, who built his reputation as a forceful opponent of non-white immigration during the 1960s, was a devout Anglican. Powell did not suggest that his political views followed from his religious convictions, maintaining rather that Christianity and politics were essentially separate spheres. He was, however, consistently unreceptive to the arguments of others, such as Bishop Trevor Huddleston, that Christian commitment implied a tolerant attitude to minorities. It was by no means clear who was closer to the majority opinion in the pew (Powell, 1973, pp.95–112).

During the 1970s and 1980s a polarization of views was apparent, symptomatic of deeper tensions over the relationship of Christianity to British identity. On the one hand, reaction against Powell and the even more blatantly racist attitudes promoted by the National Front, helped to stimulate a growing Christian anxiety during the 1970s to improve race relations.[9] On the other hand Powell continued cogently to argue for his view of Britishness as a product of a long tradition which would be fatally undermined by newcomers (Powell, 1977, pp.5, 74–82). This position was echoed in some respects by Margaret Thatcher when she spoke in 1978 of fears of being 'swamped' by an 'alien' influx (Leech, 1985, p.212). Such differences found expression in 1981 in controversy over the Thatcher government's British Nationality Bill, which removed the right of abode in Britain from some categories of British passport holders. Some church groups lobbied energetically against this measure and, although they could not prevent its central provisions from becoming law, they did obtain significant changes on minor points. The campaign against the Nationality Bill was also significant because it illustrated the potential for co-operation between the bishops in the House of Lords and other Christian bodies (Dummett, 1982).

Nevertheless, even in the 1980s, there continued to be a tendency to think in terms of racial categories to the virtual exclusion of religious ones. This was not merely a blind spot for secular commentators, but one evident within the churches themselves. For example when, in 1981, the Church of England set up a Race, Pluralism and Community group, this was within the Board for Social Responsibility and had no obvious structural

---

[9]   For instances of this process, see essay 4, pp.129–30.

connection with the work on inter-faith relations being carried out under the auspices of the Board for Mission and Unity. It was also revealing that when Thatcher, in her address before the General Assembly of the Church of Scotland in 1988, stressed her perception of the congruence between the Judaeo–Christian tradition and British identity, that portion of her speech proved relatively uncontroversial.

The tendency – even among Christians and anti-racist groups – to think in racial terms tended to increase feelings of alienation among the very people they were seeking to support and with whom they were seeking to express solidarity. It was particularly galling for Afro-Caribbeans who might strongly identify themselves as both Christian and British to be regarded as a 'problem' because they were black (Phoenix, 1991, pp.95–104). To some extent this perception proved to be self-fulfilling inasmuch as the mainstream of black political activity in Britain shifted after the Second World War away from the moderate and Christian framework in which it had operated in the inter-war period to assume a more militant and secular character (Ramdin, 1987, pp.103–22 and passim). The minority of Asian Christians struggled for recognition of their very existence in the face of an official tendency to assume that people of Asian origin were either Hindu, Muslim or Sikh. Non-Christian minorities, especially Muslims, were similarly frustrated by being classified in racial rather than religious terms: for example, in 1986 a Muslim critique of the Swann Report on the education of 'ethnic minorities' criticized its 'integrational pluralism' based on a 'secular approach to religion' (Wolffe, 1993, p.258). By the late 1980s Muslims were wavering in their previously overwhelming support for the Labour Party because of its lack of sensitivity to their confessional concerns (Caute, 1989).

The question of blasphemy provides an insight into the situation that existed in the 1980s. The *Gay News* trial of 1977 brought this seemingly obsolescent offence back into the public eye. In subsequent years there was debate over whether the common law offence should be maintained, relating as it did only to Christianity or, technically and specifically, to the Church of England. The alternatives were outright abolition, the extension of the blasphemy law to cover other traditions, or its replacement by some new offence, such as incitement to religious hatred, which already existed in Northern Ireland. In 1985 a majority of the Law Commission recommended abolition on the grounds that: 'where members of society have a multiplicity of faiths or none at all it is invidious to single out that religion [the Church of England], albeit in England the established religion, for protection' (Commission for Racial Equality (CRE), 1990, p.72).

Two out of the five commissioners dissented, however, and recommended a new offence which 'would penalize anyone who published grossly abusive or insulting material relating to religion with the purpose of outraging religious feelings'. This latter view was subsequently endorsed by a church working party set up by the Archbishop of Canterbury (CRE, 1990, pp.75, 81). The problem, in a nutshell, was whether the law should treat England as a secular society in which religion had no special protection; or as a multi-religious one in which all faiths were accorded some legal recognition. Faced with such a philosophical and sociological dilemma reflected in division among the experts, the government, not surprisingly, did nothing. It thus in effect maintained the status quo of Christian privilege.

This was how matters stood in 1988 when the publication of Salman Rushdie's novel, *The Satanic Verses,* threw the issues into stark relief. Muslims found that they had no redress in English law for their feelings of hurt and outrage.[10] Meanwhile secular politicians of the centre and left found it deeply disorientating and disconcerting to find that, where religion was involved, commitments to racial equality and to freedom of artistic expression were not necessarily always compatible. John Patten, then Minister of State at the Home Office, reiterated the government's reluctance to change the law, but affirmed that

> at the heart of our thinking is a Britain where Christians, Muslims, Jews, Hindus, Sikhs and others can all work and live together, each retaining proudly their own faith and identity, but each sharing in common the bond of being by birth or choice, British.
>
> (CRE, 1990, p.87)

Especially in the light of the then Prime Minister's declared views on the Judaeo–Christian nature of British identity, the minister's letter implied that the government still hoped that it could have things both ways.

Nevertheless there were some signs that in bringing forcefully together questions of race and religion, the Rushdie affair had a catalytic effect in pointing to new roles for organized Christianity in late twentieth-century politics and culture. It is noteworthy that Christian leaders such as Lesslie Newbigin (Newbigin, 1990) and the new Archbishop of Canterbury, George Carey (in a lecture at the University of York on 22 November 1991), were prepared publicly to express sympathy for Muslim outrage. At a local level, the Bishop of Bradford, Roy Williamson, played a key role in repairing the damage to relations between the various

---

[10] This is not to imply that if an offence on the lines of that proposed by the minority Law Commissioners in 1985 had been on the statute book in 1988, Rushdie would necessarily have been convicted under it, although there might have been a case to answer. It would have been necessary not only to prove that there had been outrage, which was undeniable, but that it had been caused intentionally, which was more debateable. For further discussion see Volume I, pp.165–9.

communities that had been caused by the controversy (as described by Philip Lewis in a lecture at Lambeth Palace on 17 November 1992). In the late 1980s and early 1990s these were still straws in the wind, but they were nevertheless indications that there was potential for the Established Church of England to find a new role in a multi-cultural society, as a bridge between the mutual incomprehensions of secular liberalism and minority religious conviction (Braybrooke, 1991).

Such is one prognosis for Establishment. However, the trends of the 1970s and 1980s also suggested other possibilities. It could be that the logic both of secular attitudes in government and the desire for even-handed treatment of all religious groups will eventually force disestablishment, the transformation of the Church of England into just another Christian denomination, and a waning of networks of Christian parliamentary influence. Conversely, the Church of England might come to be perceived as a bastion of traditional Englishness/Britishness in the face of the challenge of minority cultures, and the Establishment jealously preserved as a rallying point in a divided society (Hunter and Mackie, 1986, pp.17–19). One thing is certain: debate on the matter will continue, with wide implications for the structure of Britain in the twenty-first century, which will call for considerable statesmanship, both secular and ecclesiastical. One Free Church writer saw the issues as follows:

> The responsibility of the national church is never self-preservation but a continuous watchman's role to alert the nation on behalf of those who can only raise a small voice themselves. Past history is not happy at this point. A national church can resent religious minorities or try to ignore them. But we live in a very mixed society which holds diverse ideals and faiths. If we are to respect each person's individuality, if we are to learn from the insights of others, and if human rights are to be public policy number one, then the national church will lead the national search for justice.
>
> (Thorogood, 1988, pp.47–8)

2   Religion and nationalism in Scotland and Wales

The purpose of this section is to consider the role of religion in pressure for devolution in Scotland and Wales. The Britain that has seen the growth of ethnic and religious diversity since the Second World War was, of course, never a culturally and politically homogeneous entity. The 'United Kingdom of Great Britain and Northern Ireland' comprises three nations –

England, Scotland and Wales – and a province, Northern Ireland. Scotland, although sharing its monarch with England since 1603 and its parliament since 1707, still retains its distinct legal and educational systems, and its own national Presbyterian church, the Church of Scotland. Wales's last vestiges of true political independence were crushed in the late thirteenth century, and its constitutional and legal structures are merged with England's, but its ancient language and culture still possess significant vitality. In religious terms it has been clearly distinguished from England since its dominant Nonconformity led to the disestablishment of the (Anglican) Church in Wales in 1920.

During the period since the Second World War relationships with the British state have been a matter of – to say the least – considerable controversy in all the non-English parts of the United Kingdom. In Scotland pressure for devolution has been entirely peaceful, and in Wales largely so, but in Northern Ireland the aspirations of the minority seeking a united Ireland have, since 1969, been the seed bed for the sustained terrorist campaign of the Irish Republican Army (IRA), and have been met with comparable measures from extremist defenders of the British connection. The situation in Northern Ireland also differs fundamentally from that in Scotland and Wales in that nationalists are seeking absorption into an existing nation state in the south, rather than aiming to create (or restore) a new one. It will accordingly receive separate and more extended consideration in the next section.

Scotland provides the most convenient point of departure. The Church of Scotland remains Established in the sense that it has a formal link with the Crown expressed in the presence of the sovereign's Lord High Commissioner at the General Assembly in Edinburgh each May. It also has a parochial structure which gives it a territorial presence in all parts of the country. Unlike in the Church of England, however, legislation by the General Assembly is not subject to parliamentary ratification and the Prime Minister has no role in appointments. The Kirk is governed by a hierarchy of courts – Kirk Sessions, Presbyteries, and Synods – which culminate in the General Assembly. This body is made up of ministers and elders from all over Scotland and accordingly has been perceived by some as a kind of surrogate parliament, speaking for the nation in matters other than the strictly ecclesiastical. This function has been developed particularly by the Assembly's Church and Nation Committee, whose annual reports have provided a wide-ranging commentary on social and political affairs.

Throughout the period since 1945 the Church of Scotland has maintained qualified support for some form of devolved government within the United Kingdom. In 1946 the General Assembly called for 'a greater decentralizing of authority and an increased measure of independence'; there was strong sympathy in the church for the national covenant launched in October 1949 and calling for a Scottish Parliament; the 1950 General Assembly appealed to the government to appoint a Royal Commission. This was set up, but its report (1954) was dismissed by the Church and Nation Committee as a 'wee bit tinkering with one or two of the wheels in the machinery'. The issue receded in the late 1950s and early 1960s, but following the growth of the Scottish National Party in the mid 1960s the General Assembly of 1968 declared itself 'convinced of the need for an effective form of self-government in Scotland within the framework of the United Kingdom'. During the 1970s the church actively supported proposals for an assembly in Edinburgh, only in the referendum of 1979 to find its own credibility weakened, together with that of the whole devolution movement, by the failure of the plan to gain the support of the requisite 40 per cent of the electorate (Proctor, 1983; Sefton, 1982).

Moreover, the culmination of the campaign for devolution in the late 1970s revealed the Kirk's own divisions on the issue. On the one hand there was pressure to countenance the possibility of outright independence; on the other there was a substantial body of opinion within the Church of Scotland opposed even to devolution – at least on the basis then proposed – and led by Andrew Herron, a former moderator of the General Assembly (Proctor, 1983). There was irony in the fact that Geoffrey Shaw, a Church of Scotland minister and convenor of Strathclyde Regional Council, tipped as a likely first Prime Minister in a Scottish Assembly, had been at most lukewarm towards devolution (Ferguson, 1979, pp.246, 253). In any case Shaw died prematurely in April 1978. Continuing division was evident in the General Assembly of 1980 when a deliverance (motion) reaffirming commitment to 'an appropriate measure of devolved self-government' was only carried by a margin of fifteen votes (Sefton, 1982, p.554). It was therefore internal uncertainty as well as an unpropitious political climate at Westminster that led the Kirk again to retreat from advocacy of the issue during the 1980s. Only at the end of the decade, as other political pressures for some form of self-government in Scotland again mounted, did the Church and Nation Committee once more take an interest. This time, with memories of the difficulties of 1979 still present, the emphasis was on the general application of theological and constitutional principles, rather than the advocacy of a particular political programme. Commitment to a 'democratically elected Assembly within the United Kingdom' was nevertheless reiterated (General Assembly Reports, 1989, Part I, pp.138, 144–52).

The specific involvements of the Church of Scotland in the devolution controversy were but part of wider interconnections between religion and national consciousness. It was significant that on various occasions nationalists used religiously evocative language: the covenant of 1949 recalled the Presbyterian covenants of the seventeenth century, and the 'Claim of Right' of 1988 recalled the document of 1842 in which the General Assembly had issued an historic defiance of control by the civil courts. There were also those who saw the church itself as a repository of Scottish identity and tradition: in the eyes of one writer in the mid 1980s it was still true that 'To be a Scot is to be a Presbyterian, even though that designation may say more of cultural identity than religious persuasion' (Bisset, 1986, p.3).

This last assertion well indicates both the strength and the weakness of the Church of Scotland's position in relation to the assertion of distinctive Scottish identity. In a manner analogous to the Church of England south of the border it was able to draw on the diffuse sympathies of a substantially larger proportion of the population than the one in five or so who had a declared affiliation. At the same time, to define Scottishness in Presbyterian terms was to exclude important religious minorities. Both Roman Catholicism and Episcopalianism had had long and distinctive histories in Scotland, but even in the later twentieth century they could not wholly overcome the perception that they were 'Irish' and 'English' respectively. However, there was a dawning awareness that the strident assertion of 'Scotland' against 'England' had its dangers in fostering racist attitudes which could adversely affect attitudes to ethnic and religious minorities within Scotland (Hunter, 1991; Hunter and Mackie, 1986). It was also a significant development when in October 1988 Roman Catholic and Episcopalian representatives joined with the Church of Scotland, the Congregationalists, the Methodists and the Society of Friends, to express general support for the Claim of Right and the call for a Constitutional Convention (General Assembly Reports, 1989, Part I, pp.151–2).

A key difference of the situation in Wales from that in Scotland was the lack of a single religious institution comparable to the Church of Scotland which could serve as a focus for national feelings. Nationalist sympathies were rather diffused across most major Christian groups. During the nineteenth century the Nonconformist chapels had linked national self-assertion with the use of the Welsh language and the campaign for disestablishment, and the legacy of this was still apparent a century later. It was represented above all by Gwynfor Evans, president of Plaid Cymru, the nationalist political party, who was both a leading member of the Union of Welsh Independents (congregationalists) and the first Plaid Cymru MP, returned at the Carmarthen by-election in July 1966. In the meantime the disestablished Church in Wales[11] became a more self-consciously Welsh

---

[11] Since disestablishment in 1920 the Church in Wales has been a separate province within the Anglican communion, with its own archbishop elected from among the six diocesan bishops.

institution and some of its leaders were prepared to identify with national aspirations. Although Edwin Morris, Archbishop of Wales from 1957 to 1967, largely moved in an English cultural orbit, his two successors, Glyn Simon (1968–71) and Gwilym Williams (1971–82), were much more ready to identify themselves with Welsh linguistic, cultural and political aspirations. Meanwhile it had been a Roman Catholic, the poet Saunders Lewis, who by coming out of retirement in February 1962 to deliver a radio lecture entitled 'Tynged yr Iaith' ('The Fate of the Language') provided a major stimulus to the nationalist resurgence of the 1960s. This call for more committed and active defence of Welsh led directly to the formation later in 1962 of Cymdeithas yr Iaith Gymraeg (the Welsh Language Society) (Brown, 1979; Morgan, 1981, pp.376–408).

During the subsequent decades there was widespread support in the churches for campaigns to strengthen the position of Welsh and to gain a measure of political devolution. An Interdenominational Committee for the Welsh Language was also founded in 1962, and the Free Churches in particular proved to be enthusiastic supporters of Cymdeithas yr Iaith Gymraeg. One result of such commitments was the publication in 1975 of a new Welsh translation of the New Testament, but efforts were not confined to strictly religious matters. In 1963 the Bishop of St Davids sanctioned the use of church bells as a warning signal to villagers at Llangynderyn who were obstructing surveying work on a proposed dam; Anglican and Free Church ministers were involved in the covering of English roadsigns; Archbishop Simon visited the nationalist leader Dafydd Iwan in prison. In evidence to the Royal Commission on the constitution in 1970 the churches generally appeared sympathetic to devolution, a standpoint that was maintained in support for the proposals which were to be defeated in the referendum of 1979 (Brown, 1979, pp.44–51). Moreover, there were those who saw the nationalist cause in explicitly religious terms: the leading Congregationalist Richard Tudur Jones saw a measure of political emancipation as a necessary prerequisite for the spiritual revival of Wales (Tudur Jones, 1979); Archbishop Williams said in a sermon that 'the Bible and the Welsh language, the culture of Wales and her identity were welded together' (Rhys, 1991, p.63).

On the other hand Welsh Christians were by no means united in their support for devolution and Cymdeithas yr Iaith Gymraeg. There was quite extensive readiness to support the Investiture of the Prince of Wales in 1969 despite the manner in which this was seen as an anti-nationalist ceremony. In 1979 Archbishop Williams's calls for a 'yes' vote in the referendum were resented by many in his own church (Brown, 1979, pp.48–9, 51). The result, which showed only 11.8 per cent of the population in favour of devolution, indeed suggested that the archbishop and other religious leaders were going further than most of the people in the pews.

Specific objections to particularism were voiced in the 1970s and 1980s by those who saw the Christian vision as one that transcended Wales. The tension, it was suggested, was not so much between 'Welsh' and 'English' as between 'Welsh Welsh' and 'Welsh British', the latter seeing the material and spiritual prosperity of Wales as inextricably linked with that of Britain as a whole (Jenkins, 1979). Another writer noted with alarm a similar tendency to that apparent in Scotland, as some nationalists defined Welshness in narrow Protestant terms, and explicitly excluded not only Hindus and Muslims, but also Roman Catholics, Mormons and Jehovah's Witnesses. Here was fertile soil for the extreme political right. The antidote, it was suggested, was an alliance 'with the poor and oppressed, and with the despised minorities of the rest of Britain, of Europe, or the world' (Rhys, 1991, pp.66–71).

Scotland and Wales differ from England and resemble each other both in respect of relatively higher levels of Christian religious membership and practice and in the small scale of non-Christian religious communities. The identification of important elements in the churches with national self-assertion was therefore unsurprising. Despite the lack of concrete political and constitutional results, there were significant achievements, notably the increased status of the Welsh language and a heightened awareness of Scottish cultural and religious distinctiveness. It seems, however, that many Christians, proud of their Scottish or Welsh identity, but aware that a strident nationalism could all too easily become narrow and divisive, or even blasphemous and violent, had no desire to press things any further. From 1969 moreover they had prominently before them the example of the region of the United Kingdom with the highest levels of religious participation, the most uncompromising nationalist commitments and the most deeply seated and violent divisions: Northern Ireland.

3   Religion and the Northern Ireland conflict

Northern Ireland consists of six out of the nine counties of the ancient province of Ulster. As a political entity it was created in 1920 to meet the demands of the Unionists who were implacably opposed to the incorporation of the whole island of Ireland within the Irish Free State (Republic of Ireland from 1949). For half a century Northern Ireland had its own parliament at Stormont, but this was abolished in 1972 and direct rule from Westminster was introduced. Over a third of the population of Northern Ireland are Roman Catholics, who make up the great majority of the population of the Republic of Ireland. The 'Protestant' majority in Northern Ireland is made up of numerous denominational groups, of which the two largest are Presbyterians (themselves divided) and the (Anglican) Church of Ireland (disestablished in 1871).

Northern Ireland, in common with the Republic of Ireland, has consistently had much higher levels of religious participation and professed belief than have prevailed on the British mainland. In 1970 a survey found that 76 per cent of the population, as opposed to 46 per cent in Britain, felt that religion affected their lives a great deal; in 1971 the census showed that out of a population of just over one and a half million, less than two thousand classed themselves explicitly as atheists or agnostics; in 1973 only 1 per cent of Catholics and 11 per cent of Protestants reported that they never went to church, and 92 per cent of Catholics and 34 per cent of Protestants claimed to go at least once a week (Darby, 1976, pp.114–5; MacAllister, 1982, pp.334–50). Hence, it has been suggested, the continuing relatively great strength of traditional religious influences in Northern Ireland had its consequence in the prevalence of a kind of religious war which would be a total anachronism in most other western societies. This judgement is patronizing, over-simplistic and raises many questions, particularly relating to the mechanisms whereby religious commitment has been translated into political and social conflict, but it still provides a useful point of departure, to which we shall return.

Before doing so, however, it is necessary to allude briefly to some of the arguments used to support the view that the conflict has been essentially one about religious labels rather than religious realities. Firstly, the social geography of Northern Ireland indicates the extreme segregation of Protestant and Catholic communities. Religion, in common with culture and politics, was clearly a factor in creating such polarized communities, but their continuation, and the level of hostility between them, can also be explained in sociological terms: lack of contact results in ignorance, fear, and stereotyped prejudices, which mean that the interaction that might alleviate them is never contemplated. The separation was reinforced by an educational system that was almost entirely segregated. It was estimated in 1961 that at least 98 per cent of Catholic children attended Catholic primary schools. Polarization at secondary level was somewhat less extreme, but it is clear that the vast majority of Northern Ireland children had little or no contact with the other tradition throughout their school careers (Barritt and Carter, 1972, pp.77–92; Darby, 1976, pp.123–39).

Secondly, Northern Ireland has been economically the least prosperous part of the United Kingdom. Unemployment in the province has been substantially higher than the UK average and the gross domestic product per head substantially lower (Simpson, 1983, pp.79–99). Consequent resentments took a primarily sectarian form because there was by no means an equality of suffering: for example, in 1971, 13.9 per cent of Catholics but only 5.6 per cent of Protestants were unemployed (Darby,

1983, p.101). Moreover there is clear evidence of actual discrimination: in 1971, although Catholics made up 26 per cent of the population of Belfast, they only held 4.3 per cent of jobs in the Belfast Corporation Electricity Department, a disproportion that hardly seemed attributable to chance (Darby, 1976, pp.72–3).

Thirdly, the problem of discrimination in employment was but one aspect of a broader structure of political and social power that operated to deny Catholics effective equality of opportunity. The boundaries of the province were originally drawn with the deliberate intention of guaranteeing a secure Protestant and Unionist majority. At the local level, most notoriously in Londonderry, electoral boundaries were gerrymandered to strengthen the Protestant presence on councils. Until 1969, a property qualification for the local government franchise excluded disproportionate numbers of Catholics (Darby, 1976, p.50). It was the consequent resentments that lay behind the civil rights campaign of the 1960s which began the sequence of events leading to the outbreak of large-scale violence in 1969. Subsequent reforms were insufficient to take the sting out of Catholic resentment.

Fourthly, there has been throughout Northern Ireland's history a clash of nationalist political aspirations that is fundamentally irreconcilable. In the long term the province must either remain part of the United Kingdom or become part of a united Ireland: it cannot be both.[12] Hence the political confrontation of Nationalist and Unionist, almost but not quite co-extensive with the sectarian tension between Protestant and Catholic, was always one in which the only hope of finding an agreed answer lay in changing the question. There were some signs that this might be happening in the 1960s. Under Terence O'Neill, prime minister from 1963 to 1969, unionism became more liberal and the nationalists decided in 1965 to return to constitutional politics by becoming the official opposition at Stormont. Moreover, the civil rights movement implied that Catholics were now working for equality within the Northern Ireland state rather than seeking to subvert it. However, from 1969 onwards positions polarized again. The political loyalties of a significant proportion of

[12]   In theory a third possibility would be the creation of an independent Northern Ireland, but quite apart from the problem of the political and economic viability of such a statelet, survey evidence suggests that a 'solution' of this kind would not now command much enthusiasm even among the Protestant population (Moxon-Browne, 1983, pp.6–7). Just as this essay was about to go to press, however, the Downing Street declaration of the British Prime Minister, John Major, and the Taoiseach, Albert Reynolds, on 15 December 1993, pointed to the possibility that, given time and the development of trust between the two communities, the impasse might eventually be resolved. Nevertheless, it was still difficult to envisage how general aspirations for reconciliation – even if they could bring about a cessation of violence – were to be translated into a sustainable constitutional settlement.

Catholics shifted from the constitutional nationalism of the Social Democratic and Labour Party (SDLP) to Sinn Fein's rejection of the legitimacy of the present Northern Ireland political structure, and the outright violence of the IRA. On the Unionist side too there was a hardening of positions, symbolized inside the sphere of legitimate politics by the emergence of Ian Paisley's Democratic Unionist Party, and outside it by the promotion of paramilitary groups, including the Ulster Defence Association and the Ulster Volunteer Force.

It is awareness of these considerations that has led most analysts to concur in the view of Garret Fitzgerald, Prime Minister of the Irish Republic from 1981 to 1987, that the inter-community conflict in Northern Ireland is not a religious war, in the sense of a war about religious dogmas (Fitzgerald, 1972, p.87). Nevertheless Fitzgerald immediately went on to qualify that view, and this is a course that we must follow too, if we are to understand the enduring importance of religion as a label, symbol, and focus for the numerous other tensions at work.

Set in historical perspective, there is no doubting the reality of the extensive points of theological difference between Protestants and Catholics as they have been articulated throughout the Christian world over most of the period since the Reformation. The issues have included the role of the mass and the sacraments as channels of grace, as opposed to the Protestant emphasis on an individual response to the offer of salvation made in the life and death of Christ; the role of church authority and tradition, as against the conviction that everyone has the right to private judgement based on a reading of the Bible; and Protestant rejection of the role of saints as intercessors with God. Such specific points of dispute have been underscored, especially among more extreme Protestant groups, by a reading of the Bible in which Rome is identified with the mystical Babylon of the Book of Revelation and the papacy seen, if not as a personal Antichrist, at least as a central pivot for the forces of apocalyptic evil at work in the world (Bruce, 1986, pp.7–8, 220–31).

Views of this kind were widely held and diffused throughout the British Isles in the Victorian period (Wolffe, 1991), but in Ireland religious convictions and rivalries became particularly intense during the nineteenth century. On the Catholic side there took place what has been termed a 'devotional revolution' in which the Irish Church, initially struggling against extensive folk religion, non-practice and anticlericalism, became one of the most tightly organized, doctrinally orthodox and universally supported Catholic bodies in the world. Among Protestants too the Victorian era was a period of spiritual awakening and growth, as variously reflected in the reorganization of the Church of Ireland in response to reform and disestablishment, and movements of revivalism, most notably that of 1859, which revitalized the popular Presbyterianism of Ulster (Connolly, 1985; Parsons, 1988). The revivalist tradition continued into the twentieth century, finding expression in the Nicholson crusades of the 1920s, and, after the Second World War, had its most successful exponent in Ian Paisley (Bruce, 1986, pp.14–17). There was thus much in the relatively recent religious history of Ireland to reinforce the strength of Protestant and Catholic spiritual and doctrinal commitments.

Specifically religious divergencies played an important part in the political and cultural polarization of Ireland in the early twentieth century. The south developed a cultural and political identity which rested on the pillars of Gaelicism and Catholicism and, allegedly, marginalized the Protestant minority in the Republic (Bowen 1983; Lyons, 1979). The Catholic Church was accorded favoured status under the constitution of the Republic, and Catholic orthodoxy shaped conservative legislation on matters of personal morality such as contraception, divorce and censorship. Northern Protestants did not necessarily object to the specific moral values enshrined in that legislation, but held strongly to the view that state or ecclesiastical interference in such matters was an infringement of personal freedom, and accordingly that the southern political system was wholly unacceptable. As Fitzgerald points out, however, this position is not logically consistent in so far as the laws of Northern Ireland, like those of any other country, obviously also intervene in matters in personal morality: the underlying objection was thus not so much to statutory morality as to Roman Catholic morality (Fitzgerald, 1972, pp.92–3). A particular bone of contention was the stringent provisions of the Catholic Church on mixed marriages, which had the effect of ensuring that these took place relatively rarely and that, when they did, the children had to be brought up as Catholics. After the judgement of the Irish Supreme Court in the Tilson case in 1950 it was clear that the church had the backing of the civil law. The decline of Protestant numbers and influence in the Republic reinforced the fears of their northern counterparts regarding their own fate in a united Ireland (Barritt and Carter, 1972, pp.26–7; Bowen, 1983, pp.20–46).

From the 1960s the liberalization of Catholicism in the wake of the pontificate of John XXIII and the Second Vatican Council had its impact in Ireland, particularly in stimulating a growth in lay Catholic initiatives reflected in the civil rights movement and the development of the SDLP (MacAllister, 1977, p.9). In 1972 the clause of the Irish constitution according a 'special position' to the Roman Catholic Church was deleted; in 1983 Pope John Paul II softened the church's stance on mixed marriages. Meanwhile, by the 1990s, controversies in the Republic over abortion and homosexuality suggested that the church's influence was weakening. The Protestant response was mixed. For some the sense that the Catholic Church was reforming and changing was met by interest in ecumenism, the religious parallel to the political attempts to accommodate Catholics made by O'Neill's government in the 1960s. For others the changes in the Roman Catholic Church were seen as in no way altering its fundamental characteristics and any decline in its power in the south was held to be illusory. Ecumenism was accordingly seen as at best seriously misguided and at worst the working out of an insidious Roman plot which must be met by the forceful reassertion of traditional Protestantism (Bruce, 1986, pp.179, 224–5; Gallagher and Worrall, 1982, pp.21–38, 130–52).

The movements centred on Ian Paisley, the Free Presbyterian Church and the Democratic Unionist Party were a particularly vigorous instance of the political significance of religion in Northern Ireland. The Free Presbyterian Church originated in 1951 as a small splinter group from the Irish Presbyterian Church, which Paisley perceived as riddled with liberal apostasy. The new church grew slowly in the 1950s, but its advance gained momentum in the 1960s in the context of the challenge that O'Neill was felt to present to the Protestant traditions of the province. In 1965 there had been twelve congregations; the total increased to twenty-eight by 1970, and a further twenty-one were formed between 1970 and 1982. In the 1971 census, 7,337 people were recorded as Free Presbyterians; in 1981 there were 9,621, and Steve Bruce has estimated the 1985 figure to be 12,000 (Bruce, 1986, p.161). Although this figure, less than 1 per cent of the population of the province, might seem insignificant, the commitment of the church's membership, and its steady growth at a period when the other main Protestant groups were all in decline, secured it an increasingly important influence. Furthermore, Paisley's style of religion had an appeal to the Protestant working class, who might not attend church themselves, but still had a residual identification with evangelicalism which was most significantly expressed by sending their children to Free Presbyterian Sunday Schools (Taylor, 1984, p.67). Free Presbyterians have been characterized by their staunch adherence to traditional Protestant objections to Roman Catholicism, considered by them to be equated with the 'Mystery, Babylon the Great, the Mother of Harlots' of Revelation, chapter 17. They believe it to be working out its evil purposes not only through republican terrorist groups in Ireland, but on the international stage through the European Community (Bruce, 1986, pp.220–31). In political terms, Paisleyism is characterized by an emotive adherence to the Scottish tradition of the covenanted nation, implying compacts between God and the people and rulers and ruled. Concessions to Roman Catholic Ireland by the British government are liable to be seen as breaches of the covenant which justify civil disobedience (MacIver, 1987; Taylor, 1984, pp.74–7).

On the political front Paisley first came to prominence in the late 1960s as a vigorous critic of liberal unionism. He defeated the official Unionist candidate in a Stormont by-election in April 1970 and in June he won the North Antrim seat in the Westminster general election. By the 1980s his Democratic Unionist Party (DUP) was established as a major force in Northern Ireland politics, with three MPs at Westminster. In the 1979 European Parliament election, Paisley obtained 29.8 per cent of first preference votes, more than all the other Unionist candidates put together, a proportion that increased to 33.6 per cent in 1984 (Bruce, 1986, pp.285–91), although it fell back to 29.9 in 1989 (*The Times*, 20 June 1989). Although the DUP thus attracted an electoral support that went well beyond the boundaries of Free Presbyterianism, the majority of the party activists continued to be members of the church – for example, 125 out of 218 candidates in the local council elections of 1985 (Bruce, 1986, p.294). The association of the religious and political wings of Paisleyism was not without its tensions, for a church that feared diversion from spiritual emphases, and a party that risked a loss of popular appeal from its association with sabbatarianism and other conservative evangelical causes. Nevertheless, the success of the DUP implies that those secular Protestants who have supported it had a generalized inherited sense of commitment to religion which caused them to respect active evangelicals and accept their leadership:

> That Paisley's brand of unionism has proved popular with such a large section of the Ulster Protestant population defies any explanation other than the obvious one: evangelicalism provides the core beliefs, values, and symbols of what it means to be a Protestant. Unionism is about avoiding becoming a subordinate minority in a Catholic state. Avoiding becoming a Catholic means remaining a Protestant.
>
> (Bruce, 1986, pp.264–5)

A further dimension of the links between religion and Protestant identity is represented by the Orange Order. This quasi-masonic fraternal association celebrated – by its ideology, rituals and fraternal ethos – the 'immortal memory' of William III (of Orange) whose forces had overcome those of the Roman Catholic James II at the Battle of the Boyne on 1 July 1690. Estimates of membership in the early 1970s ranged from 90,000 to 130,000, or around a third of the adult male Protestant population of the province (Darby, 1976, pp.82–3). The qualifications for membership include explicit and detailed adherence to a Protestant Christian belief, in particular a strong reverence for the Bible, and a rejection of Roman Catholicism juxtaposed with condemnation of intolerance. Lodges routinely engage in prayer, listen to religious addresses, welcome the involvement of clergymen, and attend church services on significant days.

There has undoubtedly been a gulf between professions and reality in these respects: some Orangemen 'do get a bit rougher' and never attend church except for the annual parades on 12 July (the anniversary of the battle of Aughrim in 1691). The master of one Lodge probably reflected a widespread perception when he said, 'You don't have to go to church to believe in God's commandments'. On the other hand, Orangeism has also been perceived as a channel for diffusing Christian influences to a working-class constituency and the 'Royal Black Preceptory', an order within the order, professes to exclude less religious elements. The ambiguities are well illustrated by the 12 July celebrations, which are a curious blend of secular festivity and religious seriousness, and by the symbolism of banners which suggest a selective interpretation of biblical themes, emphasizing faithfulness to God and confrontation with alien peoples. By such mechanisms is the spiritual and historical legitimacy of the Protestant cause reaffirmed (Buckley, 1984, pp.23–4; Buckley, 1985; Gray, 1972; Hickey, 1984, pp.64–6; Roberts, 1971; Wright, 1973, pp.245–51).

On the Catholic side of the coin there have been fewer specific mechanisms linking religion and politics. It is true that Roman Catholic clergy have made significant pronouncements on political matters: for example, in 1978 Archbishop (later Cardinal) Tomas O'Fiaich called for British withdrawal from Ireland. However, although the overwhelming majority of priests identify with the SDLP, few have tried actively to influence the votes of their congregations. There is evidence of a significant degree of religiosity among IRA activists, but Sinn Fein has been the object of episcopal condemnation, and only a handful of priests have manifested any public sympathy for the IRA (McElroy, 1991, pp.56–7, 144–5, 189, 191).

It is accordingly wrong to posit a *crude* correlation between levels of active religious commitment and political sectarian identification. Questionnaire evidence suggests that religious commitment is only weakly related to political attitudes for Protestants, and unrelated for Catholics (MacAllister, 1982, p.342). Indeed, research on teenagers suggests that, in general, those most favourably disposed to religion were also those most likely to be open to the other religious tradition (Greer, 1985). Among both Protestant and Catholic clergy, sectarian political activists were outnumbered by those concerned to promote reconciliation (Birrell, Greer and Roche, 1979). There have indeed been some courageous, if unsuccessful, initiatives by leading churchmen who sought to bring an end to the violence (Gallagher and Worrall, 1982, pp.1–4, 66–84). Even Paisley has been unequivocal in his condemnation of violence, in 1975 accusing Protestant paramilitaries of committing crimes 'just as heinous and hellish as those of the IRA' (Bruce, 1986, p.109).

A brief survey such as this runs the risk of over-simplifying a very complex situation.[13] In broad terms, however, we have pointed to the inadequacies of both – on the one hand – dismissing the religious element in the Northern Ireland conflict as simply a matter of labels, and – on the other hand – portraying the situation as a religious war in which secular factors are only secondary. The truth lies somewhere between these two extreme interpretations. Non-religious factors were of considerable importance in polarizing the two communities and, generally speaking, Christian leaders had a cautious attitude towards politics and an unequivocal horror of violence. At the same time, the historic intransigence of Ulster loyalists stemmed from exaggerated, but by no means wholly unfounded, perceptions of the influence of Roman Catholicism in the south, while their own cultural and political identity owed much to Protestantism. Moreover it is striking that, at least as indicated by the associated rise of Free Presbyterianism and the DUP, these connections if anything became stronger during the first two decades of the Troubles. On the other hand, among other denominations, it was generally those with fringe church links rather than the hard core of adherents who contributed the most to sectarian militancy.

4 Conclusion: religion and the unity of the United Kingdom

How, then, does the situation in Northern Ireland relate to the wider pattern of interaction between religious and national identities in the United Kingdom? On the political front, enhanced authority and position was given to those parliamentarians such as Enoch Powell and Ian Gow who were, in a British context, the most forceful defenders of the traditional identification of the state with Christianity. On the other hand, the impact of Northern Ireland on the religious life of England, Scotland and Wales was in general limited. British churchmen usually showed little interest, whether from embarrassment or from anguished confusion. Even in areas with a history of Protestant–Catholic confrontation, notably Lancashire and the west of Scotland, sectarian conflict, although present, never assumed the ugly proportions apparent in Northern Ireland.

The case of Glasgow, which seemed to offer the greatest potential for

---

[13] An invaluable starting point for the reader requiring more detailed and nuanced discussion is John Whyte (1990) *Interpreting Northern Ireland*, Oxford University Press, Oxford. Whyte comments that 'it is quite possible that, in proportion to size, Northern Ireland is the most heavily researched area on earth' (p.viii).

an eruption, merits closer attention. Glasgow had close links with Northern Ireland and apparently polarized Protestant and Catholic communities, with separate educational systems and social organizations whose rivalries found expression in Orange marches and the 'Old Firm' (Celtic and Rangers) confrontations on the football field. Even in the late 1980s, although Catholic Celtic had been employing Protestant players for some time, the decision of Protestant Rangers to sign their first Catholic player, Mo Johnson, was a matter of controversy (*The Times*, 11 July 1989). Nevertheless such tensions did not translate themselves into politics let alone into extensive violence. To a considerable extent the explanation for this lies in the absence of many of the non-religious factors we noted in discussing Northern Ireland: housing was much more integrated; economic circumstances were rather less adverse; and discrimination much less of a problem. Above all, despite sympathy for the parties to the Irish conflict, the political confrontation was only a secondhand one: Scottish Catholics were not presenting their Protestant neighbours with the threat of an integration into a different nation state. However, contrasts in religious circumstances should also be noted. Glasgow lacked a Protestant leader of the stature of Ian Paisley, and the religious culture was in any case less receptive to such a message. The Scottish Orange Order was an organization limited to primarily social concerns and relatively lacking in Protestant religious fervour (Bruce, 1985; Gallagher, 1987).

The malleable nature of political and religious definitions of Britishness can be illustrated by juxtaposing two quotations, one from Ian Paisley's denunciation of the Anglo–Irish Agreement of 1985; the other from an article by Sybil Phoenix, a black British Christian of Guyanese origins. Paisley declared:

> I have news for the Prime Minister. God is in Heaven ... You only have to read the history of Ulster to see that time after time when it seemed humanly impossible to extricate Ulster from seeming disaster, that God intervened. Why? God has a purpose for this province, and this plant of Protestantism sown here in the north-eastern part of this island. The enemy has tried to root it out, but it still grows today, and I believe, like a grain of mustard seed, its future is going to be mightier yet. God who made her mighty will make her mightier yet in His Divine Will.
>
> (Bruce, 1986, pp.269–70)

The closing sentence has a resonance which extends beyond Northern Ireland: 'Land of Hope and Glory, Mother of the free ... God who made thee mighty, Make thee mightier yet.' The emotional and symbolic power of these words was also considerable for Phoenix, who reflected on the singing of them at the last night of the Proms:

White young people wanted to know what I wanted to go to the Proms for. I explained to them what the last night of the Proms meant to me as a British person because: 'Land of Hope and Glory, Mother of the free, How can I' – I Sybil, a British-born person – 'exalt thee, Who are born of thee?' That is my roots, that is my upbringing. How do you take away the roots of a tree and think that the tree will stand? It can't.

(Phoenix, 1991, p.100)

For Paisley Protestantism is the cord linking Great Britain and Northern Ireland, an exclusive definition which deliberately marginalizes Roman Catholics, not to mention non-Christians. For Phoenix 'Britain' is much more inclusive, still perhaps implicitly Christian, but multi-ethnic and multi-denominational. Beyond these two widely divergent perceptions, moreover, is a further range of attitudes held by those struggling to find a definition of 'Britishness' which can include them, or even asserting their own identity in their very sense of exclusion. The long-standing politico-religious differences of Scotland, Wales and Northern Ireland thus cut across the newer confessional and ethnic alignments that developed in the decades since the 1950s.

Under what circumstances does a religious group with an ambivalence towards the British state translate that tension into the assertion of an alternative identity? The comparison between Scotland and Northern Ireland is helpful here, as both have a Protestant majority and a strong Catholic minority. Despite the historic role of the Church of Scotland as a focus of Scottish national identity and its support, particularly in the 1970s, for the political campaign for devolution, Presbyterianism in Scotland never came close in the post-war period to forging that kind of intense link with the national sense of community that was apparent in the role of the Protestant churches in Northern Ireland. This failure was a reflection in part of the relatively low level of religious participation; in part of divisions in the Kirk itself which prevented the delivery of an unambiguous message; and also in part attributable to the absence of the sense of the black and white conflict of good and evil that operated in the Northern Ireland Protestant soul (Proctor, 1983).

The situation in Northern Ireland represented the most spectacular and tragic sectarian polarization in the post-war United Kingdom, all the more so as the fact that the conflict was founded in the divergence between two branches of professed Christianity would seem to suggest that the prospects for accommodation between wholly different religious creeds were bleak indeed. Such a judgement is unduly gloomy and must be substantially modified in recognition of the unusual, and in some respects unique, set of circumstances that have prevailed in the province. A more optimistic perception would find ample scope for a conception of

'Britishness' sufficiently expansive to accommodate all the religious and cultural diversity of these islands at the end of the twentieth century. One Christian writer posed rhetorical questions for those who felt traditional values were being endangered by minority groups:

> In what way does the often authoritarian family style of some West Indian communities threaten British domestic mores? How does the emphasis on tolerance and hospitality so characteristic of Indian religion subvert 'British values' of decency? Or in what sense is the Islamic duty to provide for the relief of the poor in one's neighbourhood an insult to the British way of life?
>
> (Clements, 1984, p.133)

Nevertheless, the unresolved ambivalences of a multi-national and multi-religious Britain in which institutional links remain between the state and particular religious groups are both an intriguing historical paradox and a challenging contemporary dilemma.

Bibliography

ALDERMAN, G. (1983) *The Jewish Community in British Politics*, Clarendon Press, Oxford.

BADHAM, P. (ed.) (1989) *Religion, State and Society in Modern Britain*, The Edwin Mellen Press, Lampeter.

BALLARD, P.H. and JONES, D.H. (eds) (1979) *This Land and People: a symposium on Christian and Welsh national identity*, Collegiate Centre of Theology, University College, Cardiff.

BARRITT, D.P. and CARTER, C.F. (1972) *The Northern Ireland Problem: a study in group relations*, Oxford University Press, Oxford (first published 1962).

BEBBINGTON, D.W. (1983) 'Baptists and politics since 1914' in Clements, K.W. (ed.) *Baptists in the Twentieth Century*, The Baptist Historical Society, London.

BIRRELL, D., GREER, J.E. and ROCHE, D.J.D. (1979) 'The political role and influence of the clergy in Northern Ireland', *Sociological Review*, 27, pp.491–512.

BISSET, P. (1986) *The Kirk and Her Scotland*, Handsel, Edinburgh.

BOCHEL, J.M. and DENVER, D.T. (1970) 'Religion and voting: a critical review and a new analysis', *Political Studies*, 18, pp.205–19.

BOWEN, K. (1983) *Protestants in a Catholic State: Ireland's privileged minority*, McGill/Queen's University Press, Montreal.

BRAYBROOKE, M. (1991) 'Seeking community' in Hooker, R. and Sargant, J. (eds).

BRIERLEY, P. (1991) *'Christian England': what the 1989 English church census reveals*, MARC Europe, London.

BROWN, J.F. (1979) 'Christians and nationalism in modern Wales' in Ballard, P.H. and Jones, D. H. (eds).

BRUCE, S. (1985) *No Pope of Rome: anti-Catholicism in modern Scotland*, Mainstream, Edinburgh.

(1986) *God Save Ulster: the religion and politics of Paisleyism*, Oxford University Press, Oxford.

BUCKLEY, A.D. (1984) 'Walls within walls: religion and rough behaviour in an Ulster community', *Sociology*, 18, pp.19–32.

(1985) 'The chosen few: biblical texts in the regalia of an Ulster secret society', *Folk Life*, 24, pp.5–24.

CARPENTER, E. (1991) *Archbishop Fisher – His Life and Times*, Canterbury Press, Norwich.

CAUTE, D. (1989) 'Labour's satanic verses', *New Statesman and Society*, 5 May.

CHADWICK, O. (1990) *Michael Ramsey: a life*, Clarendon Press, Oxford.

CHURCH INFORMATION OFFICE (1970) *Church and State*, Report of the Archbishops' Commission, London.

CLEMENTS, K.W. (1984) *A Patriotism for Today: dialogue with Dietrich Bonhoeffer*, Bristol Baptist College, Bristol.

COMMISSION FOR RACIAL EQUALITY (1990) *Law, Blasphemy and the Multi-Faith Society: report of a seminar*, Commission for Racial Equality, London.

CONNOLLY, S.J. (1985) *Religion and Society in Nineteenth Century Ireland*, Dundalgan Press, Dundalk.

DARBY, J. (1976) *Conflict in Northern Ireland: the development of a polarised community*, Gill and Macmillan, Dublin.

(ed.) (1983) *Northern Ireland: the background to the conflict*, Appletree Press, Belfast.

DUMMETT, A. (1982) 'Across party lines: the British Nationality Bill, the lobbyists and the churches', *The Modern Churchman*, 25, pp.36–43.

DYSON, A. (1985) '"Little else but the name" – reflections on four Church and State reports' in Moyser, G. (ed.).

DREWRY, G. and BROCK, J. (1970–71) 'Prelates in Parliament', *Parliamentary Affairs*, 24, pp.222–50.

EASTHOPE, G. (1976) 'Religious war in Northern Ireland', *Sociology*, 10, pp.427–50.

FARRELL, M. (1976) *Northern Ireland: the Orange state*, Pluto Press, London.

FERGUSON, R. (1979) *Geoff: the life of Geoffrey M.Shaw*, Famedram, Gartocharn.

FIELD, F. (1985) 'The Church of England and Parliament: a tense partnership' in Moyser, G. (ed.).

FITZGERALD, G. (1972) *Towards a New Ireland*, Charles Knight, London.

GALLAGHER, T. (1987) *Glasgow: the uneasy peace*, Manchester University Press, Manchester.

GALLAGHER, E. and WORRALL, S. (1982) *Christians in Ulster 1968–1980*, Oxford University Press, Oxford.

GARBETT, C. (1950) *Church and State in England*, Hodder and Stoughton, London.

GRAY, T. (1972) *The Orange Order*, The Bodley Head, London.

GREER, J.E. (1985) 'Viewing "the other side" in Northern Ireland: openness and attitudes to religion among Catholic and Protestant adolescents', *Journal for the Scientific Study of Religion*, 24, pp.275–92.

GUMMER, J.S., HEFFER, E. and BEITH, A. (1987) *Faith in Politics: which way should Christians vote?*, SPCK, London.

HARRIS, R. (1972) *Prejudice and Tolerance in Ulster: a study of neighbours and strangers in a border community*, Manchester University Press, Manchester.

HICKEY, J. (1984) *Religion and the Northern Ireland Problem*, Gill and Macmillan, Dublin.

HOOKER, R. and SARGANT, J. (eds) (1991) *Belonging to Britain: Christian perspectives on a plural society*, Council of Churches for Britain and Ireland, London.

HORNSBY-SMITH, M.P. (1987) *Roman Catholics in England: studies in social structure since the Second World War*, Cambridge University Press, Cambridge.

HUNTER, A.G. (1991) 'Watching from a distance: a Scottish perspective on multi-cultural Britain' in Hooker, R. and Sargant, J. (eds).

HUNTER, A.G. and MACKIE, S.G. (1986) *A National Church in a Multi-Racial Scotland*, Scottish Churches' Council.

JENKINS, D. (1979) 'A Welsh British reaction' in Ballard, P.H. and Jones, D.H. (eds).

LEECH, K. (1985) 'The church and immigration and race relations policy' in Moyser, G. (ed.).

LYONS, F.S.L. (1979) *Culture and Anarchy in Ireland, 1890–1939*, Oxford University Press, Oxford.

MacALLISTER, I. (1977) *The Northern Ireland Social Democratic and Labour Party: political opposition in a divided society*, Macmillan, London.

(1982) 'The Devil, miracles and the afterlife: the political sociology of religion in Northern Ireland', *British Journal of Sociology*, 33, pp.334–50.

McELROY, G. (1991) *The Catholic Church and the Northern Ireland Crisis 1968–86*, Gill and Macmillan, Dublin.

MacIVER, M.A. (1987) 'Ian Paisley and the reformed tradition', *Political Studies*, 35, pp.359–78.

MANTLE, J. (1991) *Archbishop: a portrait of Robert Runcie*, Sinclair Stevenson/Fount, London.

MEDHURST, K. and MOYSER, G. (1988) *Church and Politics in a Secular Age*, Clarendon Press, Oxford.

MORGAN, K.O. (1981) *Rebirth of a Nation: Wales 1880–1980*, Oxford University Press, Oxford.

MOXON-BROWNE, E. (1983) *Nation, Class and Creed in Northern Ireland*, Gower, Aldershot.

MOYSER, G. (ed.) (1985) *Church and Politics Today: the role of the Church of England in contemporary politics*, T & T Clark, Edinburgh.

(1989) 'Religion and political involvement in Britain' in Badham, P. (ed.).

MURPHY, T. (1992) 'Toleration and the law' in Horton, J. and Crabtree, H. (eds) *Toleration and Integrity in a Multi-Faith Society*, University of York, York.

NEWBIGIN, L. (1990) 'Blasphemy and the free society', *Discernment*, vol.4, no.2, pp.12–18.

PARSONS, G. (ed.) (1988) *Religion in Victorian Britain, Volume II: controversies*, Manchester University Press, Manchester.

PHOENIX, S. (1991) 'Land of hope and glory' in Hooker, R. and Sargant, J. (eds).

PLANT, R. (1985) 'The Anglican Church and the secular state' in Moyser, G. (ed.).

POWELL, E. (1973) *No Easy Answers*, Sheldon Press, London.

(1977) *Wrestling with the Angel*, Sheldon Press, London.

PROCTOR, J. H. (1983) 'The Church of Scotland and the struggle for a Scottish Assembly', *Journal of Church and State*, 25, pp.523–43.

RAMDIN, R. (1987) *The Making of the Black Working Class in Britain*, Gower, Aldershot.

REEVES, D. (ed.) (1984) *The Church and the State*, Hodder and Stoughton, London.

RHYS, G. (1991) 'The divine economy and political economy: the theology of Welsh nationalism' in Hooker, R. and Sargant, J. (eds).

ROBERTS, D.A. (1971) 'The Orange Order in Ireland: a religious institution?', *British Journal of Sociology*, 22, pp.269–79.

SEFTON, H.R. (1982) 'The Church of Scotland and Scottish nationhood' in Mews, S. (ed.) *Religion and National Identity: studies in church history*, 18, pp.549–55.

SIMPSON, J. (1983) 'Economic development: cause or effect in the Northern Ireland conflict' in Darby, J. (ed.).

TAYLOR, D. (1984) 'Ian Paisley and the ideology of Ulster Protestantism' in Curtin, C., Kelly, M. and O'Dowd, L. (eds) *Culture and Ideology in Ireland*, Galway University Press, Galway.

THOROGOOD, B. (1988) *The Flag and the Cross: national limits and the church universal*, SCM, London.

TUDUR JONES, R. (1979) 'Christian nationalism' in Ballard, P.H. and Jones, D.H. (eds).

WELSBY, P.A. (1984) *A History of the Church of England 1945–1980*, Oxford University Press, Oxford.

WHYTE, J. (1990) *Interpreting Northern Ireland*, Oxford University Press, Oxford.

WOLFFE, J. (1991) *The Protestant Crusade in Great Britain, 1829–1860*, Oxford University Press, Oxford.

(ed.) (1993) *The Growth of Religious Diversity: Britain from 1945. A Reader*, Hodder and Stoughton, London.

WRIGHT, F. (1973) 'Protestant ideology and politics in Ulster', *Archives Européenes de sociologie*, 14, pp.213–80.

4

FROM CONSENSUS TO CONFRONTATION: RELIGION AND POLITICS IN BRITAIN SINCE 1945

by Gerald Parsons

Launch of the Anglican Church report on inner cities, *Faith in the City*, 3 December 1985. Sir Richard O'Brien (Chairman of the Commission on Urban Priority Areas) speaking. Photo: Press Association.

In 1979, on the day of the first of her three consecutive General Election victories, Margaret Thatcher quoted a famous prayer, traditionally attributed to St Francis of Assisi. The opening line of the quotation was: 'Where there is discord, may we bring harmony.' In fact, the political life of Britain during the ensuing decade was notable not for its harmony but for the depth and intensity of its divisions, conflicts and discordances. Moreover, the religious origins of her quotation notwithstanding, such discord and confrontation were nowhere more noticeable than in relations between the successive Conservative governments of the 1980s and prominent and influential leaders and groups within the Christian churches of Britain. Indeed, it has been suggested that at no previous point this century had the British churches and government been so sharply and consistently at odds with each other (Baker, 1991, p.91; see also Raban, 1989, p.21; Walker and Gallagher, 1990, p.105).

Clashes between the government and leaders of the Church of England were particularly frequent and attracted the attention of the media. The catalogue of confrontations is, indeed, striking. Conflict over the terms of the British Nationality Act of 1981 was followed, in 1982, by controversy over the tone of the service and sermon in St Paul's Cathedral after the Falklands War, and tension over the unilateralist position taken in the report to General Synod entitled *The Church and the Bomb*. Further controversy ensued in 1984–85, first over comments by David Jenkins, the Bishop of Durham, who criticized the government for not caring sufficiently about poverty and unemployment and questioned government and Coal Board claims during the miners' strike; then most notoriously over *Faith in the City*, a report to the General Synod of the Church of England which was critical of government policy towards the inner cities and claimed that lack of funding and commitment by government to the inner cities was a significant factor in social deprivation. Further criticisms from bishops followed, notably over the social and moral implications of the 1988 Social Security Reform Act and its relationship to the budget of that year (again from Bishop Jenkins of Durham), and from the Archbishop of Canterbury, Robert Runcie, in 1989, over the danger that undue emphasis upon the rewards of success might lead to uncharitable judgements upon the unsuccessful. Runcie and Jenkins were by no means alone in their episcopal criticism of the government. Other bishops questioned aspects of contemporary attitudes to wealth and its acquisition, the seriousness of unemployment and of the north/south divide in British society, the social impact of the poll tax, and the alleged responsibility of 'Thatcherism' for a 'massive deterioration in community care' (Baker, 1991, pp.90–3; Clark, 1993, p.79; Patey, 1988, pp.1–8 and 142–8; Thompson, 1991, pp.280–1).

The tendency of the media to focus disproportionately upon the confrontations between the government and the Church of England undoubtedly reflected, in part, the residual prominence and influence of the Church of England not only within English life but also within the overall religious complexion of Britain as a whole – especially when viewed from the perspective of a predominantly London-based national media. However, it probably also reflected an outmoded assumption that, because it was still an established church, the Church of England remained at heart 'the Tory party at prayer' – an equation of religious and political allegiances which, though still sometimes repeated as conventional wisdom, was by then very far from being accurate. In fact, as we shall see, it was by no means only the Church of England that clashed, profoundly and repeatedly, with the Conservative governments of the 1980s. Other denominations and ecumenical groups were also similarly prompted to criticize aspects of government policy and their social consequences.

What is to be made of such conflicts between government and the churches in Britain in the 1980s? What is their immediate historical background and context in the political and religious history of Britain since the end of the Second World War? Why was it during that particular decade that government and the churches became so strikingly at odds? And what does all this suggest about the nature of the relationship between religion and politics in Britain by the last decade of the twentieth century?

1 From William Temple to Edward Norman

The confrontations between government and the churches in Britain in the 1980s stand in particularly sharp contrast to the prevailing relationship between the two during the period from the end of the Second World War until the 1970s. Whereas during the 1980s this relationship was notable precisely because of its friction and conflict, in the late 1940s and throughout the 1950s, and even for the most part through the 1960s and early 1970s, it was the remarkable degree of consensus and lack of confrontation that stood out.[1]

It is not surprising that this was so. The welfare state introduced by the post-war Labour government was, it has been observed, broadly what progressive Christian social thought had been seeking for a generation or more (Hastings, 1991, p.422). And for many – perhaps most – Christians in

---

[1] There were inevitably occasional but important exceptions to this general pattern. Thus, for example, in 1956 there was significant tension and confrontation between government and church leaders over the Suez crisis, while in the 1960s there was serious disagreement over the government's reaction to the Rhodesian declaration of UDI and again over government policy towards Asians expelled from Kenya. (For the latter, see Chadwick, 1990, pp.168–73 and 241–50. For the former, see Carpenter, 1991, pp.402–5, and also the previous essay in this volume.)

Britain since 1945, the welfare state has continued to seem one of the fairest means of ensuring the fulfilment of corporate responsibilities in society (Patey, 1988, p.138). Nor, in the 1950s, did successive Conservative governments seek to undo the social reforms which constituted the welfare state. On the contrary, it was the era of 'Butskellism' – a term coined from the names of the prominent Conservative and Labour politicians, R.A. Butler and Hugh Gaitskell, to convey the broad agreement which then existed on the need for 'fair shares', 'equality of opportunity' and 'meeting needs regardless of ability to pay'; on the rightness of some redistribution of income in order to achieve such ends; and on the commitment to full employment (Preston, 1983, p.59).

This was, indeed, in broad terms what progressive and prominent Christian social thought in Britain had been arguing towards from as early as the 1920s. The point may be illustrated by reference to William Temple's short but immensely influential book *Christianity and Social Order*. Temple had been a prominent participant in Christian debates over social and economic policies throughout the 1920s and 1930s (Kent, 1992, ch.3). *Christianity and Social Order* was published in 1942, the year that Temple became Archbishop of Canterbury. A short text, originally published as a 'Penguin Special', it quickly sold 150,000 copies and was subsequently regularly reissued during the 1940s and 1950s.

Christianity and Social Order has been described as 'one of the foundation piers of the welfare state' (Munby, 1960, p.157; Preston, 1976, p.6; Wilding, 1992, p.40). It is not hard to see why. Temple was an immensely popular and influential Christian leader, and the publication of a concise and persuasive summary of his perception of the social and economic implications of Christian faith occurred in the midst of the Second World War, just at the point at which thoughts were turning to the question of what social issues and policies should be the priorities for a post-war government. In December 1942 the Beveridge Report was published, setting out the 'assumptions' that there should be a national health service, that economic policy should be geared to securing full employment, and that there should be a concerted attack upon want, sickness, squalor, ignorance and idleness.

Comparison of these aims with those set out in the concluding pages of *Christianity and Social Order* is instructive. At the end of the final chapter, 'The task before us', Temple concluded that Christians were entitled to call upon government to set itself six objectives which should be pursued as steadily and rapidly as possible. These were: that every child should be part of a family housed 'with decency and dignity' and free of 'underfeeding and overcrowding'; that every citizen should possess an income sufficient to maintain such a home; that every child should have the opportunity of education 'till years of maturity, so planned as to allow for his [sic] peculiar aptitudes and make possible their full development'; that every citizen should have a voice in the conduct of business; that every citizen should have sufficient weekly leisure and annual holidays with pay; and that every citizen should have freedom of worship, speech, assembly and association (Temple, 1942, pp.96–7).

The concurrence between the aims of the Beveridge Report and those of Temple's *Christianity and Social Order* goes far towards explaining the broad consensus that existed throughout the late 1940s and 1950s between church leaders and successive governments. Both were engaged in exercises in reconstruction, and the building of the welfare state provided a benevolent and reforming context within which – in social and economic matters – fundamental conflicts simply did not occur. There were, of course, individual Christians whose stances, either in general or on particular issues, witnessed to a specifically radical political or social interpretation of their religion. Thus, for example, figures such as the prominent Methodist minister, Donald Soper, or the Anglicans, Mervyn Stockwood, John Collins and Michael Scott, continued to speak on behalf of a self-conscious Christian Socialism and radicalism (Hastings, 1991, pp.422–3 and 428–32). In so doing they could claim to be legitimate heirs of the more radical side to Temple and his views. But so too could those whose politics were far from socialist – Christian or otherwise. Thus when *Christianity and Social Order* was again reissued in 1976 – some three decades after its first appearance – it was accompanied by a commendatory Foreword from Edward Heath, Conservative prime minister from 1970 to 1974. Temple's impact on Heath's own generation, Heath observed, had been immense. Nor was it limited to those who shared Temple's own way of thinking: 'It embraced the whole spectrum of those who were seriously concerned with the social, economic and political problems of the day' (Heath, 1976, p.1).

How long did such consensus last? In retrospect, it is possible to see the years from, roughly, the mid 1960s to the mid 1970s as the period during which a number of important developments paved the way for the subsequent collapse of the prevailing consensus between government and the churches on social and economic matters, and its replacement by increasingly sharp confrontation. The process involved was by no means clear cut. Nor is it easy to disentangle. However, a number of strands may be discerned.

It is significant that during the decade from the mid 60s to the mid 70s the principal context of the British churches' discussion and thinking about political and social issues shifted from a primarily domestic focus to a determinedly international one. International developments impinged increasingly dramatically upon the social and political thinking and awareness of the British churches. On the one hand, the ecumenical movement – and especially the World Council of Churches (WCC) –

entered upon a markedly politicized phase of its history. As 'third world' churches increasingly took their places within the WCC, similarly third world issues assumed new prominence. In particular, the issue of racism and of support for the 'liberation movements' in Angola, Mozambique, Namibia, Rhodesia and South Africa became a central concern of the WCC, culminating in the setting up of a Programme to Combat Racism in 1969.

More generally, however, issues of third world poverty and inequality also moved to the centre of WCC debate and activity. Theologically, such developments found expression in the reinterpretation of traditional understandings of 'salvation' in terms of the contemporary realization of the 'Good News' of liberation and social justice – a trend that perhaps reached its clearest expression during this period at the international missionary conference in Bangkok in 1973 on the theme of 'Salvation Today'. The themes and ideas of the 'Salvation Today' conference were summarized for British Christians in a brief book of the same title by Pauline Webb, a British Methodist who participated in the event (Webb, 1974). This, however, was but one example of such events and trends feeding back into the life of the British churches. Of equal importance was the general diffusion of such ideas among British participants in the intense international ecumenical activity of this period as a whole.

Nor was it only the impact of the WCC that helped to transform the context of the British churches' discussion of social and economic issues during this decade. International developments in the Roman Catholic Church also tended to the same end. Within the more general ferment of the Second Vatican Council and its legacy, the 1960s and 1970s witnessed the emergence – particularly from Latin America – of 'Liberation Theology', with its emphatically left-wing political stance and its emphasis upon the biblical text as a narrative of God's liberation of his people from oppression and injustice. Moreover, with the ecumenical contacts between Roman Catholics and Protestants made possible by Vatican II, the influence of Liberation Theology was not confined to Roman Catholic circles.[2]

Such international developments changed the context and ethos of debate and discussion of social and economic issues within the British churches. Perhaps the most obvious instance was, indeed, in the area of race relations. As pointed out in the previous essay, the British churches were, in general, slow to recognize and respond to the worsening of race relations which occurred in Britain from the early 1960s onwards. Despite the important and courageous contributions to debates over race relations, immigration policy, and the situation in Rhodesia and South Africa of

---

[2] For similar but more detailed assessments of the impact of developments in both the WCC and the Roman Catholic Church, see Clark, 1993, pp.20–1; Medhurst and Moyser, 1988, pp.67–8; Preston, 1983, pp.81–92.

individuals such as Archbishop of Canterbury Michael Ramsey (Chadwick, 1990, pp.165–76, 241–50 and 255–66), it was not until the beginning of the 1970s that such issues attracted the concerted attention of the British churches. During the 1970s, however, issues of race and race relations rapidly became a major concern of the British churches, both within individual denominations and in interdenominational groups (Leech, 1985).

Interdenominational initiatives included the British Council of Churches Community and Race Relations Unit, the Evangelical Race Relations Group founded in 1974, and the militantly anti-racist organization, Christians Against Racism and Fascism, formally launched in 1978. The particular issue of apartheid in South Africa also produced interdenominational pressure groups and collaboration in groups such as Christian Concern for Southern Africa and End Loans to South Africa (Ecclestone, 1985, pp.39–40; Perman, 1977, pp.166–8). Denominationally based initiatives included the Catholic Commission for Racial Justice, and increasing research and involvement in issues of race and racism by, for example, the Church of England General Synod's Board for Social Responsibility and the Methodist Church Division of Social Responsibility. The work of such groups – denominational and interdenominational – included both the fostering of local projects and the more general promotion of awareness of the issues raised by the emergence of an increasingly multi-racial society in Britain. The pursuit of the latter task resulted in a steadily increasing number of surveys and reports, which called upon the churches to address both their specifically Christian contribution to the wider issues of race and racism in modern Britain as a whole and the question of their own attitudes towards such issues within the Christian community.[3]

Concern over race relations and racism was, however, by no means the only example of the way in which international perspectives prompted a reorientation of the British churches' perspectives on social and economic issues. The more general concern – both within the WCC and among advocates of Liberation Theology – over third world poverty, inequality and 'issues of justice and peace', also influenced developments within the British context. The remarkable growth in both the scale and diversity of the work of Christian Aid was perhaps the most striking example – the annual Christian Aid week became a part of the British Christian calendar, a regular occurrence in the rhythm of the churches' year. By the 1970s, it has been observed, the concerns of Christian Aid had moved from the periphery to near the centre of church life in Britain (Hastings, 1991, p.585).

---

[3] For the development of concern within the churches over attitudes to race and racism within the Christian community, see also Volume I, essay 6.

Nor was Christian Aid alone in thus demonstrating a heightened Christian awareness of issues of third world poverty, injustice and inequality from the mid 1960s onwards. The Catholic Fund for Overseas Development (CAFOD), together with its Scottish equivalent SCIAF, and both the Catholic Institute for International Relations (CIIR) and Pax Christi were further examples of such concern (Hornsby-Smith, 1987, pp.155 and 178–9). From the evangelical wing, meanwhile, came the foundation of The Evangelical Alliance Relief (TEAR) Fund, which provided a vehicle for concern over third world poverty among evangelical Christians who were unwilling to support Christian Aid because of its association with the theologically more liberal British and World Councils of Churches (Bebbington, 1989, p.265).

Nor was such concern for the more radical application of Christian principles and insights to social, economic and political matters confined to third world issues. It also found expression in the context of domestic social issues and political concerns. During the later 1960s and the 1970s a striking variety of groups and trends emerged within British Christianity, again both within and across denominations, some more overtly left-wing and radical, some more cautious and moderate, but all of them representative of a widespread sense that the social and political implications of Christian faith required more explicit expression within contemporary Britain.

At the more politically radical and left-wing end of the spectrum, the ferment of the 1960s produced a number of short-lived experiments, such as the attempted fusion of Catholic and Marxist insights in the journal *Slant*, and the more broadly and ecumenically left-wing Christian journal *New Christian* – both of which had folded by the 1970s (Hastings, 1991, pp.549, 571–3 and 583). The Student Christian Movement, meanwhile, once an influential focus for liberal Christian social thought, came perilously close to politically radicalizing itself out of existence during the late 1960s and early 1970s (Hastings, 1991, pp.542–3; Preston, 1986, pp.435–7). Despite their short-lived nature, initiatives such as *Slant* and *New Christian* were none the less significant for the way in which they contributed to a more general raising of political consciousness and awareness in the churches from the mid 1960s onwards. Moreover, other more enduring politically radical Christian groups also emerged during these years. Organizations such as the Alliance of Radical Methodists, the Anglo-Catholic Jubilee Group, or the Sheffield based and thoroughly ecumenical Urban Theology Unit, were numerically small but exercised an influence quite disproportionate to their size. Between them, these and other similar groups and organizations sought to explore the concepts of 'political' and 'liberation theology' in a British context and to place such exploration firmly on the agenda of the British churches. A sense of their aims and ethos may be gained from the titles – and still more from the contents – of two avowedly ecumenical collections of essays from the early and mid 1970s: *Seeds of Liberation: spiritual dimensions to political struggle* (edited by Kee, 1973) and *Stirrings: essays Christian and radical* (edited by Vincent, 1976); and from a further collection of essays from 1980 which reflected on the development of 'political theology' in Britain up to that point, *Agenda for Prophets: towards a political theology for Britain* (edited by Ambler and Haslam, 1980).

Less overtly left-wing, but no less significant in the more general increase in debate over the social, political and economic implications of Christianity during this period, were developments within evangelical thinking. Thus one of the significant developments at the National Evangelical Anglican Congress at Keele in 1967 was the way in which it acknowledged a need for a greater emphasis upon the social implications of the Christian gospel among evangelicals. This trend was then maintained and extended at the next National Evangelical Anglican Congress at Nottingham in 1977 – by which time evangelical debate over such issues had been further stimulated by the publication of Bishop David Sheppard's book, *Built as a City* (Sheppard, 1974).

Nor should the scale of practical Christian participation in other organizations and initiatives such as War on Want, Oxfam, Shelter, the Cyrenians, Amnesty International, the Samaritans, and numerous local housing associations and similar projects, be overlooked. Such participation again tended to run across the theological and denominational spectrum and linked Christians significantly into a burgeoning subculture of social, political and economic pressure groups. At an institutional level, meanwhile, both ecumenically and within particular denominations, the British churches during the later 1960s and the 1970s developed increasingly extensive and influential departments and boards charged with researching and reporting on social, economic and political issues. Bodies such as the General Synod Board of Social Responsibility of the Church of England, the Church and Nation Committee of the Church of Scotland General Assembly, the Methodist Church Division of Social Responsibility, and the various departments of the British Council of Churches, produced surveys, assessments and reports on an increasingly wide range of social and political issues.

It would be an exaggeration to argue that the period from the mid 1960s to the late 1970s constituted, in itself, an end to the era of broad consensus between government and the churches in post-Second World War Britain. Indeed, it has been argued that the most solid achievements of these years were based squarely on the legacy that stemmed, perhaps above all, from William Temple (Hastings, 1991, p.654). It was, however, an important period of transition. By the mid to late 1970s the overall ethos of Christian discussion of social and political issues in Britain had undergone a significant change. *Within* the churches there was now more active and more widespread debate on such matters than there had been fifteen or so years earlier. There were more pressure groups of more radical kinds pressing such issues to the fore. There were more frequent reports from official departments. And in the process of debate, attitudes within the churches on social and political issues had already begun to become more varied, less consensual and potentially open to a new polarization of opinion. An early example of such polarization was the fierce controversy within the British churches in the early 1970s over the decision by the World Council of Churches Programme to Combat Racism to set up a special fund to support liberation movements in Southern Africa. Since some of the movements concerned were committed to armed struggle, a sharp controversy ensued over the morality of 'grants to guerrilla movements'. The WCC had been assured that such financial support as was received would be used only for humanitarian and not military ends, but many British Christians remained either uneasy or overtly hostile to the grants – an opinion in which they were sustained by sensationalized reports in the press (Perman, 1977, pp.208–11).

The controversy over the Programme to Combat Racism was, in retrospect, part of the beginning of a much more profound transformation of political debate within both the British churches and Britain as a whole. As the economic situation steadily worsened, so in the mid to late 1970s conservative thinkers and politicians began to lay the theoretical and intellectual foundations of the policies that were to be followed by successive Conservative governments during the 1980s – and significantly these foundations included a profound hostility towards the perceived legacy of the 1960s and an equally profound scepticism about the welfare state and its alleged social, economic and moral consequences (Clark, 1993, pp.7–10; Leech, 1991, p.162; Weeks, 1989, pp.278–9). At the same time, however, the social boards and committees of the British churches were engaged in their own analyses of the social implications of Christian belief in a society in which a declining economic situation posed painful dilemmas about social responsibility, inequality and the appropriate policies to ensure both economic recovery and continued commitment to social justice.[4]

By the mid to late 1970s, therefore, the scene was thus set for the transition to the period of sharp conflict between government and the churches which subsequently occurred during the 1980s. Indeed, in the year before the first of Margaret Thatcher's election victories, a fierce

---

[4] Thus, for example, some of the most important Church of England Board for Social Responsibility texts on economic issues and their social implications were published during these years (Clark, 1993, pp.35–6).

controversy over the appropriate attitude of the churches towards social and political matters provided a foretaste of the confrontation to come. In the 1978 Reith Lectures, Edward Norman, an Anglican clergyman and historian, delivered a swingeing attack upon recent social and political trends within the major Christian churches in the western world.

Subsequently published under the title *Christianity and the World Order* (Norman, 1979), the lectures argued that, as western society had become increasingly secularized, the churches, instead of continuing resolutely to uphold their eternal and supernatural message and perspective had, in fact, increasingly translated their beliefs and message into secular moral, social and political values. This in turn, Norman argued, had further contributed to the secularization of society and the decline of the churches themselves. Christianity, in Norman's view, had become disastrously politicized. Whereas the churches had made social, moral and political action increasingly central to their message and activity, they should have continued to emphasize worship and personal piety as the heart of Christianity. Christianity was by nature concerned primarily with the soul and its relation to eternity. Individual Christian action in the social and political sphere should be distinguished from the corporate witness of the church – and the church should in any case be reluctant to become involved in such matters since, in a fallen world, there is little hope of securing any real or lasting improvement in the situations addressed.

Edward Norman's *Christianity and the World Order* has been described, appropriately enough, as an attempt to rebut that whole line of thinking of which Temple's *Christianity and Social Order* had been such an influential example (Hastings, 1991, pp.653–4; see also Suggate, 1991, p.152). Not surprisingly, it prompted a sharp controversy. Representatives of the tradition of Christian social and political involvement which Norman so fiercely attacked rallied to its defence and criticized Norman for oversimplifying the relationship between Christianity and social and political activity, for neglecting the specifically Christian and theological roots of the churches' recent engagement with such issues, and for caricaturing the nature and complexity of such recent engagement.[5] Norman's argument drew much popular support, however, thus

[5] See, for example, the collection of essays by Christians of various denominations in *Christian Faith and Political Hopes: a reply to E.R. Norman* (edited by Willmer, 1979); the essays by members of the Anglo-Catholic Jubilee Group in *Christianity Reinterpreted: a critical examination of the 1978 Reith Lectures* (edited by Leech, 1979); the Roman Catholic response, *Catholicism and the World Order: some reflections on the 1978 Reith Lectures* (Dummett, 1979); and the even more markedly interdenominational survey and interpretation of contemporary radical Christian political commitment in *Agenda for Prophets: towards a political theology for Britain* (edited by Ambler and Haslam, 1980). The editors of the latter collection suggested that the whole of their book was an answer to Norman's thesis.

indicating that – whatever the historical or theological rights and wrongs of the matter – there was indeed already a significant body of opinion which disliked the more overtly committed tone of much of the comment by the churches on social and political matters since the mid 1960s. Such support, moreover, was also a sign – as, arguably, were Norman's lectures themselves – of the imminent assertion of a new and radical strand of right-wing opinion both within national life in general and within the spectrum of specifically Christian social and political thought. Thus, the controversy over Edward Norman's 1978 Reith Lectures was the curtain-raiser to a far more sustained and bitter sequence of exchanges and confrontations during the 1980s between consecutive Conservative governments and their supporters on the one hand, and a substantial number of prominent church leaders and groups on the other.

2 The 1980s and beyond

It is not possible in this essay to examine in detail the various specific confrontations between government and the churches in the 1980s. Nor, in any case, would such detailed examination of specific cases be appropriate in the present context. The point here is to focus on the overall shifts that occurred in government/church relations and in debate within the churches on social and economic issues – and to do so, moreover, in a way that relates these changes to the broader developments in the religious life of Britain since 1945 which all the essays both in this volume and its companion are intended to address.

As the introduction of this essay noted, the sequence of clashes was both sustained and wide ranging. The 1981 Nationality Act; the Falklands memorial service; nuclear weapons; aspects of the conduct of the police and security forces in Northern Ireland; the Birmingham Six, Guildford Four and Maguire cases; the operation of the rules governing the granting of refugee status and political asylum; community and race relations; inner-city poverty and social deprivation; unemployment; the poll tax; reforms in benefits; the alleged tendency of the adverse effects of government policy to fall disproportionately upon the already disadvantaged; the social effects and impact of reforms in the National Health Service – in all of these areas there was criticism of government policy from within the churches and hence tension between government and church leaders, pressure groups and official bodies.

Inevitably the most prominent confrontations centred – with the active help of the news media – upon controversial figures such as the Bishop of Durham, or on particular texts such as the 1985 Church of

England report, *Faith in the City*. In reality, however, the most significant aspect of Christian criticism of government policies during the 1980s and into the 1990s was the fact that it was not only continuing, but that it gathered pace steadily and became increasingly diffused among the various denominations. Whatever the cruder stereotypes of the popular press might suggest, such criticism was not simply a matter of a few controversial left-wing bishops and a Church of England whose leadership had somehow gone softly and mildly pink. Christian misgivings and criticisms over government policies were not isolated incidents; they increased steadily as the 1980s progressed and included contributions from the British Council of Churches and other interdenominational groups, and from members of various churches including, notably, the Church of Scotland and the Methodist and Roman Catholic Churches.

Thus, for example, as early as 1981 the outgoing Moderator of the Church of Scotland General Assembly described the monetarist policies of the government at that time as 'immoral and blasphemous' because of the way they increased unemployment (Bradley, 1992, p.130), while the General Assembly itself, through its Church and Nation Committee, maintained a critical commentary on government policy (Montefiore, 1990 pp.74–5 and 111–15; Walker and Gallagher, 1990, p.104–5). Senior Roman Catholic leaders spoke out over security issues in Northern Ireland and over the Birmingham Six, Guildford Four and Maguire cases (Baker, 1991, p.93; Stanford, 1993, pp.112–17), and also questioned the ethics and morality of other government social and economic policies (Bradley, 1992, p.137; Martin, 1989, p.338; Stanford, 1993, pp.106–12). And the Methodist Church demonstrated its continued commitment to its own well-established historical tradition of social awareness and criticism (Baker, 1991, p.93; Martin 1989, p.339; Vincent, 1990).

In addition to such protests from particular denominations, there were also ecumenical protests as well. Thus, the poll tax produced a statement of opposition from the London Churches Group which represented Anglican, Methodist, Roman Catholic, United Reformed and Baptist churches in Greater London (Patey, 1988, p.146). And in 1989, the interdenominational group, Church Action for Poverty, published a pamphlet *Hearing the Cry of the Poor*, which criticized the impact of a whole range of government policies during the 1980s and argued that many current social and economic policies simply could not be morally right: the signatories included twelve Anglican bishops, the Moderator of the Church of Scotland and prominent Methodists, Baptists and Roman Catholics (Baker, 1991, p.93). Meanwhile, the Sanctuary Movement, which sought to provide places of refuge in religious buildings for people facing the threat of deportation, came into increasing conflict with government in the later 1980s. The movement was particularly notable for the way in which it was not only ecumenical in eliciting support and involvement from a variety of Christian denominations, but also inter-faith in its involvement of Hindus, Sikhs, Jews and Muslims as well as Christians (Johnson, 1988, pp.93–4; Weller, 1990).

As well as the much publicized clashes between government and the churches, however, there were also increasingly fierce debates over these issues *within* the Christian community as well as between Christians and government. The 'Conservative revolution' of the 1980s had ardent supporters within the churches as well as opponents. The Conservative MP and Church of England General Synod member, John Selwyn Gummer, and Professor Brian Griffiths, for some time head of Margaret Thatcher's policy unit, were perhaps among the best known examples of such overtly Christian support for 'Thatcherism', but they were by no means unique.[6] Moreover, for many Christians sympathetic to the policies of the successive Thatcher governments of the 1980s, support for her radical brand of conservatism was combined with – and in part expressed through – a concerted protest against the allegedly 'politicized' and 'simplistic' nature of the majority of recent and contemporary social and political statements by church leaders, pressure groups and reports.

Thus, for example, a collection of essays entitled *The Kindness that Kills: the churches' simplistic response to complex social issues* (edited by Anderson, 1984) argued that many of the increasingly frequent reports and pronouncements on social and economic issues from church bodies contained little theology and merely repeated fashionable secular ideas and arguments. Such reports, it was argued, tended to be: 'sloppy, ill-thought out, ignorant, one-sided, addicted to secular fashions, uncritical of conventional 'progressive' wisdom, hysterical, unmethodical in the use of sources and evidence, theologically desiccated and, most deplorable, uncharitable to those who disagree' (Anderson, 1984, p.2).[7] A subsequent attack on the alleged 'politicization' of the Church of England in particular similarly alleged that General Synod reports increasingly reflected a one-sided (and left-wing) political stance, that the Church of England's policies on racism were virtually indistinguishable from those of left-wing councils, that the increasing appeal to 'theologies of liberation' was transforming theological concepts into political ones, and that the church's bureaucracy was increasingly infiltrated by activists from Christian

---

[6] For a summary of the positions of both Gummer and Griffiths, see their contributions to the collection of essays *Christianity and Conservatism* (edited by Alison and Edwards, 1990), a volume that also includes a number of other Christian defences of the Conservative policies of the 1980s, together with several dissenting voices.

[7] For brief and blunt restatements of the case and a review of a number of subsequent publications, see also Anderson, 1990 and 1992.

pressure groups which were part of an 'aggressively leftist and anti-western network' (Tingle, 1988).

Not surprisingly, those thus attacked complained, conversely, that such criticisms were themselves 'poorly researched' (Leech, 1988, p.134) and 'not merely abusive, but grossly unfair' (Montefiore, 1990, p.80). Which side in the debate people sympathized with was almost certainly as much – and perhaps more – a matter of instinctive loyalties and prior convictions as it was sober and dispassionate reflection. Moreover, the instinctive loyalties and prior convictions involved were *both* theological *and* political – when thus combined, the resulting clashes were, indeed, characteristically impassioned and frequently bitter.

Behind the confrontations over specific issues, however, there was also a deeper clash over the theoretical bases of government policies in social and economic matters during the 1980s. Thus supporters of the successive Conservative governments extolled not only the practical effects but also the moral virtues which might be fostered by capitalism and 'the market', by an 'enterprise culture', and by an emphasis upon 'wealth creation'. Such advocacy included the theory that the most effective way to help the poor and disadvantaged in society was not through the 'handouts' and 'politicized welfare' of the 'nanny state', which allegedly fostered a 'dependency culture' inimical to the preservation of the work ethic but, rather, by means of the encouragement of sturdy self-reliance and the 'trickledown effect' of increased prosperity in society as a whole. The wisdom and morality of such theories were, moreover, argued not only on the basis of political and economic philosophies, but also on specifically Christian grounds, by appeal to biblical and theological principles and precepts. (See, for example, Alison, 1990; Griffiths, 1982, 1984a and b, 1985 and 1990; Harris, 1984 and 1990.)

By contrast, Christian critics of government policies challenged both their practical consequences and their moral bases. Practical experience of pastoral ministry – especially but not only in the inner cities – was a significant influence in the formulation and expression of much of the criticism by church leaders of the actual effects of government social and economic policies during the 1980s (Leech, 1991, pp.165–7). This in turn prompted church leaders to challenge the morality of 'the market' alone, and the emphasis upon the moral virtues of an 'enterprise culture' in which the importance of 'wealth creation' and the celebration of individual effort and success were so central that the very existence of 'society' could seriously be questioned by the prime minister (in an interview in *Woman's Own* in 1987, quoted in Eyre, 1991, p.45). Such emphases led the Archbishop of Canterbury Robert Runcie to warn of the danger of regarding 'success as a sort of blessing or reward for righteousness', which in turn could lead to uncharitable and untrue judgements upon the unsuccessful and hence to being dismissive of their value as fellow human beings (in an interview in *Director*, the magazine of the Institute of Directors, in 1989, quoted in Bradley, 1992, p.137).

The protests of church leaders were characteristically rooted in a combination of pastoral experience and reflection on the biblical text and the Christian tradition (Baker, 1991, p.98). Thus, for example, David Sheppard, the Bishop of Liverpool, argued that it was 'some of the most central teachings of orthodox Christianity' that led him to the conclusion that 'there is a divine bias to the poor, which should be reflected both in the Church and in the secular world' (Sheppard, 1983, p.10). Similarly, the prominent Methodist minister John Vincent, in his inaugural address as President of the Methodist Conference, spoke of 'the poor and their concerns' having 'an absolute priority in the work of Jesus' and of 'the rising of the poor to new dignity, wholeness and acceptance' being a mark of the presence of the Kingdom of God (Vincent, 1990, p.3; see also Vincent, 1992a and 1992b). Or again, a careful reading of David Jenkins' various discussions of social and political issues in the mid and late 1980s also reveals a characteristic combination of an appeal to biblical themes and an awareness of the pastoral realities of his diocese of Durham (Jenkins, 1988, chs 1–7, and 1991, chs 7–8).

Outright confrontation and controversy were not, however, the only form of Christian engagement with social, political and economic issues during the 1980s. In the later 1980s there also emerged an increasing number of more theoretical reassessments of Christian social and economic thought. These at once sought both to recognize weaknesses in earlier church pronouncements on social and economic issues, and also to maintain a critical and sceptical attitude towards the social and economic theories of Thatcherism and the 'new right' (see, for example, Atherton, 1992; Hay, 1989; Preston, 1987, chs 7–9 and 1991, especially chs 6–7). On the practical level, meanwhile, in the later 1980s and early 1990s there were significant experiments in co-operation between inner-city churches and government agencies such as the Manpower Services Commission and the Home Office. Such initiatives included, notably, collaboration with government by Black-led as well as 'historic' churches and also a major initiative, 'Evangelical Enterprise', between the government and both the Evangelical Alliance and the West Indian Evangelical Alliance (Arnold, 1992; Johnson, 1988, pp.95–6). The latter initiatives were, moreover, significantly extended following a meeting in 1990 between Margaret Thatcher and the directors of the Evangelical Alliance and the largest of the evangelical social work agencies, the Shaftsbury Society, at which, according to press reports, Thatcher observed that she was 'fed up with woolly, liberal clergymen' and therefore thought it time to 'see what the evangelicals can do' (quoted in Bradley, 1992, p.143).

Such co-operation was itself controversial, however, and further illustrated the sheer complexity of Christian engagement with social and political issues during the 1980s and early 1990s. Thus, the involvement of the Evangelical Alliance and West Indian Evangelical Alliance with the government in 'Evangelical Enterprise' *can* be presented as one more example of the development of a socially conscious, actively socially committed outlook within evangelicalism as a whole – a further addition to the trend represented by aspects of the National Evangelical Anglican Conferences of 1967 and 1977; by contributions such as David Sheppard's *Built as a City* and *Bias to the Poor,* and the pamphlet *Hope in the City* by five evangelicals in response to the 1985 report *Faith in the City;* and by the foundation of groups such as the Evangelical Coalition for Urban Mission and Evangelical Christians for Racial Justice (Forster, 1986; Sheppard, 1974 and 1983). But this particular style of co-operation with government has also been criticized – by other evangelicals – for its 'close alignment with the Tory corridors of power', its 'tendency to equate biblical teachings of creativity, stewardship and hard work with enterprise culture', and its failure to address the underlying causes of social deprivation in order to avoid confrontation (Nelson, 1990, p.9; and see also Grant, 1990, pp.51–3). Conversely, by the late 1980s some evangelicals were beginning to question whether the evangelical turn to social ethics and social action in the 1970s and 1980s had in fact already gone too far, perhaps even involving a 'betrayal of the Gospel' (Sinton, 1990).[8]

The 1980s thus brought a decisive end to the broadly consensual approach to political, social and economic issues which had characterized the position of the churches from 1945 until the late 1970s – albeit with increasing tension during the last decade of that period. In the 1980s, consensus was decisively replaced by confrontation, both between government and the predominant group within the leadership of the churches and between various strands of opinion within the churches. Indeed, within the churches the political diversity – and the variety of combinations of political and theological opinion – was as marked as any of the other diversities within contemporary British Christianity. It simply was not possible to make straightforward equations between theological positions and political allegiances. Neither denominational membership nor commitment to a particular theological position – whether 'catholic', 'evangelical' or 'liberal' – constituted in itself an even tolerably reliable guide to the likely political, social or economic position of any individual Christian. The various social and political positions adopted and advocated by Christians in Britain during the increasingly polarized 1970s

---

[8] For a concise discussion of the variety of particular political and economic policies advocated by evangelicals in the late 1980s and early 1990s, see Hay, 1993.

and 1980s all self-consciously drew upon the historical legacy of Christianity and upon the Bible in particular. But the biblical witness and the Christian tradition were themselves contested concepts in the articulation of an equally contested contemporary Christian social witness: thus both advocates of the market economy and enterprise culture and exponents of political and liberation theology appealed to the biblical tradition for inspiration and support.

Nor was such diversity in the interpretation of the implications of scriptural and theological tradition confined to Christianity. During the 1980s representatives of different strands of the Jewish community in Britain demonstrated that there was a similar variety of perspectives on contemporary social and economic issues among British Jews. Thus, in response to the appearance of the Church of England report *Faith in the City*, the Chief Rabbi, Immanuel Jakobovits, published a brief pamphlet entitled *From Doom to Hope* (Jakobovits, 1986), also setting out his position in the *Jewish Chronicle* of 24 January 1986. Jakobovits defended the assumption of *Faith in the City* that religious leaders should address the social issues of the day – including if necessary 'questioning the morality of economic policies in the light of their effects' – and also acknowledged that the report was impressively researched. He also argued, however, that the report's conclusions and recommendations embodied 'at times, a measure of patent political bias'. He then set out an alternative approach 'derived primarily from Jewish teachings and from the Jewish experience' (Jakobovits, 1986, p.3).

The alternative that Jakobovits proposed emphasized the Jewish experience of deploying ambition, education and hard work as the means to social and economic advancement, and escape from the inner-city poverty and deprivation which had been the historic lot of many previous generations of Jewish immigrants. He also emphasized the ways in which the Jewish tradition valued the virtues of work, noting that while no work 'was too menial to compromise human dignity and self-respect', yet 'idleness is an even greater evil than unemployment'. 'Cheap labour', he asserted, 'is more dignified than a free dole, and industriousness generates greater wealth than increased wages for decreasing hours of work' (pp.9–10). He also stressed that while Jewish tradition insisted upon both rectitude in the acquisition of wealth and due provision for charity, yet it did not frown on wealth as such or demand 'that wealth be shared or distributed to equalize rich and poor by some artificial balance, unrelated to effort and skill' (p.11).

Not surprisingly, this alternative to the approach of *Faith in the City* was popular with the government and with Margaret Thatcher in particular – and, indeed, in 1988 the Chief Rabbi became a member of the House of Lords. It did not, however, command universal assent from other members of the Jewish community in Britain. On the contrary, it stimulated a lively debate within the Jewish community and prompted other interpretations of the significance of the Jewish religious tradition and experience for the discussion of contemporary British social and economic issues. Thus, for example, it was argued that Jakobovits' approach was unduly narrow in its account of the Jewish perspective on questions of work, poverty and deprivation. There were, it was urged, other aspects of the Jewish tradition such as 'the Exodus experience', 'the prophetic message' and 'the kingdom of God' which, together, constituted a 'focus on moral action'. In this view, Judaism implied an active commitment to work for the overcoming of poverty, deprivation and powerlessness and the recovery and reconstruction of the inner cities (Cohn-Sherbok, 1989a; see also Cohn-Sherbok, 1989b; Friedman, 1986; Neuberger, 1992).[9]

Granted the diversity and complexity of both Christian and Jewish social and political thought in Britain in recent years, there still remains, however, the further question of why the polarization between government and the churches become *so* marked in the 1980s. At one level the explanation may be thought almost ludicrously obvious. It was, after all, as we have noted already, the deliberate and clearly stated aim of the successive Thatcher governments to shatter what remained of the previous political consensus, and repudiate above all what they perceived to be the weaknesses inherent in the welfare state and the debilitating legacy of the 1960s. Since, as we have seen, the Christian churches had welcomed the welfare state and its broad aims, it was hardly surprising that conflict should now arise between them.

It is also possible, however, to press somewhat further than this. It has been suggested that the intensity of the confrontations between government and the churches during the 1980s was also due to the degree and nature of Conservative predominance during that decade, and to the fact that the majority of church leaders in the 1980s were themselves products and defenders not merely of the post-war welfare state consensus in general, but also of the particular 'left-liberal establishment consensus' of the 1960s and 1970s (Baker, 1991; Martin, 1989).[10] Thus, it is argued, the lack of effective political opposition and the consequent dominance of policy by one party at once prompted the churches to speak for those who

---

[9] For a further Jewish perspective on these issues, more dispassionate than that of Jakobovits, but less radical than that of Cohn-Sherbok, Friedman or Neuberger, see *Wealth and Poverty: a Jewish analysis* by Jonathan Sacks, subsequently Jakobovits' successor as Chief Rabbi (Sacks, 1985).

[10] It has also been argued that this is especially true of the leadership of the Church of England and their collective sense of 'Anglican norms' (Medhurst and Moyser, 1988, pp.90–1 and 125–31) which, if correct, would further explain the particular intensity of clashes between the government and that church and its bishops.

were increasingly disadvantaged and – in the absence of other effective opposition – made their speaking appear all the more overtly political and radical (Baker, 1991, pp.95–8; Stanford, 1993, pp.105–6). A similar process has been observed at work in the response of Britain's charitable agencies: faced with the attempt to shift more of the burden of welfare work away from the state and back to voluntary philanthropy, they too have become increasingly 'political' in campaigning against the causes as well as the consequences of poverty and inequality (Eyre, 1991, p.50). And at the same time, the churches, while remaining essentially wedded to the post-war consensus line, also developed a more radical tone as a result of their participation in wider debates over 'issues of justice and peace', 'liberation theology', and so forth.

To this, however, must be added the significance of Margaret Thatcher's personal style and opinions. It is a commonplace that she was above all a 'conviction politician' and apt to divide the world into those who were 'one of us' and those who were not. Dissent against her successive governments (within her own party as well as without) was characteristically opposed, pursued and rooted out with considerable vigour. It has also been noted that she was distinctive among recent British prime ministers and political leaders precisely because she not only took religion so seriously, but also sought to justify her government's policies on explicitly religious grounds (Bradley, 1992, p.126; Clark, 1993, p.10; Leech, 1991, p.159). Indeed, it has even been argued that her own programme may best be understood as 'a religious crusade' (Clark, 1993, pp.10–12), and that both 'Thatcherism' and the 'enterprise culture' themselves exhibited characteristics of a 'quasi religious' kind, not the least of which were its triumphal language, its demand for a veritable 'conversion' from the previously prevailing social and political consensus, and a 'belief' in the renewing and revitalizing power of 'enterprise' (Roberts, 1992; see also Thompson, 1991). Margaret Thatcher, then, saw herself as a crusader, as the 'preacher' of a new 'doctrine' of economic realism (Crewe, 1989, p.240).

Not surprisingly, she also espoused a quite specific perception of the proper relationship between religion and social and economic issues. This was nowhere made more clear than in her speech to the 1988 General Assembly of the Church of Scotland (Thatcher, 1990, pp.333–8). Having explained that 'the distinctive marks of Christianity ... stem not from the social but from the spiritual side of our lives', she then discussed her 'personal belief in the relevance of Christianity to public policy' and the possibility that the Bible might provide a 'view of the universe, a proper attitude to work, and principles to shape economic and social life'. Those principles, she went on, included the injunction to 'work and use our talents to create wealth', quoting also the biblical text 'if a man will not work, he shall not eat'. Abundance rather than poverty had 'a legitimacy which derives from the very nature of creation' – the spiritual dimension, however, came in deciding what to do with wealth. She acknowledged that none of this pointed to 'exactly what kind of political and social institutions we should have', but continued that 'What is certain, however, is that any set of social and economic arrangements which is not founded on the acceptance of individual responsibility will do nothing but harm ... intervention by the state must never become so great that it effectively removes personal responsibility.'

The overall thrust of her speech was the conviction that the heart of Christianity lay in spiritual redemption, not social reform, and that the proper role of the churches, therefore, is spiritual and personal. Social and economic obligations are not irrelevant, but they flow from – and must never be allowed to overshadow – personal and individual responsibility.[11] It was, in effect, a prime ministerial version of the position set out a decade earlier by Edward Norman in his Reith Lectures attacking the 'politicization' of Christianity; a position subsequently endorsed and elaborated upon, as we have seen, by other fierce internal critics of the predominant trends in contemporary Christian social and political thought. Given this, and given also that conservative sections of the press were only too keen to dramatize the conflicts involved (Baker, 1991, pp.90 and 94, Jenkins, 1991, pp.103, 107 and 113; Leech, 1988, pp.134–5; Montefiore, 1990, pp.77 and 80; Thompson, 1991, pp.282–5 and 289), perhaps the real surprise is not that sharp confrontations between government and the churches occurred during the 1980s, but rather that they were not sharper and more frequent still.

3 Grassroots and other issues

This examination of the interaction between religion and politics in Britain since 1945 has focused upon the changing relationship between government and the leadership of the Christian churches in attitudes to social and economic issues. There remain, however, at least two further important issues to consider.

---

[11] Immediately after giving her speech Thatcher was presented with a report by the Moderator of the General Assembly. Entitled *Just Sharing*, it hoped for 'the beginnings of a renewed Christian social vision rooted in the neighbour' (Bradley, 1992, p.131). The chairman and general secretary of the Church of England's Board for Social Responsibility subsequently issued a joint response to the speech which similarly emphasized the 'essentially social character of human life' (Clark, 1993, pp.40–1). For a sustained and highly critical 'deconstruction' of the General Assembly speech and its significance as a symbol of the 'religiousness' of Thatcherism, see Raban, 1989.

First there is the relationship between the political and social stance of church leaders and that of the grassroots within the churches, namely, the lay majority in the pews. 'Most Christians', it has been observed, 'do not involve themselves in … high ideological battles. Their Christianity is local, moral and personal, rather than political and doctrinal. Many of them are theologically liberal and politically conservative (whereas some clergy are just the reverse!)' (Martin, 1989, p.338).There is, indeed, a good deal of evidence to suggest that during the period addressed in this essay – and probably increasingly in its latter decades – the clergy, on the whole, stood significantly more to the left politically than the majority of the laity in their respective churches. (See, for example, Bradley, 1992, pp.135–6; Davie, 1990, p.410; Medhurst and Moyser, 1982, p.186, and 1988, pp.225–31; Montefiore, 1990 pp.68–9.) The general tendency for the clergy to be further to the left politically than the laity was further accentuated, moreover, among the leading clergy and those who were particularly involved in specialized or 'sector' ministries (to industry, for example), in ecumenical activity, in the running of denominational departments and boards, or in the life of central bodies such as the Church of England General Synod or the Church of Scotland Church and Nation Committee (Bradley, 1992, pp.135–6; Brown, 1990, pp.82–4; Medhurst and Moyser, 1988, pp.139–40 and 231; Montefiore, 1990, p.70; Walker and Gallagher, 1990, p.105).

In noting the *relative* conservatism of the laity, however, the contrast between lay and clerical attitudes should not be exaggerated. On the one hand, it is likely that the 'conservatism' characteristic of the laity in general was predominantly of a relatively 'soft', 'unideological', 'pre-Thatcherite' kind (Baker, 1991, p.99; Bradley, 1992, p.136). On the other hand, it should not be overlooked that along with the clergy there were also substantial bodies of highly 'activist' laity who participated vigorously in the running of their churches and in the debates over their policies on specific issues. In general terms, it has been noted that the laity who are most 'activist' – those Anglicans, for example, who become members of General Synod, or Roman Catholics who become members of national or diocesan commissions – are also likely to be more to the left politically than their less 'activist' fellow laity (Hornsby-Smith, 1987, pp.175–9; Martin, 1989, p.337; Medhurst and Moyser, 1982, p.186 and 1988, p.231; Montefiore, 1990, pp.69–70). Similarly there were also numerous lay Christians for whom the most effective expression of the politically left-of-centre commitments and conclusions which they drew from their personal faith was to be found not in 'church-based activism', but in participation in 'secular' agencies such as Shelter, Amnesty International, War on Want, and CND (Hornsby-Smith, 1987, p.179; 1989, p.189). And there were also many examples of specifically local expressions of a socially and politically radical understanding of the implications of Christian faith in which laity and clergy co-operated at the parish or neighbourhood level (see, for example, Dunn, 1986; Vincent, 1992a; Wheale, 1985).

Nor, finally, should it be forgotten that, despite the generally left/liberal stance of such lay activists, there were also influential lay activists of conservative or right-of-centre opinion – John Selwyn Gummer's membership of the Church of England General Synod being a pertinent but by no means unique illustration of the point. Indeed, in matters of politics – as also in matters of theology and liturgy – the fundamental contrast was not that between the majority of the laity and a leftward-leaning clerical leadership, but rather that between the 'passive majority' and at least two competing 'activist minorities', one 'conservative' and the other 'radical'. The latter minorities were composed of *both* clergy and laity, shared a common conviction that Christianity should involve support for distinctive social values, but divided sharply over what those values actually were. Moreover, as with similar theological and liturgical parallels, it was in the ferment of the 1960s that the emergence of such 'activist minorities' crucially began to take shape; a process that continued in the 1970s, and was then made dramatically evident in the 1980s as successive Thatcher governments deliberately radicalized political debate so sharply that even those Christians who simply believed themselves to be contemporary representatives of the post-war welfare state consensus began to be portrayed as distinctively 'left-wing'.[12]

The second issue that remains to be considered is whether it is likely that the relationship between politics and religion in Britain in the mid and late 1990s and beyond will continue, as in the 1980s and early 1990s, to be dominated principally by debates and controversies over social and economic issues such as poverty, unemployment, social deprivation, 'communal needs versus individual enterprise', 'welfare versus wealth creation', and so forth. Or is it likely, rather, that the ongoing political and religious life of the nation may produce a significantly different agenda for the interaction of religion and politics? Judgements on such matters can be no more than tentative, but there are aspects of recent British religious history and debate that indicate at least the possibility of some significant adjustments to the future agenda of political–religious debate in Britain.

---

[12] For the way in which this situation reflects arguably a much more general tension within the traditional Christian churches of Britain between 'passive majorities' and more peripheral believers on the one hand, and competing 'activist minorities' on the other, see Volume I, essay 1, pp.85–8. For the view that it was less a matter of the churches moving to the left than of the government moving radically right, while the churches sought to uphold the values of the post-war consensus, see also Clark, 1993, p.2; Davie, 1990, p.412; Leech, 1991, p.160; Thompson, 1991, p.291.

At the time of writing, it remains impossible to tell whether the removal of Margaret Thatcher as prime minister will produce, in due course, a return to a more consensual and less confrontational relationship between church leaders and government over social and economic issues. It is clear that active concern over the implications of Christian theology for social issues is now firmly on the agenda of the British churches; is well established as a central concern of leaders, synods, committees, and boards and divisions of social responsibility; and is increasingly and diversely expressed in numerous local contexts and communities. It is also the subject of lively and intense debate within the churches and will almost certainly continue to be so. In the early 1990s, moreover, such debate was further stimulated by a newly confident reassertion of the historic links between Christianity and socialism – an attempt, in effect, to 'reclaim' the ethical code of Christianity as a key element within democratic socialism (Smith et al, 1993).

If political debate in the post-Thatcher era eventually becomes less polarized, if a more consensual 'one-nation Toryism' is reasserted within the Conservative Party, and if the dismantling of the post-war welfare state is not pressed even further, then it is possible that the confrontations between government and church leaders will once more recede. But if the general trend in social policies of the 1980s continues, accompanied by further increases in the social disparities within British life, then it is likely that government and church leaders will continue to clash. It is also possible, however, to suggest two trends from the mid and late 1980s and the early 1990s which may point at least to an important extension of the political–religious agenda in Britain in the last years of the twentieth century, even if not to an outright reordering of priorities within political–religious debate.

In the mid and late 1980s it became clear that, alongside the ongoing debates over the social and economic implications of Christianity for contemporary British political life, there was also an increasingly vocal network of Christian groups concerned to reassert their version of 'traditional Christian *moral* values' within society, and prepared to mobilize politically to achieve this end. Thus, in January 1987, an article in *The Times* provided a review of groups concerned to promote a 'moral resurgence' in British life. The organizations listed included both new pressure groups such as the National Campaign for the Family, the National Council for Christian Standards in Society, and the Conservative Family Campaign, and older well-established groups such as the anti-abortion group, Society for the Protection of the Unborn Child (SPUC), and Christian Action Research and Education (CARE) (Bradley, 1992, p.147; *The Times*, 15 January 1987, p.14). Such groups were characteristically concerned about a broad range of moral issues. These included, most notably, abortion, homosexuality, sexually explicit literature, films and television programmes; the nature and availability of advice and education concerning sex and contraception; the rising divorce rate and the resulting threat to 'the family'. These concerns amounted to a generalized opposition to what such groups perceived as the moral decadence of British life consequent upon the 'permissive' legislation and legacy of the 1960s, together with a conviction of the need for a reassertion of 'traditional' Christian and 'family' values.

The roots of this increasingly prominent trend in the mid and late 1980s may be discerned clearly in the 1960s and 1970s. As early as the mid 1960s, the campaigning of Mary Whitehouse and the National Viewers and Listeners Association signalled the emergence of an 'anti-permissive' Christian lobby. Subsequently the foundation of SPUC (in opposition to the legalization of abortion in 1967), and the emergence in the early 1970s of groups such as the Order of Christian Unity, the Community Standards Association and the Nationwide Festival of Light (from which CARE later emerged), began to focus conservative Christian opposition to the reforming legislation of the late 1960s and to consolidate the basis for a restatement of moral conservatism.[13]

Significantly, such groups were often predominately led by laity and frequently cut across conventional denominational lines, combining theologically conservative Christians from various denominations. Perhaps most significantly, they notably combined those Roman Catholics who retained a conservative stance on issues of personal and sexual morality and the increasingly self-confident evangelicals, who also characteristically tended to maintain a markedly conservative position on such matters (Bradley, 1992, pp.144–9; Stanford, 1993, pp.175–84). By the 1980s such groups – together with newer pressure groups and organizations of a similar kind – were actively exploring their political potential and flexing their political muscles – and not only in matters such as abortion or sexual morality. Thus in 1985–86, government proposals to allow Sunday trading were defeated by a coalition of interests which extended to trade unions as well as religious groups, but among whom Christian campaigners were prominent (Bradley, 1992, pp.143–4; Patey, 1988, pp.52–3). Perhaps even more strikingly, evangelical pressure groups scored a significant political victory in the parliamentary debates which led to the passing of the 1990 Broadcasting Act. The religious broadcasting

---

[13]   For a fuller discussion of this theme and its significance within broader religious and theological debates in Britain, from the 1960s onwards, over personal morality and the appropriate approach to moral decision making, see essay 7 in this volume. (See also Capon, 1972; Perman, 1977, ch.11; Thompson, 1992; Wallis, 1979, chs 7–9; Weeks, 1989, chs 14 and 15.)

'establishment' – including the BBC, ITV and leading representatives of 'mainstream' religious opinion on broadcasting in the form of the Central Religious Advisory Council – argued against sanctioning religious advertising or the ownership of television stations by churches and religious bodies. Skilled and persistent lobbying by evangelical Christians, however, persuaded the government to amend the Act as originally proposed in order to extend the possibilities for specifically evangelistic broadcasting (Bradley, 1992, pp.199–201; Maitland, 1992, pp.42–3).

For an increasing number of commentators, developments such as these suggested the emergence – or at least the attempt to foster the emergence – of a British version of the 'moral majority' which, through tele-evangelism and high-profile, professionally targeted pressure-group lobbying, sought so decisively to influence American politics during the 1980s (Bradley, 1992, pp.146–7; Maitland, 1992; Martin, 1989, p.340; Thompson, 1992; see also Carroll, 1991, ch.3; Weeks, 1989, chs 14 and 15). Because of the very different political and social cultures of Britain and America, it is unlikely that a moral majority would emerge in Britain in the same way or to the same extent that it did in the USA in the 1980s – and even in the American context, it should be noted, there is much debate as to just how effective a force it was (Thompson, 1992, pp.65–7). On the other hand, the fact that it may not prove as *prominent* a force in British politics as it does in America does not mean that it will not exert an influence – and perhaps a significant one – upon the political agenda in Britain. What is clear, however, from the remarks of both historians of recent evangelical campaigning initiatives and representatives of some of the groups concerned, is the desire so to influence British political life.

Thus, for example, it has been observed of the resurgence of social and political campaigning in general among evangelicals since the 1960s that 'the widest enthusiasm for public campaigns ... appeared when the target, in Evangelical eyes, was sin. Much of the renewed impetus for socio-political action sprang from an eagerness to take up broadly moral issues' (Bebbington, 1989, p.265). Or again, it has been noted that bodies such as CARE provide advice and guidelines 'for positive action on moral issues like abortion, single-parent families and the bias perceived towards homosexual preference in community and educational services' (Calver, 1987, p.35). Those involved have also remarked upon the sheer number of potential votes available to be mobilized, citing for example, '1,000,000 evangelical believers' (Calver, 1987, p.39) or 'two million believing Christians prepared to consider their vote' (cited in Bradley, 1992, p.147; see also, Thompson, 1992, p.79). Thus, significantly, in the mid 1980s, both the CARE organization and the Evangelical Alliance – arguably the two most influential co-ordinating agencies in evangelical campaigning in Britain – signalled a new determination to go beyond local initiatives and private lobbying of local and national government and to intervene directly in the British party political and electoral process.

CARE members were encouraged to form core groups in local constituencies, to join local political parties and to question candidates on their position on 'vital moral issues'. The list of 'vital moral issues' included such matters as the law on abortion, homosexuality, obscene publications, moral and sex education in schools, Sunday trading, financial reforms in relation to marriage and the family, and both embryo research and surrogacy. Phrases such as 'God's Agenda' indicated a belief that government should create a society based on 'God's laws'. To facilitate such political activism by individuals, CARE produced a quarterly magazine, a handbook and a wide range of briefing papers on both individual issues and the best methods to organize and lobby politicians and local government. At the national level, CARE in due course employed a full-time parliamentary secretary (Thompson, 1992, pp.77–8 and 88). The Evangelical Alliance, meanwhile, called upon its members to take decision making back from 'politicians, doubters and secularists', and sought to co-ordinate the political action of both individual members and a whole range of affiliated and umbrella groups. The Evangelical Coalition on Sexuality, for example, aimed to co-ordinate churches and Christian groups concerned with medicine, education, sociology and the family in order to 'speak and act on sexually related issues that affect society' (Thompson, 1992, p.79).

It is true that those involved in such activities have argued strongly that the diversity of party political opinion among such Christians in Britain will prevent the emergence of a 'moral majority'. Similarly they have argued that, in the British context, there is no straightforward alignment between Christian campaigners on moral issues and the political and economic 'new right' – thus some evangelicals have criticized aspects of 'new right' economic policies and of 'Thatcherism' (Thompson, 1992, p.79), while the anti-abortion campaigns of SPUC and CARE in the late 1980s were not only defeated, despite a large Conservative majority in parliament, but were vigorously opposed by, among others, Conservative MPs from the 'new right' (Alton, 1991, pp.11–13; Calver, 1987, p.39).

On the other hand, however, it is also clear that the increasingly organized and confident political activity of those who wished to bring their version of 'biblical Christianity' and 'God's Agenda' to bear on British political and social life coincided with the sustained period of Conservative government which began in 1979 (Weeks, 1989, pp.292–6). Although the Conservative governments of the 1980s did not embark on a concerted repeal of the reforms of the laws governing personal and sexual morality passed in the late 1960s, yet the Conservative manifestos for the 1979, 1983 and 1987 general elections included significant concessions in the areas of censorship and media reform (Thompson, 1992, pp.88–9). Similarly, the putative British moral majority and the Conservative governments of the 1980s shared a common concern with 'family values', and a common disposition to oppose 'permissiveness' and to blame it for all manner of social and moral dilemmas and difficulties in contemporary British society (Weeks, 1989, pp.279–80 and 293–6).

This, moreover, was a long-standing sympathy and similarity of interest clearly discernible as early as the mid and late 1970s (Perman, 1977, p.191; Tracey and Morrison, 1979, pp.197–9; Weeks, 1989, p.278). Such common interests, in addition, were apt to issue in campaigns for legislation which, if passed, would have interfered significantly with personal liberties by reimposing upon society as a whole a particularly conservative and restrictive version of Christian sexual morality in relation to a whole range of activities and aspects of life (Kent, 1992, p.189; Tracey and Morrison, 1979, pp.38 and 187–8). The broad thrust of such campaigns, it has been observed, may be described as nothing less than an attempt to 'recapture British society for Christianity' and 'recolonize social life for God', by resisting and reversing the steady liberalization and secularization of personal and sexual morality in Britain since the 1960s and returning to an essentially 'theocratic' conception of the relationship between Christian morality – conservatively understood – and the laws of the land (Tracey and Morrison, 1979, pp.38, 184–5 and ch.10). During the 1980s, therefore, as so many areas of British life became increasingly polarized and the emergence of AIDS cast a long shadow over both sexual practice and debates over sexual morality, so sexual issues became increasingly prominent in political debate (Weeks, 1989, ch.15). And, as they did so, so the 'new moral right' emerged, with increasing clarity.

Moreover, to deny the existence (or possible emergence) of a 'moral majority' in Britain, on the grounds that there is no explicit link between such a 'moral majority' or 'new moral right' and a particular political party, is to assume that a 'moral majority' must, by definition, operate by means of alliance with a specific party and with the economic and political 'new right'. That, however, is surely not the case. The Movement for Christian Democracy, for example, provides an alternative model for the operation of a 'new moral right' in Britain. Initially founded by three MPs on a cross-party basis in 1988, and subsequently publicly launched in 1990, the MCD stated that it would aim to endorse specific candidates in general elections, providing them with a letter of endorsement which could be used in their campaigning. Such endorsement was not intended to be party specific but, rather, to increase the number of Christians in Parliament.

One of the leading figures in the founding of the MCD was the Roman Catholic MP, David Alton, a leading and passionate anti-abortion campaigner. In a book designed to introduce the MCD and its principles,

Alton wrote of the need for a 'new Christian consensus, based on biblical values and Holy-spirit led priorities' (Alton, 1991, p.x). In the light of such sentiments, it is not surprising that representatives from CARE, the Evangelical Alliance and the London Institute for Contemporary Christianity also served on the MCD's steering committee (Bradley, 1992, pp.148–9). The open alliance between conservative Roman Catholic and conservative evangelical perspectives and the cross-party nature of the MCD indeed serve to reinforce the fact that any British 'moral majority' will be significantly different from its American counterpart. But the desire for a new Christian consensus; for 'biblical values' and 'Holy-Spirit led priorities'; for the promotion of a conservative Christian standpoint on matters of sexual morality and the family; and for the endorsement (or not) of candidates according to their stand on specific moral issues – all of these features suggest that the MCD is at least a potential vehicle for the political aims and aspirations of the 'new moral right' in Britain[14] (Maitland, 1992, p.43).

The eventual extent and impact of such campaigning remains to be seen. It may or may not result in a fundamental transformation of the agenda of religious–political debate in Britain in the last years of the twentieth century and the opening years of the twenty-first. At the very least, however, it seems likely to extend the range of such debate, when compared with the issues that dominated during the 1970s and 1980s. A second trend from the 1980s and early 1990s, however, was similarly – perhaps, indeed, even more significantly – suggestive of possible additions and adjustments to the future shape and agenda of political–religious discussion and controversy in Britain.

As various other essays in this volume and its companion demonstrate, during the 1980s and early 1990s a succession of issues steadily served to pose the question 'how will the modern British state cope with the issues raised by the development of an increasingly thoroughly religiously plural society?' In particular, how will British governments and political parties respond to a variety of religious minorities (including ardently and assertively Christian minorities) who insist on taking distinctively religious claims upon life, morality and conduct more seriously than the majority of the modern British population, and who also insist, moreover, upon seeking to translate such religious claims into social and political realities? (Beckford, 1991, p.198). How will British governments and political parties respond when some religious groups wish to oppose freedoms that others either take for granted or no less passionately demand for themselves?

---

[14] For a more extended and rather different – though still necessarily tentative – assessment of the Movement for Christian Democracy see Fogarty, 1992.

Such issues were raised most forcefully and dramatically by the Rushdie affair and its complicated involvement in conflicting notions of the meaning and implications of 'freedom of expression', 'blasphemy', 'religious equality' and 'pluralism' – to say nothing of its significance for the even more contentious and complex notion of 'multi-culturalism'.[15] But, as others have also pointed out, it was by no means only the Rushdie affair and the Muslim community that were involved in the wider range of questions noted in the preceding paragraph (Davie, 1990, p.417). The discussion of New Religious Movements in Britain in the early 1980s extended, crucially, into their legal status and the 'right to be religious' of their members and adherents.[16] The debates over education in the mid and late 1980s – and especially those surrounding the 1988 Education Act and its provision for religious education and religious worship in state schools – similarly revealed complex and deeply felt issues arising from the religious convictions and aspirations of a variety of groups, of whom some Christians and Muslims were undoubtedly the most vociferous, but by no means the only groups to be concerned.[17]

Or again, from 1985 onwards there was a significant political–religious debate over the fundamental conflict between the recommendations of the Farm Animal Welfare Council concerning the religious slaughter of animals and the practices and religious requirements of both the Jewish and Muslim communities in Britain. Although much less publicized than the controversies over Rushdie and education – and perhaps less publicized even than those over New Religious Movements – it has been pointed out that what has been termed 'the politics of religious slaughter' is in fact strikingly relevant to debate over the nature and extent of British tolerance, the role of the state and public opinion in relation to religious minorities, and the political strategies of religious minorities themselves (Kaye, 1993; Kushner, 1989).

Finally – but not therefore any less importantly – it has also been emphasized that while most of the debates over minority religious rights in Britain tend to focus on issues raised by the demands of respect for the integrity of the religious customs, values and practices of distinct ethnic and religious communities in Britain, yet there are also important but often neglected issues of minority rights *within* those communities. Thus, in

---

[15] For brief accounts of the development of an increasingly assertive political stance among British Muslims, especially in the wake of the Rushdie affair, see Beckford, 1991, pp.196–8; Hiro, 1992, ch.10 and pp.312–13; Modood, 1990, pp.153–60; Nielsen, 1987 and 1992, pp.52–9 and 156–62.

[16] For a fuller discussion of this see Volume I, essay 7, pp.289–94.

[17] For a fuller discussion of the 1988 Education Act and the debates prompted by it, see essay 5 in this volume.

1989, a number of women from a variety of religious backgrounds and ethnic minority groups within Britain formed the organization Women Against Fundamentalism in order to campaign on behalf of women from various religious backgrounds (including the Christian, Jewish, Muslim, Hindu and Sikh traditions) whose roles and rights are prescribed or proscribed by the male leaders of their communities who, in turn, often appeal to the right to tolerance of 'their' cultural and religious norms to justify non-interference in the control of the women within those communities (Connolly, 1991; Sahgal and Yuval-Davis, 1990 and 1992; Yuval-Davis, 1992).

Whatever may transpire in respect of the possible extension of the specifically Christian political–religious agenda into a wider range of 'moral' issues, it is certain that the political–religious issues raised by religious pluralism and the competing rights and claims of religious groups and individuals will make increasing demands upon the attention of British politicians and political parties in coming years. This being so, it is appropriate for us to ask whether the political culture of Britain is equipped to handle such matters in an informed and thoughtful way.

The political and media reactions to the clashes between government and the churches in the 1980s, complete with caricaturing dismissals of 'trendy left-wing bishops' and 'Marxist theology' and calls for the clergy to keep out of politics and stick to matters spiritual, are not a happy precedent. It may be that in the years ahead, religious leaders and politicians, religious groups and political parties, will all make the effort to understand the subtleties and complexities of the interactions to which their various commitments give rise. With such effort the religious–political debates of the near future in Britain may prove both rich and fascinating. Without such effort, the alternative is the reduction of increasingly complex issues to the convenient slogans of competing religious-cum-political pressure groups – a bleak and unhappy prospect indeed.

Bibliography

ALISON, M. (1990) 'The feeding of the billions' in Alison, M. and Edwards, D. (eds).

ALISON, M. and EDWARDS, D. (eds) (1990) *Christianity and Conservatism*, Hodder and Stoughton, London.

ALTON, D. (1991) *Faith in Britain*, Hodder and Stoughton, London.

AMBLER, R. and HASLAM, D. (eds) (1980) *Agenda for Prophets: towards a political theology for Britain*, The Bowerdean Press, London.

ANDERSON, D. (ed.) (1984) *The Kindness that Kills: the churches' simplistic response to complex social issues*, SPCK, London.

(1990) 'The church's debate on social affairs' in Cohn-Sherbok, D. (ed.).

(1992) 'How can we discharge our obligations to the poor?' in Cohn-Sherbok, D. and McLellan, D. (eds).

ARNOLD, S. (1992) *From Scepticism to Hope: one Black-led church's response to social responsibility*, Grove Books, Nottingham.

ATHERTON, J. (1992) *Christianity and the Market: Christian social thought for our times*, SPCK, London.

BAKER, D. (1991) 'Turbulent priests: Christian opposition to the Conservative Government since 1979', *The Political Quarterly*, 62, pp.90–105.

BEBBINGTON, D. (1989) *Evangelicalism in Modern Britain: a history from the 1730s to the 1980s*, Unwin Hyman, London.

BECKFORD, J. (1991) 'Politics and religion in England and Wales', *Daedalus*, 120, pp.179–201.

BRADLEY, I. (1992) *Marching to the Promised Land: has the church a future?*, London, John Murray.

BROWN, C.G. (1990) '"Each take off their several way?" The Protestant churches and the working classes in Scotland' in Walker, G. and Gallagher, T. (eds).

CALVER, C. (1987) *He Brings Us Together*, Hodder and Stoughton, London.

CAPON, J. (1972) '... and there was light: the story of the Nationwide Festival of Light*, Lutterworth, London.

CARPENTER, E. (1991) *Archbishop Fisher – His Life and Times*, Canterbury Press, Norwich.

CARROLL, R. (1991) *Wolf in the Sheepfold: the Bible as a problem for Christianity*, SPCK, London.

CHADWICK, O. (1990) *Michael Ramsey: a life*, Oxford University Press, Oxford.

CLARK, H. (1993) *The Church under Thatcher*, SPCK, London.

COHN-SHERBOK, D. (1989a) *'Faith in the City*: a Jewish response' in Harvey, A. (ed.) *Theology in the City: a theological response to* Faith in the City, SPCK, London.

(1989b) 'Judaism in modern Britain: a new orientation' in Badham, P. (ed.) *Religion, State and Society in Modern Britain*, Edwin Mellen Press, Lampeter.

(ed.) (1990) *The Canterbury Papers: essays on religion and society*, Bellew, London.

COHN-SHERBOK, D. and MCLELLAN, D. (eds) (1992) *Religion in Public Life*, Macmillan, London.

CONNOLLY, C. (1991) 'Washing our linen: one year of women against fundamentalism', *Feminist Review*, 37, pp.68–77.

CREWE, I. (1989) 'Values: the crusade that failed' in Kavanagh, D. and Seldon, A. (eds).

DAVIE, G. (1990) 'An ordinary God: the paradox of religion in contemporary Britain', *British Journal of Sociology*, 41, pp.395–421.

DUMMETT, M. (1979) *Catholicism and the World Order: some reflections on the 1978 Reith Lectures*, Catholic Institute for International Relations, London.

DUNN, J. (ed.) (1986) *The Kingdom of God and North-East England*, SCM, London.

ECCLESTONE, G. (1985) 'Church influence on public policy today', *The Modern Churchman*, New Series 28, pp.36–47.

ELLIOT, A. and FORRESTER, D. (eds) (1986) *The Scottish Churches and the Political Process Today*, Centre for Theology and Public Issues and Unit for the Study of Government in Scotland, University of Edinburgh, Edinburgh.

EYRE, A. (1991) 'Faith, charity and the free market' in Gee, P. and Fulton, J. (eds) *Religion and Power, Decline and Growth*, British Sociological Association, London.

FOGARTY, M. (1992) 'The churches and public policy in Britain', *The Political Quarterly*, 63, pp.301–16.

FORSTER, G. (ed.) (1986) *Hope in the City*, Grove Books, Nottingham.

FRIEDMAN, E. (1986) 'Faith in the city: an alternative Jewish view', *The Jewish Quarterly*, 33, pp.20–5.

GRANT, P. (1990) 'If it happened to you, tell me, what would you do?' in Grant, P. and Patel, R. (eds).

GRANT, P. and PATEL, R. (eds) (1990) *A Time to Speak: perspectives of black Christians in Britain*, A Joint Publication of Racial Justice and the Black Theology Working Group, Birmingham.

GRIFFITHS, B. (1982) *Morality and the Market Place: Christian alternatives to capitalism*, Hodder and Stoughton, London.

(1984a) *The Creation of Wealth*, Hodder and Stoughton, London.

(1984b) 'Christianity and capitalism' in Anderson, D. (ed.).

(1985) *Monetarism and Morality*, Centre for Policy Studies, London.

(1990) 'The Conservative quadrilateral' in Alison, M. and Edwards, D. (eds).

HARRIS, R. (1984) 'The folly of politicized welfare' in Anderson, D. (ed.).

(1990) 'Poverty and wealth creation' in Alison, M. and Edwards, D. (eds).

HASTINGS, A. (1991) *A History of English Christianity 1920–1990*, SCM, London.

HAY, D. (1989) *Economics Today: a Christian critique*, Appollos, Leicester.

(1993) 'Evangelicalism and economic issues' in France, R. and McGrath, A. (eds) *Evangelical Anglicans: their role and influence in the church today*, SPCK, London.

HEATH, E. (1976) 'Foreword' in Temple, W., *Christianity and Social Order*, Shepheard-Walwyn/SPCK, London.

HIRO, D. (1992) *Black British White British: a history of race relations in Britain*, Paladin, London.

HORNSBY-SMITH, M. (1987) *Roman Catholics in England: studies in social structure since the Second World War*, Cambridge University Press, Cambridge.

(1989) *The Changing Parish: a study of parishes, priests and parishioners after Vatican II*, Routledge, London.

JAKOBOVITS, I. (1986) *From Doom to Hope: a Jewish view on 'Faith in the City'*, Office of the Chief Rabbi, London.

JENKINS, D. (1988) *God, Politics and the Future*, SCM, London.

(1991) *Free to Believe*, BBC Books, London.

JOHNSON, M. (1988) 'Resurrecting the inner city: a new role for the Christian Churches', *New Community*, 15, pp.91–101.

KAVANAGH, D. and SELDON, A. (eds) (1989) *The Thatcher Effect*, Clarendon Press, Oxford.

KAYE, R. (1993) 'The politics of religious slaughter of animals: strategies for ethno-religious political action', *New Community*, 19, pp.235–50.

KEE, A. (ed.) (1973) *Seeds of Liberation: spiritual dimensions to political struggle*, SCM, London.

KENT, J. (1992) *William Temple: church, state and society in Britain 1880–1950*, Cambridge University Press, Cambridge.

KUSHNER, T. (1989) 'Stunning intolerance: a century of opposition to religious slaughter', *The Jewish Quarterly*, 36.

LEECH, K. (ed.) (1979) *Christianity Reinterpreted: a critical examination of the 1978 Reith Lectures*, The Jubilee Group, London.

(1985) 'The church and immigration and race relations policy' in Moyser, G. (ed.).

(1988) *Struggle in Babylon: racism in the cities and churches of Britain*, Sheldon Press, London.

(1991) 'The Christian critique of Thatcherism' in Linzey, A. and Wexler, P. (eds).

LINZEY, A. and WEXLER, P. (eds) (1991) *Fundamentalism and Tolerance: an agenda for theology and society*, Bellew Publishing, London.

MAITLAND, S. (1992) 'Biblicism: a radical rhetoric' in Sahgal, G. and Yuval-Davis, N. (eds).

MARTIN, D. (1989) 'The churches: Pink Bishops and the Iron Lady' in Kavanagh, D. and Seldon, A. (eds).

MEDHURST, K. and MOYSER, G. (1982) 'From princes to pastors: the changing position of the Anglican Episcopate in English society and politics', *West European Politics*, pp.172–91.

(1988) *Church and Politics in a Secular Age*, Clarendon Press, Oxford.

MODOOD, T. (1990) 'British Asian Muslims and the Rushdie Affair', *The Political Quarterly*, 61, pp.143–60.

MONTEFIORE, H. (1990) *Christianity and Politics*, Macmillan, London.

MOYSER, G. (ed.) (1985) *Church and Politics Today: the role of the Church of England in contemporary politics*, T&T Clark, Edinburgh.

MUNBY, D. (1960) *God and the Rich Society*, Oxford University Press, Oxford.

NELSON, C. (1990) 'The churches, racism and the inner-cities' in Grant, P. and Patel, R. (eds).

NEUBERGER, J. (1992) 'The prophetic tradition and human rights' in Cohn-Sherbok, D. and McLellan, D. (eds).

NIELSON, J. (1987) 'Muslims in Britain: searching for an identity?', *New Community*, 13, pp.384–94.

(1992) *Muslims in Western Europe*, Edinburgh University Press, Edinburgh.

NORMAN, E. (1979) *Christianity and the World Order*, Oxford University Press, Oxford.

PATEY, E. (1988) *For the Common Good: morals public and private*, Mowbrays, Oxford.

PERMAN, D. (1977) *Change and the Churches: an anatomy of religion in Britain*, Bodley Head, London.

PRESTON, R. (1976) 'Introduction: thirty-five years later 1941–1976' in Temple, W. *Christianity and Social Order*, Shepheard-Walwyn/SPCK, London.

(1983) *Church and Society in the Late Twentieth Century: the economic and political task*, SCM, London.

(1986) 'The collapse of the SCM', *Theology*, 89, pp.431–40.

(1987) *The Future of Christian Ethics*, SCM, London.

(1991) *Religion and the Ambiguities of Capitalism*, SCM, London.

RABAN, J. (1989) *God, Man and Mrs Thatcher*, Chatto and Windus, London.

ROBERTS, R. (1992) 'Religion and the "Enterprise Culture": the British experience in the Thatcher era (1979–1990)', *Social Compass*, 39, pp.15–33.

SACKS, J. (1985) *Wealth and Poverty: a Jewish analysis*, The Social Affairs Unit, London.

SAHGAL, G. and YUVAL-DAVIS, N. (1990) 'Refusing Holy Orders', *Marxism Today*, March, pp.30–5.

(1992) 'Introduction: fundamentalism, multiculturalism and women in Britain' in Sahgal, G. and Yuval-Davis, N. (eds) *Refusing Holy Orders: women and fundamentalism in Britain*, Virago, London.

SHEPPARD, D. (1974) *Built as a City: God and the urban world today*, Hodder and Stoughton, London.

(1983) *Bias to the Poor*, Hodder and Stoughton, London.

SINTON, V. (1990) 'Evangelical social ethics: has it betrayed the gospel?' in Tinker, M. (ed.) *Restoring the Vision: Anglican Evangelicals speak out*, Marc, Eastbourne.

SMITH, J., et al. (1993) *Reclaiming the Ground: Christianity and socialism*, Spire, London.

STANFORD, P. (1993) *Cardinal Hume and the Changing Face of English Catholicism*, Geoffrey Chapman, London.

SUGGATE, A. (1991) 'William Temple and British society today' in Linzey, A. and Wexler, P. (eds).

TEMPLE, W. (1942) *Christianity and Social Order*, Shepheard-Walwyn/SPCK, London.

THATCHER, M. (1990) 'A speech by the Prime Minister' in Alison, M. and Edwards, D. (eds).

THOMPSON, K. (1991) 'Transgressing the boundary between the sacred and the secular/profane: a Durkheimian perspective on a public controversy', *Sociological Analysis*, 52, pp.277–91.

THOMPSON, W. (1992) 'Britain's moral majority' in Wilson, B. (ed.) *Religion: contemporary issues*, Bellew Publishing, London.

TINGLE, R. (1988) *Another Gospel: an account of the growing involvement of the Anglican Church in secular politics*, The Christian Studies Centre, London.

TRACEY, M. and MORRISON, D. (1979) *Whitehouse*, Macmillan, London.

VINCENT, J. (ed.) (1976) *Stirrings: essays Christian and radical*, Epworth Press, London.

(1990) *Gospel in the 90s*, Methodist Publishing House in association with Cliff College Publications and the Urban Theology Unit, Peterborough.

(1992a) 'Christianity as a movement of the poor' in Willmer, H. (ed.) *20/20 Visions: the future of Christianity in Britain*, SPCK, London.

(1992b) 'Christian discipleship and politics' in Cohn-Sherbok, D. and McLellan, D. (eds).

WALKER, G. and GALLAGHER, T. (1990) 'Protestantism and Scottish politics' in Walker, G. and Gallagher, T. (eds) *Sermons and Battle Hymns: Protestant popular culture in modern Scotland*, Edinburgh University Press, Edinburgh.

WALLIS, R. (1979) *Salvation and Protest: studies of social and religious movements*, Frances Pinter, London.

WEBB, P. (1974) *Salvation Today*, SCM, London.

WEEKS, J. (1989) *Sex, Politics and Society: the regulation of sexuality since 1800*, Longman, London.

WELLER, P. (1990) 'The multi-faith dimensions of sanctuary in the United Kingdom' in Cohn-Sherbok, D. (ed.).

WHEALE, G. (1985) 'The parish and politics' in Moyser, G. (ed.).

WILDING, P. (1992) 'Re-Review: William Temple's *Christianity and Social Order*', *The Modern Churchman*, New Series 34, pp.40–9.

WILLMER, H. (ed.) (1979) *Christian Faith and Political Hopes*, Epworth Presss, London.

YUVAL-DAVIS, N. (1992) 'Fundamentalism, multiculturalism and women in Britain' in Donald, J. and Rattansi, A. (eds) *'Race', Culture and Difference*, Sage Publications, London.

5

THERE AND BACK AGAIN? RELIGION AND THE 1944 AND 1988 EDUCATION ACTS

by Gerald Parsons

A multifaith primary school in Bradford. Photo: Carlos Reyes-Manzo, Andes Press Agency.

In 1944 the wartime coalition government passed an Education Act designed to function as one of the cornerstones of post-war recovery and reconstruction in England and Wales. The Act included provision for religious education, including the key requirements that in all schools the day was to begin with an act of collective worship, attended by all pupils, and that all pupils were also to receive religious instruction (subject only to the right of parents to withdraw their children from such worship and such classes). At the same time the Act sought finally to resolve the long-standing religious and denominational rivalry over education which had bedevilled the development of educational policy and provision in England and Wales since the early nineteenth century.

In the latter aim it was largely successful. Although the 'dual system' of state schools and church schools continued, the 1944 Education Act did not prompt widespread opposition or resistance from particular denominations or churches: on the contrary, it secured a hitherto unprecedented degree of approval and support across the range of Christian churches and denominations, while also securing an overall extension in the amount – and also an enhanced recognition of the status – of religious instruction and worship within state schools. Although the development of religious education was not to be without controversy during the next few decades, the 1944 Education Act thus appeared to have brought an end to the long sequence of bitter religious rivalries and confrontations which had dogged education over the previous century.

Forty-four years later, in 1988, the Conservative government of Margaret Thatcher passed an Education Reform Act. A major reform of the structure and content of educational provision in England and Wales, the 1988 Act also both reaffirmed and sought to clarify the clauses relating to religious education in the 1944 Act. In so doing, however, the 1988 Act prompted a sharp and ongoing debate over the significance and implications of this reaffirmation and would-be clarification of the requirements, terms and content of religious education. Although by no means the most controversial or most hotly disputed aspect of the 1988 Education Reform Act, the debate over the religious elements of the Act nevertheless returned religious education in particular – and the place of religion in education in general – to the centre of national political debate in a way not seen for more than a generation. The rights and sensibilities of different religious groups; the privileging of some groups over others; the value of 'confessional' as against 'non-confessional' religious education; the difference (and the potential tensions) between 'worship' and 'religious education'; and the implications of the Act for wider questions of 'identity' and 'belonging' within modern British society as a whole – all of these issues were brought back onto the agenda of public and political debate as a result of the 1988 Education Reform Act.

Had anything really changed at all, then, between 1944 and 1988? Was it not, perhaps, simply a case – as far as religious education and the place of religion in education were concerned – of going 'there and back again' in the intervening years? A matter of enjoying some forty years of relative calm in this whole area as a result of a particularly effective compromise in the 1944 Act, while not having resolved various underlying issues, which then resurfaced in 1988 when the earlier Act was reaffirmed and made more specific? Or is that so absurdly over-simplified a way of approaching the matter that it can only obscure the real issues and developments involved?

The aim of this essay is to explore these questions and, in so doing, to consider how the particular issues of religious education and the place of religion in education in English and Welsh schools are related to more general trends in the history of religion in Britain since 1945. The essay is not, therefore, a study of the changing attitudes towards the theory and practice of religious education, nor a survey of the professional debates among practitioners and theorists of religious education – although some mention will necessarily be made of such matters. Nor is it a comparative survey of the developments in religious education in England and Wales, Scotland and Northern Ireland. In both Scotland and Northern Ireland, religious education and the place of religion in education in the decades following 1945 were the product of distinctive histories, different legislative frameworks, contrasting denominational groupings and relationships, and pressing contemporary circumstances. It would, therefore, be impossibly over-ambitious to attempt a comparative treatment of these issues in a single essay of this length.[1] In examining religious education and the place of religion in education in England and Wales, however, and in focusing in particular upon the respective impacts of the 1944 and 1988 Education Acts, the essay will, nevertheless, provide a case study of a number of underlying issues that are also, by implication and extension, of relevance to debates about the relationship between religion and education in Britain as a whole.

---

[1] For accounts of the historical background and more recent history of the relationship between religion and education in Scotland see, for example, Fitzpatrick, 1988; Millar, 1971; Walls, 1990, pp.38–40. For the same themes in Northern Ireland, see Darby et al, 1977; Greer, 1988; and Murray, 1983.

I From 1944 to the 1960s

The 1944 Education Act required that in all schools the day should begin with a collective act of worship and that all children should receive regular religious 'instruction'[2] . Unless the schools were 'aided schools' – that is schools in which one of the churches continued to exercise a major role, albeit in partnership with government in return for substantial state funding – the religious instruction was to be according to an 'Agreed Syllabus'. (In 'aided schools', the particular church concerned retained control over the content of the religious instruction.[3]) The Agreed Syllabus, in turn, was to be formulated by an Agreed Syllabus Conference consisting of four 'panels' representing, respectively, the Church of England (except in Wales where the Anglican church was disestablished); such other religious denominations as the Local Education Authority thought appropriate (having regard for the circumstances of the area); the local authority; and teachers' associations. An Agreed Syllabus had to receive the approval of all four panels. A local Agreed Syllabus Conference could either prepare its own syllabus, adopt one from another authority, or combine elements from several other examples. In addition, if it wished to do so, a Local Education Authority might set up a Standing Advisory Council on Religious Education (SACRE) to assist it in fulfilling the requirements of the Act (Cox and Cairns, 1989, pp.2–3; Hull, 1984, p.73).

These provisions placed religious education in a unique position: it was the only specific subject that schools were legally required to teach under the 1944 Act. And yet, paradoxically, despite making religious education a required subject, to be taught according to an Agreed Syllabus, beyond this the 1944 Act was remarkably imprecise about what religious education was actually to consist of. The long-standing requirement (in force since the Education Act of 1870) that religious teaching in state schools would be non-denominational and would not reflect teaching characteristic of a particular church or denomination still applied. But the Act made no positive statement as to what was to be included. Indeed, despite requiring a regular act of worship as well as regular religious instruction, it did not even specify which religion (or religions) were to provide the basis of the worship and teaching.

---

[2] It was significant that the 1944 Act referred to both 'religious education' and 'religious instruction', apparently seeing no tension between the two terms. Indeed, far from tension between them, the Act regarded 'religious education' as the overall entity, comprising of, on the one hand, 'collective worship' and, on the other, 'religious instruction'.

[3] The majority of 'aided' schools was either Anglican or Roman Catholic, although there was also a much smaller number of Nonconformist and Jewish 'aided' schools.

In reality, such apparent reticence simply reflected an unquestioned and unquestioning assumption that – the small minority of Jewish schools apart – the worship and teaching provided would be Christian in basis and character. The constitutions of the Agreed Syllabus Conferences reflected this assumption and, significantly, made no specific provision for representatives of religions other than Christianity. Christianity clearly, it was assumed, was the historically predominant and crucial formative influence in British religious life. An undenominational Christianity, therefore, was the obvious basis for the religious worship and education of schoolchildren. The details of the syllabus, however, could be left to local conferences, thus avoiding the potentially contentious business of defining the content of religious education by Act of Parliament just at the point when government had apparently overcome the long sequence of denominational controversies and confrontations over the subject in general.

The kind of Agreed Syllabus that resulted from the 1944 Education Act has been characterized as actually dealing entirely with the past, while seeking to nurture the religious lives of pupils in the present. The religious past that was studied was also predominantly – if not exclusively – Christian. The predominant themes in the syllabus were the history of Israel (but conceived as the background to Christianity, not as the early history of Judaism); the life and teaching of Jesus; Paul and the growth of the early church; and aspects of the history of Christianity (Hull, 1984, pp.75–6). The underlying approach and assumptions of such a syllabus may conveniently be illustrated, it has been suggested, by reference to the stated aims of the Surrey Agreed Syllabus of 1945. The aim of the Surrey syllabus was that children would 'gain knowledge of the common Christian faith held by their fathers [sic] for nearly 2,000 years ... seek for themselves in Christianity principles which give a purpose to life and a guide to all its problems ... and find inspiration, power and courage to work for their own welfare, for that of their fellow creatures, and for the growth of God's kingdom' (cited in Hull, 1984, p.76).

Even more explicitly, the Sunderland syllabus of 1954 stated that the school 'ought to do its positive best to guide children into church membership' (cited in Earl, 1984, p.90), while the Derbyshire syllabus of 1948 hoped to 'bring the pupil into such contact with the personalities and teaching of the Bible that he [sic] will be led to fashion his own life and his relations with other people on the examples set before him and supremely on the pattern of the life of Christ, who perfectly fulfilled the will of God' (cited in Day, 1985, p.58). Given such openly stated aims it is hardly surprising that the Agreed Syllabuses of the late 1940s and 1950s should have been described as 'the biblical phase' in the development of Agreed Syllabus construction, and as overt 'instruments of Christian nurture', designed to elicit a religious response and commitment from children, not merely to impart religious knowledge of a textual or historical kind (Day, 1985, p.58; Earl, 1984, p.89). Similarly – in an era when the concept of 'multi-faith' worship was not even on the agenda of debate – the daily act of worship required by the 1944 Education Act was bound to have an essentially confessional and committed character (Day, 1985, pp.55 and 57).

Such aims, however, were no more than specific embodiments of the basic role envisaged for religious education by those who planned, in the early 1940s, for the overall 'Educational Reconstruction' of post-war Britain. Thus the influential White Paper of 1943, itself entitled *Educational Reconstruction*, had included the observation that there was a 'a very general wish, not confined to representatives of the Churches, that religious education should be given a more defined place in the life and work of the schools, springing from the desire to revive the spiritual and personal values in our society and in our national tradition' (cited in Day, 1985, p.57). The detailed aims of particular Agreed Syllabuses in this period also reflected the outlook and attitudes of the leading theologians, clergy and church leaders who were prominent within the Agreed Syllabus Conferences, and highly regarded by the other members. The strongly biblical and ecclesiastical content and ethos of the syllabuses were a natural consequence of the interests and perspectives of the 'religious experts' who advised upon their framing (Cox and Cairns, 1989, pp.10 and 15).

The overtly Christian aims and assumptions of the Agreed Syllabuses of this period were supported and fostered by the energetic and influential school of 'Christian Educationists' who flourished between, roughly, the mid 1930s and the late 1950s and early 1960s. This group of avowedly Christian educational theorists produced books, lectures and articles on religious education on a hitherto unprecedented scale. At the heart of their conception of an agenda for religious education lay the conviction that schools were to be essentially Christian communities preparing children for Christian living in the wider society. Christian education was thus to combat the secularism, materialism and humanism which – in the Christian Educationists view – threatened the very fabric of a fondly idealized traditional Christian culture and society. The Christian character of the nation's schools – embodied and sustained by daily acts of worship and regular religious instruction – was to be a prophetic bastion and bulwark against the secularizing and potentially anarchic and chaotically corrosive forces of modernity (Michell, 1984).

The religious assumptions of the 1944 Education Act thus brought together the hopes of those who, in the midst of war, had assigned a key role to religion within 'Educational Reconstruction'; the hopes of theologians and church leaders; and the ambitious visions of 'Christian Educationists' who sought to stem the tide of secularism, humanism and scientific materialism by a reassertion of the values of a Christian civilization and society. But how far did the assumptions of the Act correspond to reality? How far was the apparent coherence and confidence of this merging of educational and religious ideals a genuinely stable solution and resolution of long-standing ambiguities and tensions?

In so far as the 1944 Education Act sought to lay to rest the long and distracting saga of destructive inter-denominational conflict over education, it was largely successful. The 1944 Act was not accompanied or followed by renewed inter-denominational controversy or conflict between particular denominations and the government. Instead, the churches were given greater financial support from the state for the schools which they ran, and the place of religion and religious education within *all* schools was made more secure and more extensive than ever before. From the point of view of the Church of England in particular, it has been suggested, the 1944 Act may be seen as a kind of 'treaty': a bargain by which the established church accepted a significant reduction in the scale of its own direct influence over education (by allowing a large number of its schools, many of which were in any case in poor condition and becoming beyond the means of the Church of England to maintain, to be effectively taken over by the state) in return for the proposed diffusion of Christian values and teaching throughout the education system as a whole (Earl, 1984, p.88; Hastings, 1991, pp.418–20).[4] In denominational terms, the principal beneficiary of the 1944 Act was the Roman Catholic Church. The Catholic Church had in any case a long-standing policy of providing as many schools as possible for the Catholic community. The funds made available by the 1944 Act for schools with 'aided' status therefore represented a substantial gain for the Catholic Church and its educational policy – although the extent of the financial burden which the policy still involved was substantial and demanded an extremely high level of commitment from the Catholic community.

The 1944 Education Act was arguably less realistic and successful in its assumptions about the nature of the religious education which was appropriate and suitable for the post-war world. Although the Christian Educationists emphasized the need for schools to be prophetic witnesses

---

[4] It can also be argued, however, that the 'treaty' or 'bargain' between the state and the churches left religious education in an exposed and ambiguous position over its academic status as a subject. Thus, while compulsory, it nevertheless lacked the taken-for-granted professional and intellectual standing enjoyed by most other subjects. On the one hand, this left religious education vulnerable to the predilections and preferences of head teachers. Meanwhile, on the other hand, it left the door open for the teaching of 'RE' by enthusiastic non-specialists, often untrained in the subject and frequently undertaking the task as a consequence (and extension) of their personal religious belief and commitment.

against the allegedly corrosive effects of secularism, materialism and humanism, they did so from an essentially optimistic standpoint. The task assigned to schools of nurturing Christian values and Christian life was conceived as not only appropriate but also viable. The daily worship and religious instruction prescribed by the Education Act were conceived as the basis of the nurturing and consolidation of a Christian 'identity' and legacy which were commonly and securely established within British culture and society. It is by no means clear, however, that this was indeed the case.

Granted that the respect for and residual allegiance to formal Christian commitment and belief were undoubtedly much greater in the late 1940s than they were some forty years later, yet even in the late 1940s and 1950s the extent of that commitment and allegiance was already markedly less than the 1944 Education Act had assumed implicitly in its provision for religious instruction and worship. By the mid twentieth century, it has been observed, Christianity had already ceased to have a prior, determining hold upon the affections of the majority of the British population. It continued to exert a residual influence and to command a residual respect – especially in terms of its commonly perceived ethical core, conceived in terms of tolerance, neighbourliness and kindliness. But such residual Christian allegiance did not require or entail 'a fully developed theological and liturgical system' (Cox and Cairns, 1989, pp.3–4). Although favourably disposed to 'Christian values', by 1944 the majority of the population was unlikely to construe such values as implying formal ecclesiastical commitment, and still less likely to associate them with traditional doctrinal orthodoxy (Day, 1985, p.59).

Had this situation been recognized, there might, perhaps, have been some possibility of framing an approach to religious education which addressed the already uneasy balance between a variety of explicitly committed Christian communities, a residual Christianity and Christian cultural heritage, and an emergent post-Christian humanism. Such an approach to religious education might conceivably have allowed for a critical – and hence effective – engagement with the claims and values of both the Christian tradition and other contemporary philosophies and world views. Such possibilities remained, however, unrecognized and hence unconsidered. As a result, and in retrospect, the years after the passing of the 1944 Education Act have been characterized – from the standpoint of religious education – as a period of 'missed opportunities' and of 'a failure to communicate' (Cox and Cairns, 1989, pp.5–16). However, it was not until the late 1950s and the early 1960s that serious doubts actually began to be voiced as to the adequacy of the religious education provided in the wake of the 1944 Education Act.

2 From 'Christian nurture' to 'world religions'

By the end of the 1950s and the beginning of the 1960s there was a growing recognition that the religious education provided under the Agreed Syllabuses then operating was failing to fulfil the aims of the 1944 Education Act. An increasing number of reports and studies were beginning to indicate clearly that pupils did not find the religious education that they were being given relevant to their lives and concerns – despite the fact that they recognized the importance of many of the underlying issues which such teaching was intended to address (Cox and Cairns, 1989, pp.14–16). During the next two decades the contemporary state and proposed future development of religious education gave rise to a series of lively debates and new initiatives. These ranged over the methods, content and aims which might be deemed appropriate for the treatment of religion and issues of religious belief and practice in English and Welsh schools in the later twentieth century. Two particularly significant trends and stages are discernible in the development of such debates. Both initially emerged during the 1960s. However, while the first remained predominantly associated with that decade, the second did not reach its clearest expression or achieve its main impact until the 1970s.

The first stage in the concerted attempt to reassess the aims, content and methods of religious education and to make its presentation more effective was associated, above all, with an influential sequence of books, dating from the early and mid 1960s, by Harold Loukes (*Teenage Religion*, 1961, and *New Ground in Christian Education*, 1965), R.J. Goldman (*Religious Thinking from Childhood to Adolescence*, 1964, and *Readiness for Religion*, 1965) and Richard Acland (*We Teach them Wrong*, 1963, and *Curriculum or Life*, 1966). Although these authors differed in their detailed analyses and proposals for the reorientation of religious education in schools, they nevertheless shared a common aim of seeking to make such religious education more child-centred and child-related, more focused on themes, values, feelings and issues relevant to pupils' everyday lives, and less centred on abstract religious ideas or the essentially academic study of the Bible or church history (Cox and Cairns, 1989, pp.16–18; Jackson, 1990, p.107; Schools Council Working Paper 36, 1971).

The debates and new initiatives to which the work of these educationists gave rise were characterized by a distinctive vocabulary. An 'open-ended approach'; 'exploration of life themes'; 'learning through experience'; 'finding religion in the depths of human experience'; emphasis upon dialogue and discussion between teachers and pupils – such were the keynotes of the changes proposed for religious education in the early and mid 1960s. Above all there was an overwhelming emphasis upon 'experience' and 'the experiential': it was from children's own experiences that religious education was to proceed and to build. Such an orientation was the result not only of critical and empirical studies of the actual state and effectiveness of religious education in the late 1950s and early 1960s, but also of the application to religious education of contemporary research and thinking about educational psychology and the ways in which children learn (Goldman, 1964; Jackson, 1990, pp.105–6). And it was also, in addition, entirely appropriate to and consonant with the broader cultural and intellectual ethos of the 1960s and the characteristic turn in that decade towards the personal, the experiential and the expressive. Similarly, it was highly compatible with the kind of theological re-thinking called for by figures such as John Robinson and symbolized above all by *Honest to God* (Cox and Cairns, 1989, pp.16–18; Mathews, 1966).

This entire approach found formal expression in both the titles and the structure and contents of a new generation of Agreed Syllabuses formulated and issued in the mid and late 1960s. The West Riding Agreed Syllabus of 1966, *Suggestions for Religious Education*, was the first of the new generation of Agreed Syllabuses. It was also probably the single most influential example of the new style, subsequently adopted by a number of other Local Education Authorities, quite apart from providing a model for others to work from. The West Riding Syllabus acknowledged the importance of the changing stages in a child's development, structured the content of the syllabus principally on 'Themes and Activities', and included much more material directly concerned with the present than had hitherto been customary. The three 'Underlying Principles' of the syllabus were also highly significant: namely, that the material 'must satisfy the religious needs of children and young people at all stages of their development'; that the material must be 'related to life and experience'; and that the syllabus must 'provide opportunities for shared experiences to be enjoyed' (West Riding Agreed Syllabus, 1966, pp.1–2). Other significant new Agreed Syllabuses of this period included that of the Inner London Education Authority, published in 1968 and entitled *Learning for Life*; the Lancashire syllabus of 1968 entitled *Religion and Life*; and the Northampton primary and secondary syllabuses entitled, respectively, *Fullness of Life* and *Life and Worship*, both again dating from 1968.

Such syllabuses not only sought to embody an 'open-ended' and specifically non-dogmatic approach to religious education, but also characteristically included recognition of the need to include at least some material both on world religions other than Christianity and also on non-religious philosophies and attitudes to life. In this, moreover, they were supported implicitly by the Newsome and Plowden Reports of, respectively, 1963 and 1967 (Schools Council Working Paper 36, 1971, pp.30–2). Despite such concessions to religious pluralism and to a less monolithically and evangelistically Christian conception of the aims and purposes of religious education, however, the whole approach represented by the work of Loukes, Goldman, Acland and the new Agreed Syllabuses remained, in the end, fundamentally Christian in orientation, assumptions and world view. Thus the 'open-endedness' was still essentially open-endedness towards Christianity, not an open-ended engagement with a whole range of religious options. Similarly, there remained a presumption that leading pupils towards a personal spiritual appreciation of Christianity and its relevance was one of the key purposes of religious education. The attention given to other religious traditions therefore remained marginal: they were, as one critical assessment expressed it, 'regarded as tolerated extras to the officially approved viewpoint' (Schools Council Working Paper 36, 1971, p.30).

The still firmly Christian assumptions of such syllabuses, reports and proposals – together with the fact that until the late 1960s it was still all but universally assumed that religious education should be 'a vehicle for fostering Christian faith and morality' (Jackson, 1990, p.107) – led to their being described as examples of 'neo-confessionalism' in religious education. 'Neo'-confessional because, in contrast to the straightforwardly evangelizing and dogmatic assumptions of the pre 1960s Agreed Syllabuses, the 'new RE' being advocated in the early and mid 1960s was indeed open-ended and questioning; 'confessional' none the less, however, because – open-endedness notwithstanding – the 'new RE' remained committed to nurturing Christian faith, albeit in liberal and progressive terms, and by means of experience rather than straightforward instruction (Hull, 1984, p.29; Schools Council Working Paper 36, 1971, pp.30–6).

Such continuing commitment to the active nurturing of faith was one of the key features of the 'new RE' of the early and mid 1960s which sharply differentiated it from the second trend and stage in the questioning of the aims, methods and content of religious education during that decade. From the mid to late 1960s onwards, and with increasing vigour and success in the 1970s, this second strand of innovation in thinking about religious education sought to respond to the growing demands and challenges posed by, on the one hand, the growing secularity of British society and, on the other hand, the increasingly plural nature of British religious life, arising not least from the development of significant Muslim, Sikh and Hindu communities in Britain, alongside the long-established Jewish and Christian communities.

The latter development naturally posed particularly acute questions and dilemmas for religious education in areas with a significantly multi-ethnic and multi-cultural population. To present religious education with an implicitly Christian basis – and with the aim of nurturing faith on this basis – in schools attended only by children of at least nominally 'Christian' background was already, in itself, open to serious questioning in a society in which an increasing number of people explicitly rejected even nominal Christian belief. But to present such religious education in a plural and multi-cultural context in which numbers of pupils might actively profess a variety of quite different religious faiths was immediately to raise ethical, moral and indeed religious questions of an even more profound kind. Moreover, quite apart from the sensibilities of individuals and communities with other than Christian beliefs, the steady emergence of an increasingly plural society in Britain raised a further question. Should not religious education seek to teach pupils about the diversity of religious traditions which they might now encounter in Britain, and thereby seek to facilitate the emergence of a population whose perceptions of fellow citizens of various religious backgrounds were based on informed understanding rather than ignorance, misconception, or whatever knowledge they might pick up from their own efforts and interest?

Just as the emergence of the 'new RE' of the early and mid 1960s was associated with a particular group of books by Loukes, Goldman and Acland, so also the initial development of the movement away from religious education as a means of fostering faith and towards giving greater attention to a variety of world religions was similarly associated with a group of three key books. In 1966 Edwin Cox published *Changing Aims in Religious Education* in which he argued that – in state schools at least – any confessional approach to religious education was now unacceptable and that only a genuinely 'open-ended' method of religious education was justifiable. In order to be genuinely open-ended, Cox argued, such an approach would require that children were presented with a religious view of life but left to make up their own minds about its value. Religion was to be presented as 'a vital reaction to the mystery of life', 'an open search for truth and a matter of personal choice', and as 'a personal search for meaning' (Cox, 1966).[5]

Two years later Ninian Smart published *Secular Education and the Logic of Religion*, arguing that the appropriate approach to religious education in schools was a phenomenological and strictly non-dogmatic study of major world religions. Attempts to use religious education for confessional ends or as a deliberate means of nurturing a particular kind of faith were, in Smart's view, inappropriate both on educational grounds and in view of

[5] It has been argued that Cox failed, in fact, to remove all traces of confessionalism even from his own vigorous presentation of the case for 'open-ended' religious education (Greer, 1985, pp.14–15). In the 1970s and 1980s Cox stressed the need for religious education to be justified on strictly educational grounds, not residually or implicitly religious ones. He also explored the thesis that the best stance for actually teaching an open-ended, pluralistic religious education might be 'a searching agnosticism' which 'allows respect for all beliefs and admits the possibility that any of them could lead to truth' (Cox, 1977 and 1983).

the religiously plural nature of modern British society. Smart's ideal was that religious education should develop the pupil's understanding of the religious beliefs and practices of a variety of religious traditions, individuals and groups, using scholarly methods to generate empathy and an appreciation of a wide range of viewpoints and faiths, both religious and non-religious. The task of the teacher was thus to treat and portray a variety of religious positions and beliefs sympathetically, displaying an imaginative grasp of their significance, content and claims while not advocating one religious tradition rather than another. Such religious education would thus be, in essence, an academic – but not therefore dry or non-experiential – dialogue with both particular religions and with religion as an overall phenomenon (Smart, 1968).

Thirdly, in 1969, J.W.D. Smith published *Religious Education in a Secular Setting* in which he argued that the *de facto* secularization of British society and consciousness had become so extensive as to render the kind of 'Christian education' implicitly endorsed by the 1944 Education Act no longer viable. (Indeed, Smith was one of the early exponents of the view that the 1944 Act was already anachronistic in its assumption of a 'Christian culture' even as it was passed into law.) Christian educators, he argued, must therefore begin to think in more strictly educational terms and to formulate – in dialogue with other teachers and educationists who were not Christians – a policy for religious and moral education which was viable in the context of a contemporary Britain which did not possess the familiarity or manifest the general acceptance of Christianity and Christian values which the 1944 Education Act had taken for granted. Such religious and moral education, Smith argued, should be grounded in the examination of fundamental existential questions and issues which confront believers and non-believers alike (Smith, 1969).[6]

As with the earlier work of Loukes, Goldman and Acland, there were numerous and often important differences between the respective positions of Cox, Smart and Smith. At the same time, however, they collectively symbolized and expressed a more general shift towards the advocacy and articulation of a model of religious education which at once disclaimed any overtly religious or spiritual function, yet firmly emphasized the significance of religion as a distinctive and important area of human experience (Jackson, 1990, p.107). Of the three, Smart's ideas

---

[6] As with the suggestion that Edwin Cox failed to eliminate all traces of confessionalism from his work, so also even sympathetic critics have detected a residual privileging of – and perhaps even a concealed apology for – Christianity in Smith's detailed proposals for the actual content of religious education, most notably in the prominence afforded to specifically Christian examples and the justifications offered for this (Bates, 1992; Hull, 1984, pp.97–101).

were to prove particularly influential because of his role as Professor and Head of Department in what was then the newly founded Department of Religious Studies at Lancaster University. The department – which approached the study of religion at university level in the same phenomenological and non-dogmatic way that Smart advocated for religious education in schools – was also the location, from 1969 onwards, for the prestigious Schools Council Secondary Project on Religious Education. Run under Smart's overall direction, the Project produced a number of important publications including, in 1971, the widely influential Working Paper, *Religious Education in Secondary Schools* – a text that embodied and argued the case for Smart's conception of religious education (Schools Council Working Paper 36, 1971).

The movement towards an essentially phenomenological approach to religious education, based upon the study of a variety of world religions, was aided by two further factors during the late 1960s and the 1970s. On the one hand, it was supported implicitly by the more general development of the discipline of 'Religious Studies' (as opposed to the traditional emphasis upon 'Theology', which in practice meant 'Christian Theology') in higher education from the later 1960s onwards (Cunningham, Walls, Williams and Thomas, all in King, U., 1990; Gates, 1990). On the other hand, it was also explicitly fostered by the development of an increasing number of professional groups, centres and organizations for teachers of religious education, often aimed specifically at those 'RE specialists' who were frustrated by traditional confessional approaches and wished to develop the subject in a more thoroughly academic and rigorously educational direction (Jackson, 1990, pp.113–15). Among such groups, probably none was more influential than the Shap Working Party on World Religions in Education. Founded in 1969, it has since provided an increasingly rich and wide-ranging variety of conferences, mailings and publications. It has sought to foster and encourage the phenomenological, non-dogmatic, world religions based approach at grassroots level among teachers of religious education (Wood, 1989).[7]

The shift away from religious education as the nurturing of Christian faith and towards religious education as the study of a variety of world religions and religious and non-religious world views was also reflected in the development of a further 'generation' of Agreed Syllabuses. The most famous of the post 1970 Agreed Syllabuses was that of Birmingham, finally published in 1975 after a period of consultation dating back to the late

---

[7] For an indication of the way in which the influence of the West Riding Agreed Syllabus, the development of religious studies within higher education, and the foundation of the Shap Working Party all interacted to stimulate new thinking in respect of religious education, see the collection of papers, *Comparative Religion in Education*, edited by Hinnells, 1970.

1960s. The process of consultation had involved representatives of the various religious traditions present in modern Birmingham – going beyond merely Christian representation and including, for example, Jews, Muslims, Hindus, Sikhs and humanists. The syllabus was markedly controversial, exciting criticism both from some humanists (who considered even its avowedly non-confessional approach to represent, nevertheless, a form of religious indoctrination) and from some Christians (who objected, conversely, that it failed to develop a genuine appreciation of the meaning of religious commitment and amounted to an endorsement of agnosticism and a positive invitation to non-commitment).[8]

The introduction to the Birmingham Syllabus acknowledged explicitly that, whereas a generation ago religious education had aimed to nurture Christian faith, the present syllabus saw religious education as 'subject to the same disciplines as other areas of study'. The syllabus therefore aimed to enable pupils to develop 'a critical understanding of the religious and moral dimensions of human experience' but disavowed any attempt to 'foster the claims of particular religious standpoints'. These aims were to be achieved by studying world religions and 'exploring all those elements in human experience which raise questions about life's ultimate meaning and value' – an approach that therefore included study of secular alternatives to religious ways of understanding the world. The introduction to the syllabus also explained that this approach was a direct response to the increasingly diverse range of religious groups present in contemporary Birmingham (City of Birmingham, 1975, pp.4–5). It was also significant that the syllabus itself was only a few pages long, indicating broad areas of study at various stages in a pupil's school career but refraining from supplying detailed content for every stage and aspect of the curriculum. The syllabus was accompanied, however, by a substantial handbook for teachers providing several hundred pages of articles and detailed courses, lists of resources and bibliographies for every level of school life.

In its disavowal of any attempt to promote the claims of any particular religion, its emphasis on cultivating an understanding of what it is to be religious by means of the study of several world religions, and its combination of a short formal syllabus with a substantial handbook of

---

[8] For discussions of the controversies surrounding the origins and publication of the Birmingham Agreed Syllabus, see Hull, 1984, pp.29–38, 82–86 and 103–16. For examples, from the mid 1970s, of the sharply contrasting views on religious education of committed humanists on the one hand and conservatively minded Christians on the other, see *Objective, Fair and Balanced: a new law for religion in education* (British Humanist Association, 1975) and *Ways Whereby Christian Education in State Schools Should be Saved* (Order of Christian Unity, 1976). For the particular charge that the Birmingham Syllabus encouraged agnosticism and non-commitment, see Taylor, 1976.

supplementary material, the Birmingham Syllabus embodied the three major characteristics which have been identified as typical of the Agreed Syllabuses of the 1970s and early 1980s (Earl, 1984, pp.89–90). Other statements of the aims of new Agreed Syllabuses were similarly emphatic. Thus the Northamptonshire Syllabus of 1980 stated that 'Religious Education is most appropriately seen as an introduction to an individual's religious quest and some of its contemporary expressions in belief and practice rather than an induction into a particular religion', while that for Hampshire, dating from 1978, stated boldly that 'It is no part of the responsibility of a county school to promote any particular religious standpoint, neither can an exclusive Christian content do justice to the nature of the subject' (both quoted in Cox and Cairns, 1989, p.27). Similarly, it has been observed that even where it was affirmed that Christianity would remain the religion studied in greatest detail – on the grounds that it had most decisively influenced British culture and society – yet the trend here too was firmly towards the study of Christianity as 'one of the world's religions' (Cox and Cairns, 1989, p.28).

One aspect of the legacy of the 1944 Education Act upon which the 'third generation' of Agreed Syllabuses were apt to be notably – and significantly – silent was the whole question of the requirement for a daily act of worship in schools. The silence was not surprising. Until the mid to late 1960s there was relatively little questioning of either the propriety or the credibility of the 'daily act of worship'. From the late 1960s onwards, however, disquiet with the received tradition of daily school worship rapidly gained ground. As religious education became more oriented to the non-confessional study of world religions and eschewed the nurturing of any particular faith as an aim, as both pupils and teachers in general became more secular and less likely to identify themselves as Christians in even a residual sense, and as numbers of pupils from other religious traditions began to increase, so the daily act of worship became increasingly problematic (Cole, 1990, pp.118–19; Cox and Cairns, 1989, pp.32–3; Hull, 1975 and 1984, pp.5–24).

Since worship, on most definitions, would imply an intrinsically 'committed' religious stance – a personal apprehension of some transcendent 'other' to whom (or to which) the worship was a personal response – what did a specifically Christian act of worship mean for that majority of pupils for whom personal Christian belief was not part of their lives? What was to happen in schools with an increasingly diverse religious complexion? Were multi-faith acts of worship to become the norm? Or were assemblies to be distinctive of particular religious traditions, and pupils of other religious backgrounds absent? How was 'committed' worship to be reconciled with non-confessional teaching of religious education in the classroom? And what was daily worship to be if it was not 'committed' or distinctive of a particular religious tradition? Simply to articulate the questions was to recognize the complexity of the issues involved. It was also to suggest the virtual impossibility and genuine incredibility of the 'traditional' school assembly based on a straightforward act of Christian worship. It was not surprising that one of the most influential critical discussions of the subject was entitled *School Worship: an obituary,* or that the author should have argued that the most that schools without a specifically religious foundation might achieve in this area was to bring pupils to 'the threshold of worship' (Hull, 1975).

A variety of more or less practical solutions to the problems involved was increasingly deployed, with more or less success. These included strategies such as the holding of assemblies for different age groups within the school; the use of the 'assembly' as a means of 'celebrating' shared values within the school community; the exploration of religious themes in an experimental and devotional yet 'open' and as far as possible non-dogmatic manner; and the practice of inviting representatives of different religious faiths into the school to participate in, or lead, assemblies which thus introduced pupils to a variety of types of religious worship and devotion (Hull, 1984, pp.9–15). While such strategies were certainly not without value, they posed at least two unresolved questions. On the one hand, were schools ready (or able) to invest the substantial input of effort required to make such thematic, exploratory assemblies a potentially successful venture? On the other hand, was this what the 1944 Education Act meant by a daily act of worship? Or was this, rather, essentially an evasion of a key requirement of that Act – albeit, perhaps, an evasion on the justifiable grounds that the acts of worship imagined by the proposers of the 1944 Act had become, for many (perhaps a majority), both educationally unacceptable and religiously objectionable?

How, then, might the developing pattern of religious education in England and Wales by the early 1980s – and the residual legacy of the 1944 Education Act – best be summed up? Clearly tensions remained, especially in relation to the question of worship. There was still plenty of scope for controversy and opposition to the trends which had come to predominate within the teaching of religious education from the mid 1960s onwards – as the sometimes bitter exchanges over the 1975 Birmingham Agreed Syllabus had demonstrated. There also remained the long-standing lack of adequate resourcing (especially in terms of the provision of sufficient specialist teachers) and the problem over the perceived status of the subject: a compulsory subject it might be, a high-status one it still was not. Where particular schools and head teachers were sympathetic these problems might be overcome – but such good fortune was by no means the norm. Similarly, despite the efforts of groups such as the Shap Working Party on World Religions, the spread of non-confessional and world religions based religious education was far from universal and was subject to marked variations at the local level.

On the other hand, there were also considerable signs of promise and a number of causes for optimism. Local variations notwithstanding, an increasingly professionalized and professionally self-conscious body of teachers, with access to a steadily increasing range of innovative and stimulating teaching materials, was nevertheless developing the teaching of a style of religious education which eschewed confessionalism, advocated the value of studying a variety of world religions, possessed an increasing sense of its own identity as a distinct and genuinely academic subject, and was self-consciously responsive and relevant to the increasingly religiously plural nature of late-twentieth-century Britain.

There was, moreover, in general terms, a continuing lack of denominational rivalry. As long ago as 1970, the report of a major Church of England commission on religious education in schools, *The Fourth R*, had expressed a readiness to accept change and greater flexibility in religious education in any future revision of the 1944 Education Act, had welcomed the use of the term 'religious education' and the dropping of the older term 'religious instruction', had endorsed the study of secular alternatives to religion within religious education, and had affirmed that religious education must, above all, be justified on strictly educational grounds – although, unsurprisingly, the report also argued for the retention of regular worship within school life (Durham Report, 1970). It was observed in the early 1980s that even Anglican aided schools used Agreed Syllabuses, sometimes with additional material, although by law they were not required to do so. Roman Catholic schools still remained, in general, more strongly committed to nurturing the children of the Catholic community in the beliefs and values of the Catholic Church. But significantly, by the mid 1980s, a leading authority on the development of English Catholicism since 1945 suggested that the immense effort which had been made by the Catholic community in the 1940s and 50s to expand the number of Catholic schools would probably not be repeated. The Catholic community, it was intimated, would no longer regard the distinctiveness thus gained worth the effort involved (Hornsby-Smith, 1987, pp.161–2).

It was also clear that many teachers of religious education, although themselves Christian believers, were professionally committed to the non-confessional, phenomenological tradition of religious education embodied in, for example, Schools Council Working Paper 36, the Shap conferences and mailings, and the 'third generation' of Agreed Syllabuses. The changing title of the journal, published from 1934 onwards by the Christian Education Movement, provided a significant, if minor, illustration of the point. From 1934 until 1961 it was entitled *Religion in Education* (and we may safely assume that the religion involved was Christianity). From 1961 to 1978 the title was *Learning for Living* – a reflection of the turn to the experiential and the thematic so characteristic of the 1960s. But from 1978 onwards the title became the *British Journal of Religious Education* – and the essays and articles within it steadily reflected the turn to world religions and the development of school religious education – at least among 'RE specialists' – in the direction of the discipline of religious studies.

In 1984, an edition of the *British Journal of Religious Education* included a series of articles looking back forty years to the 1944 Education Act and its legacy. One of the articles included the observation that 'no changes in the law on religious education appear to be likely – except, possibly, in the clause on worship – because the Act is working remarkably well and all governments prefer to let well alone' (Earl, 1984, p.91). At the time it was a sensible enough assessment of the situation, but by the end of the decade it had been proved wildly over-optimistic – and the whole position of religious education had once more been thrown into question.

3 The 1980s: debate renewed

In 1985 an official Committee of Inquiry into the Education of Children from Ethnic Minority Groups, chaired by Lord Swann, published its findings. The Swann Report, officially entitled *Education For All*, included a substantial section on the role of religion in schools, religious education and the already growing debate over whether it was desirable for ethnic minority communities – and especially Muslim, Sikh and Hindu groups – to found their own 'Separate Schools', thus extending the range and variety of 'denominational' schools within the English and Welsh educational system.

The Swann Report came down decisively in favour of non-denominational, non-dogmatic religious education, arguing that such an approach was the 'best and only means of enabling all pupils, from whatever religious background, to understand the nature of religious belief, the religious dimension of human experience and the plurality of faiths in contemporary Britain' (Swann, 1985, p.518). With respect to the daily act of collective worship required under the 1944 Education Act, the Swann Report considered this to be no longer justifiable 'with the multiplicity of beliefs and non-beliefs now present in our society' (Swann, 1985, p.497). As for separate schools, the report affirmed the existing right of minority communities to found schools and to seek voluntary aided status, but argued that, on balance, this was not in the long-term interests of the ethnic minorities themselves. The report also called upon Local Education Authorities and schools to be more aware of, and sensitive to, the particular needs of ethnic and religious minorities and to be willing to preserve the option of single sex schools in a given area (Swann, 1985, pp.519–20). *Education For All* thus affirmed that whole phenomenological, world religions based line of development which had steadily gained ground in religious education since the early 1970s.[9]

It was significant, therefore, that some of the sharpest criticisms of the Swann Report came from within the Muslim community. Thus, for example, a joint statement by the Islamic Academy in Cambridge and the Islamic Cultural Centre in London protested, on the one hand, that while the Swann Report treated Muslims in Britain as an ethnic group, in reality they are a multi-ethnic *religious* group. On the other hand, they protested that, precisely as a religious group, Muslims could not accept the 'extremely secular philosophical basis' of the Swann Report which would, in turn, endorse the 'prevalent secularist approach in schools to all branches of knowledge', and aggravate the conflict which Muslim children therefore experienced between the ethos of their schools and 'the religious approach to life and events which they learn at home' (*News of Muslims in Europe*, 36, 1986; see also, for further Muslim responses to the Swann Report, Ashraf, 1986; Council of Mosques, 1986; and National Muslim Education Council of UK, 1987).[10]

Such Muslim responses to the Swann Report were but a part of the development of a much longer and broader Muslim endeavour both to articulate, and to secure facilities to accommodate, their strongly felt needs with regard to education in Britain. Moreover, such needs were less concerned with specifically religious education or collective worship in schools – the existing mechanism for withdrawing children from such activities on grounds of conscience was in theory sufficient to resolve these particular issues – but rather with the need to meet Muslim requirements in respect of diet, dress, religious observance (including the possibility of Islamic acts of worship), the content of the curriculum in areas such as art, music, science and sex education, and the perceived need to observe segregation of the sexes for physical education and, after puberty, for all

[9] The report included a convenient and perceptive overview of many of the issues dealt with in the preceding section of this essay (Swann, 1985, pp.465–539). In discussing official government responses on the *de facto* diversity in Agreed Syllabuses and school worship, it also confirmed the reasonableness of the assessment in 1984, quoted above, that no legislative changes in these matters then seemed likely (pp.482 and 485).

[10] It should be noted that Muslims were not alone in responding negatively to the Swann Report. For a non-Muslim response – albeit prompted by discussion of the educational alternatives available to Muslims in Britain – which expresses consistent and intense hostility to both Swann in particular, and the entire phenomenological, world religions approach to religious education, see Hiskett, 1989.

purposes. All these issues, in turn, constituted elements in a much wider and more comprehensive attempt to ensure the availability of single sex schools, to secure voluntary aided status for Muslim schools, and to present and sustain the case for a specifically Islamic approach to, and concept of, education and the entire curriculum. (See, for example, Ashraf, 1988a and b, 1992; Halstead, 1986; Halstead and Khan-Cheema, 1987; Iqbal, 1975; Mabud, 1988; Sarwar, 1983, 1989b, 1991).

Nor was it only Muslims who, by the mid 1980s, were reasserting the cause of distinctively religiously based education and pressing the case for an expansion of specifically confessional and denominational schools back onto the agenda of religious educational debate. Even as the mainstream of Christian educationists were articulating contemporary versions of the meaning of Christian education in a religiously plural society, which spoke the same language and worked within the same overall context as the post sixties phenomenological, world religions tradition of religious education,[11] so other Christians asserted the claims for a 'Christian education' of a quite different kind. From the late 1970s onwards there was a modest but steady growth in the number of newly founded Christian schools. Such schools were, characteristically, strongly evangelical in their inspiration and theological background. They were founded on the conviction that a biblical and evangelical Christianity demanded a corresponding approach to education, including the presentation of a curriculum informed throughout by specifically evangelical perspectives, the presentation of distinctively evangelical moral principles and responses to moral issues, and the centrality of Christian nurture and preparation for Christian commitment. The founders and supporters of such schools were also convinced that the state system of education was so compromised by secular and non-Christian values that it simply could not supply an adequate or appropriate education for the children of evangelical Christians (Hughes, 1992, ch.5; O'Keefe, 1992).

Indeed, by implication the state system could not – according to this particular view of the relationship between religion and education – supply a genuinely adequate education for any children, since a proper education involved recognition of, and respect for, a quite specific and particular Christian understanding of the world. Moreover, by the mid 1980s, there were increasing attempts – as for example in the foundation and activities of organizations such as Christians in Education – to carry the principles and perspectives expressed in the new Christian Schools

---

[11] For an example from the later 1980s of such 'mainstream' Christian educationists engaging constructively with a wide range of issues in contemporary religious education, see the collection of essays *Christian Education in a Pluralist Society* edited by McClelland (1988), especially those in the first part of the book.

Movement into the state sector as well (Hughes, 1992, pp.90–1). Thus, for example, Christians in Education, founded in 1986, described itself as a charitable trust established to address the increasing secularization of the British educational system by encouraging a biblical perspective on education. Developments in 'children's literature, the occult, sex education, and multi-faith RE' were all cited as aspects of such alleged secularization (Murdoch, in the Preface to King, J., 1990). Similarly, a publication sponsored by Christians in Education set out to 'unmask' the secular, humanist and enlightenment assumptions and values that allegedly lie within, and effectively dominate, the curriculum in state schools, urging instead a particular Christian and biblical view of both education as a whole and the various subjects across the curriculum (Roques, 1989).

Although based upon quite different religious traditions, there was thus a striking and suggestive similarity – at one level – between the concerns of many Muslims and those of a significant number of evangelical Christians. For both groups, the predominantly secular values of the state system of education in modern Britain were not only inadequate but fundamentally objectionable and damaging.[12] After forty years, therefore, the kind of religious controversy over education which the 1944 Education Act had tried to resolve – and which subsequent developments in religious education had also sought to avoid by a steady broadening of the subject – was coming firmly back onto the agenda. By the mid 1980s, however, the controversies were no longer between different Christian denominations but, rather, between an essentially liberal, secular and pluralist educational establishment and a number of religiously conservative groups. The latter resisted the liberal, secular and pluralist ethos and values thus presented by the mainstream of British education and advocated, instead, the virtues of a return to confessionalism.

The various issues involved in this clash of assumptions about the purposes and bases of education, and of the role of religion in education, were made explicit and brought forcefully into public debate by the religious aspects of the 1988 Education Reform Act. When the proposed Act reached the House of Lords in April 1988, its direct engagement with the question of religious education and the place of religion in schools was limited to no more than a few lines. These reasserted that Local Education Authorities, school governing bodies and head teachers were to ensure that the requirements of the 1944 Education Act in respect of religion were, indeed, complied with – including those relating to a daily act of worship.

---

[12] Significantly, both groups also exhibited a particular concern and anxiety over the place and nature of sex education in state schools, for which see, for example, Christians in Education, 1988, and Islamic Academy, 1991.

By the time the Bill re-emerged from the Lords, the clauses relating to religious education and the place of religion in state schools had been significantly extended, strengthened and made more specific as a result of amendments originally prompted by the intervention of a determinedly Christian lobby led by Baroness Cox. In the first section of the first chapter of the Act it was now stated that the various authorities responsible for schools were to exercise their functions 'with respect to religious education, religious worship and the National Curriculum'. More specifically, the 1988 Education Reform Act, as finally passed into law, went considerably further than the 1944 Education Act in defining what was required in respect of collective worship, religious education and the local mechanisms for the regulation and oversight of these aspects of school life.

The 1988 Act not only required that all pupils should take part in a daily act of collective worship but, in addition, specified that 'the collective worship required in the school … shall be wholly or mainly of a broadly Christian character'. Worship of a 'broadly Christian character' was, in turn, defined as worship that reflected 'the broad traditions of Christian belief without being distinctive of any particular denomination'. Moreover, not every single act of collective worship had to be even 'of a broadly Christian character', provided that 'taking any school term as a whole, most such acts' were so. It was also possible for individual schools to obtain exemption from this particular requirement in the light of the multi-religious nature of the school's population. As for religious education, the 1988 Act reaffirmed the use of Agreed Syllabuses, but specified that any Agreed Syllabus which came into effect after the Act 'shall reflect the fact that the religious traditions in Great Britain are in the main Christian while taking account of the teaching and practices of the other principal religions represented in Great Britain'.

The 1988 Act also made the establishment of a Standing Advisory Council on Religious Education (SACRE) a requirement in every Local Education Authority. The membership of the SACREs thus set up was to consist of four panels representing, respectively, 'such Christian and other religious denominations as, in the opinion of the authority, will appropriately reflect the principal religious traditions in the area'; the Church of England (except in Wales, Anglicanism there being disestablished); local teachers' associations; and the local authority itself. Such SACREs were not only empowered to review any Agreed Syllabus currently in use but were also responsible for considering applications from head teachers and governing bodies for exemption from the requirement to provide collective worship of a specifically Christian character. The 1988 Act also restated the long-established 'conscience clauses' whereby – at the request of parents – pupils could be withdrawn from either the daily act of worship or periods of religious education, or, indeed, from both.

How, then, did the 1988 Education Reform Act actually change or define more precisely the requirements regarding religious education and religious worship inherited from the 1944 Education Act? Clearly the requirements for a daily act of collective worship and compulsory religious education according to an Agreed Syllabus (albeit not as one of the core or foundation subjects within the newly created National Curriculum) were, in themselves, continuations of the 1944 model. Similarly, provisions for conscientious withdrawal of pupils (including the admirably humane but strictly illogical paradox of a compulsion that was in the end voluntary and optional) and the basic structure and mechanism of both SACREs and Agreed Syllabuses were retained and reaffirmed. Within these broad continuities, however, there were several new and significant features.

The particular religions which were to be included in the religious education and worship provided in schools were now specified – whereas the 1944 Act had said nothing on this point. Thus, on the one hand, the requirements that the daily collective worship should be 'wholly or mainly of a broadly Christian character', and that the Agreed Syllabuses should 'reflect the fact that the religious traditions in Great Britain are in the main Christian', meant that Christianity was now *formally* and *officially* given a prominence which it had not enjoyed under the previous legislation. On the other hand, there was also explicit recognition of the possibility that other religious traditions should be represented within (at least some of) the acts of collective worship, and a specific requirement that the Agreed Syllabuses take account of 'the teaching and practices of the other principal religions represented in Britain' – thus also making the inclusion of religious traditions other than Christianity a *formal* requirement for the first time. The membership of local SACREs was similarly required to include representation of such 'Christian and other religious denominations' as reflect the 'principal religious traditions' of an area in question: this too constituted a *formal* recognition of the right to participation in SACREs of a wider constituency of religious groups than was strictly required by the 1944 Act. Similarly, the requirement that all Local Education Authorities set up a SACRE was more demanding than the 1944 Act, as was the process of annual reporting also required of them. Last, but not least, it should be noted that the 1988 Act always uses the term 'religious education' and never uses the term 'religious instruction' which had appeared in the 1944 Act.[13]

But what did these changes in wording actually mean? How was the Act – and equally importantly, how were the intended aims of the Act – to

[13]   For the text of the 1988 Act see Liell, 1988. For more detailed analyses and discussions of the implications of the various clauses relating to religious education and religion in schools, see especially Cox and Cairns, 1989, chs 4–9 and Hull, 1989.

be interpreted, both in respect of overall intentions and for the impact of particular clauses and requirements? It is not the aim of this essay to attempt to supply a definitive – or even a specific – answer to these questions and a host of others which follow in their train. Rather, the aim here is to suggest and evoke the sheer quantity of uncertainties and ambiguities which clustered around (or, perhaps better, lurked within) the Act, and to illustrate the radically different assessments and interpretations of its significance which have been offered.

We may begin by considering some of the specific phrases used. What exactly did it mean to speak of the daily act of worship having to be 'wholly or mainly of a broadly Christian character'? Even if 'wholly' was taken to be essentially permissive (allowing that such worship *might* be entirely Christian), what exactly did 'mainly' mean? The next clause admittedly explained that 'most' acts of worship in a given term should be 'wholly or mainly' of a 'broadly' Christian kind, but this by no means resolved all the ambiguities. How many was 'most'? More than 50 per cent clearly; but would 60 per cent be enough? Or must it be at least 70 or 80 per cent? And what, anyway, was worship of a 'broadly Christian character'? Again, this was glossed subsequently as worship that reflected the 'broad traditions of Christian belief ... without being distinctive of any particular denomination' – but still the question remained, what did this mean? Just how broad was Christianity in this instance? Did it mean that as long as it was characteristic of the traditional mainstream of Christian denominations that was acceptable? As long as it was something that the majority of late-twentieth-century Protestants, Anglicans and Roman Catholics could all share in, then that was fine? Or did it mean that the worship must be so unspecific, so broad, in a generalized sense, that even more heterodox elements of the Christian tradition, such as Quakers and Unitarians, would also feel equally 'at home' with it? Did the exclusion of worship distinctive of a particular denomination simply rule out use of, say, a particular denominational form of service? Or did it also rule out the presentation of particular theological emphases and teachings (of, say, a generally 'evangelical' or generally 'catholic' kind) even if these were found in several formal denominations and not exclusive to just one?

Simply to articulate such questions was to begin to perceive the intractability of the issues involved. Moreover, quite apart from such problems of definition *within* the Christian tradition, the reassertion of the essentiality of a collective act of worship, together with the requirement (however construed in detail) that this mostly be specifically Christian, posed yet further problems. In particular, it reactivated and rendered even more acute all those dilemmas over school worship that had led to a crisis over this requirement in the 1970s, and to a steady reduction in the overtly religious nature of school 'assemblies'. It is true that the 1988 Act offered important scope for elasticity and flexibility of interpretation by also speaking of the need for the daily act of collective worship to be appropriate to the ages, aptitudes and 'any circumstances relating to the family backgrounds of the pupils'. But just how broad was the scope and discretion offered here intended to be? And – quite apart from schools granted dispensations from the letter of the Act by local SACREs – was it legitimate to use some acts of worship as self-consciously multi-faith events, while a minority of others were wholly or mainly of a broadly Jewish, Muslim, Sikh or Hindu character, and the majority remained 'wholly or mainly of a broadly Christian' kind?

Future arrangements for Agreed Syllabuses presented a similar set of ambiguities. The requirement that they reflect the fact that the religious traditions of Britain are 'in the main' Christian, while also taking account of the other principal religions present in Britain, *could* be taken to constitute an endorsement of the world religions approach which had gained so much ground in Agreed Syllabuses since the 1970s. The qualifying emphasis on Christianity then becomes no more than a cautionary attempt to ensure that the *historically* predominant religion in British culture and society received adequate treatment, suited to both its historic and contemporary significance.[14] Similarly, the fact that the Act did actually *require* the inclusion of the study of other religious traditions present in Britain *could* be read as a further implicit endorsement of the world religions approach and a recognition that study of these traditions was not to be allowed to remain an optional extra. Or again, the requirement that representation on SACREs should extend to all local religious groups – and not just, by implication or omission, Christian ones – could be construed as a further recognition of the now intrinsically religiously plural nature of modern Britain and the need for this to be reflected in provision for religious education. The fact that the Act spoke only of 'religious education' and never of 'religious instruction' was likewise open to interpretation as an implicit endorsement of the development of a non-confessional approach to the subject. Read in such ways, the 1988 Act could be seen as offering considerable scope for – and little or no threat to – the future development of 'world religions style' Agreed Syllabuses.

On the other hand, however, it was also possible to interpret the 1988 Act as an attempt to stem the advance of the non-confessional,

---

[14]   Thus it has been observed that, by the mid to late 1980s, even among those who personally favoured a non-confessional approach to religious education, there was evidence of significant concern that the reaction against 'Christian indoctrination or subliminal evangelism' in religious education was in danger of producing – in some cases at least – an unsatisfactory and disproportionate ignorance of the Christian tradition and its heritage (Watson, 1991, p.148).

phenomenological, world religions orientated approach to religious education. It was not difficult to interpret the Act as allowing – perhaps even requiring – the more or less radical diminution of the amount of space allowed in Agreed Syllabuses for religions other than Christianity, and the corresponding inclusion of much more material on the Christian tradition. Read thus, and bearing in mind also the reassertion of the requirement that most worship must be of a Christian character (albeit, broadly so), it was quite possible to interpret the 1988 Act as an attempt to reassert the specifically Christian identity of British culture and society and, in particular, to 're-Christianize' a tradition of religious education which had once been pleased to play an important role in the nurturing of religious – and specifically Christian – faith among the nation's children, but had latterly, especially since the 1960s and 70s, forsaken this role in favour of a (on this view) faithless and wishy-washy relativism.

That some of those who supported the 1988 Act did so on such grounds is clear from the debates and amendments that were proposed in the course of the Bill's passage through the House of Lords. Indeed, as a careful reading of the debates reveals, the 'Christianizing' clauses which were eventually included in the Act were in fact deliberately and skilfully rendered less absolute and more qualified, tentative and ambiguous than the original amendments which had been proposed by an overtly Christianizing lobby. Thus, for example, the amendments originally proposed sought to establish the requirement that religious education in all maintained schools would be '*predominantly* Christian', with further and separate provision being made for 'the religious education of children of other faiths, according to their own faiths'. Similarly, an amendment in respect of the requirement for a daily act of worship had originally sought to establish that this would be simply (and specifically) 'collective Christian worship'.

Graham Leonard, who was then the Bishop of London, spoke on behalf of the Church of England in the debates on the Bill, and was a key figure in the eventual compromise solution of the clauses actually passed into law, with their studiously ambiguous use of 'wholly or mainly', 'broadly', 'in the main', and having regard to 'ages', 'aptitudes' and 'family backgrounds'. It is, perhaps, a measure of both the complexity of the political manoeuvring involved and the convoluted nature of the eventual Act itself that Bishop Leonard – himself a noted theological conservative within the Church of England – should have led the opposition to the inclusion of the most overtly and assertively Christianizing amendments that were proposed. It is similarly significant that Leonard was subsequently variously praised and criticized from both sides for his role in the debate. For some he was guilty of (and for others he was to be credited for) causing the insertion of clauses which asserted the special place of

Christianity in the new Act. For others again he was guilty of resisting the inclusion of properly assertive clauses in favour of Christian teaching and worship; and for yet others, he was to be thanked for that act of resistance and the strategic compromises which he secured instead (Alves, 1991, p.168).[15]

It is also clear that for some speakers in the debates in the Lords, the issue at stake was not only one of religion, but also concerned the relationship between religion and notions of national identity. For some speakers, the case for the priority afforded to Christianity in the proposed Act was expressed not merely in terms of the historic predominance of Christianity within British society and culture, but also in terms of Britain still being essentially a 'Christian nation' or a 'Christian country'. Such remarks, Lord Beloff observed, made people like himself, who practised a different religion, appear in some way to be second-class citizens. Significantly, one of Bishop Leonard's clearly stated reasons for opposing the original, strongly Christianizing, amendments was precisely the difficulties these might cause in discussions with leaders of other religious communities (cited in Hooker, 1991, p.1). At the same time, however, the debates also included contributions from the then Chief Rabbi, Lord Jakobovits, to the effect that religious education 'must be a transmission of a commitment even more than of mere knowledge' and against the presentation of multi-faith worship and education which amounted to 'a cocktail of faiths' – itself a more elegant version of the dismissive term 'mish-mash' which many speakers used to describe and deride what they took to be the consequence and result of a world religions approach to religious education (Copley, 1989, p.17; Cox and Cairns, 1989, p.76; Homan and King, 1993, pp.8–10).

The parliamentary debates over the religious aspects, aims and implications of the 1988 Education Reform Act – together with the examination of what, in principle, the clauses relating to religious education and worship in schools might actually mean – thus suggest, above all, the complexity of the issues involved. But what evidence is there concerning the way(s) in which the Act has actually been interpreted in the short period between 1988 and 1994, the year in which this essay was written? Assessments here must, inevitably, remain impressionistic, but it is already possible to discern a number of different reactions and trends in responses to the 1988 Act.

---

[15] Alves provides a useful and revealing analysis of the various stages in the Lords' debates. For an assertion of Leonard's positive achievement from a supporter of the 'world religions' tradition of religious education, see Cole, 1990, p.123. For a critical verdict on the Bishop's role from a supporter of the spirit of the original amendments, see Hiskett, 1990, p.13.

The predominant response of the religious studies professionals – the body of 'RE specialists' who increasingly developed the phenomenological, world religions based approach from the late 1960s and early 1970s onwards – was to construe the Act in as promising and positive a manner as possible, and to emphasize its potentially supportive implications for the type of religious education to which they were committed. Thus, the reference to religious 'education' not 'instruction'; the requirement that religions other than Christianity be studied; the broader rights of representation on SACREs and the latitude and breadth implied by words and phrases such as 'wholly or mainly', 'broadly' and 'in the main' were all stressed and exploited to the full (see, for example, Cole, 1990; Cox and Cairns, 1989; Hull, 1989; Palmer, 1992; and also the ongoing sequence of editorials in successive issues of the *British Journal of Religious Education* from 1988 onwards). The overall tenor of such responses may be characterized as perceiving the Act to have endorsed key aspects of the world religions approach, while also leaving sufficient scope and flexibility – even in its apparently more restrictive and explicitly Christianizing clauses – to allow thoughtful and imaginative teachers to exploit the Act's requirement in a creative and non-confessional manner. On this view, the explicit recognition and requirement of the study of religions other than Christianity is more significant and decisive than the explicit assertion of a relative priority for Christianity.

Not surprisingly, a range of attitudes can be discerned among religious groups. Among Christians, for example, some specifically church based and ecumenical publications concerned with worship in schools after the 1988 Act similarly emphasized the creative possibilities offered by the Act. At the same time they recognized that a collective act of worship in a modern state school will continue to pose acute problems relating to religious pluralism, to widespread non-belief among pupils, and to the question of the meaning of worship under such circumstances (see, for example, British Council of Churches, 1989; Copley, 1989). However, other Christians saw the 1988 Act as a major opportunity to reassert a determinedly Christian influence within and upon schools, especially through involvement in worship in local schools (King, J., 1990), but also through the general extension of parental involvement and influence over schools envisaged by the 1988 Education Reform Act as a whole (Cooling and Oliver, 1989).

The Act also served to focus yet further Muslim educational aims and concerns, both in respect of the tension between secular and religious – and in this instance specifically Islamic – perceptions and concepts of education and the curriculum, and in connection with both provision for Muslim pupils within state schools and the case for Muslim voluntary-aided schools. Muslim writers on education thus urged their fellow Muslims to use the machinery set up by the 1988 Act not only to secure exemptions from religious education and non-Islamic worship under the conscience clauses, but also to press for the provision of facilities for Muslim children to receive Islamic education and hold Islamic assemblies within state schools. At the same time Muslims were urged to participate in school life as much as possible and to become school governors and serve on SACREs (see, for example, Mabud, 1992; Sarwar, 1989a). Muslims also continued to press the case for voluntary-aided schools, pointing to the anomaly of the state accepting various Christian and Jewish schools of this kind but refusing to extend the system to include Muslims – an inconsistency and inequality to which the Commission for Racial Equality also drew attention, despite itself retaining a preference for a solution along the lines suggested by the Swann Report (CRE, 1990).

Meanwhile, signals from government as to what it thought the Act meant and required remained ambiguous and open to widely different interpretations. Thus, in 1989, a substantial circular from the Department of Education and Science set out to clarify the meaning of the clauses in the 1988 Act (DES, 1989). Its overall effect was to emphasize the flexibility, breadth and permissive character and intention of the 1988 Act as eventually passed. Indeed, so much was this its tone that one supporter of the distinctively Christianizing aims of the original amendments proposed in the House of Lords debate on the Bill described the 1989 DES circular as 'a tortuous compilation of checks and balances designed to avoid any change to the existing state of affairs' (Hiskett, 1990, p.13). Not surprisingly, supporters of the world religions approach to religious education viewed the circular in question in a quite different and much more positive light. And in 1991, after some newly adopted Agreed Syllabuses had faced complaints that they were insufficiently Christian in emphasis to meet the terms of the 1988 Act, the then Secretary of State for Education reiterated to Local Authority Chief Education Officers that an Agreed Syllabus could not now confine itself to Christianity or 'exclude from its teaching any of the principal religions represented in Great Britain'. Education officers were also advised that new Agreed Syllabuses should not be evaluated simply in terms of shorthand phrases such as 'mainly Christian' or 'multi-faith' (Palmer, 1992, p.28).

Such evidence might be taken to suggest that the 'optimistic' interpretation of the 1988 Act by the religious education professionals was entirely and unproblematically justified. But that would itself be too sanguine a view of the ongoing position and debate, for between 1992 and 1994 the meaning of the 1988 Act and the interpretation of its wording was again the subject of controversy and disquiet. By then a number of Christian groups had begun to campaign for the formal and official interpretation of the 1988 Act in a manner that required a defined percentage of the syllabus (and of worship) to be specifically Christian – some groups pressing for as much as 80 per cent of the syllabus to be so designated. In 1993 a further draft circular was duly issued by the Department for Education (DFE, 1993). It carefully side-stepped the pressure for a definition of just how much time should be devoted specifically to Christianity. But its attempts to further gloss and interpret the meaning of the 1988 Act aroused renewed concern and protest from religious studies experts and representative bodies. Thus, the new draft circular was criticized as a further attempt – again prompted by pressure from conservative Christian groups – to narrow the range of permissible interpretations of the 1988 Act, to further foster the priority of Christianity within both collective worship and the Agreed Syllabuses, and to sharpen the distinctions between the 'Christian' and 'non-Christian' aspects of religious education in state schools.

Distinctions such as those proposed between obtaining a 'thorough grounding in the country's Christian heritage' while simply obtaining 'knowledge' of other religions were – it was suggested – indicative of a renewed intention to promote Christianity above other religious traditions. Similar objections were raised to the draft circular's reintroduction of the notion that Christianity was to be 'predominant' – a word, we may recall, which the parliamentary debates over the 1988 Act explicitly chose not to adopt – and to the addition of further glosses concerning collective worship, including the suggestion that in collective worship pupils should 'accord some special status to the person of Jesus Christ'. At the same time, the draft circular also reaffirmed that syllabuses were not to be designed 'to convert pupils or to urge a particular religion or religious belief on pupils'. It is not difficult to perceive that the according of 'some special status to Jesus Christ' in an act of collective worship, and the simultaneous requirement to avoid urging any particular religious beliefs in the RE syllabus, must inevitably stand in some considerable tension with each other. Some professional groups even went so far as to assert that circulars were now increasingly being used to 'promulgate ministers' personal predilections'. The essentially ambiguous state of affairs was compounded by the fact that the draft circulars for England and Wales were themselves different, that for Wales being largely free of the terms and phrases which were causing anxiety and controversy in England – a difference reflected in the more positive response to the draft from Welsh religious education specialists.[16]

[16] For the debate over the Engish draft circular – and the sources of all quotations referred to above – see *The Times Educational Supplement*, 15 October 1993, 26 November 1993, and 10 December 1993, and the editorial in the Spring 1994 issue of the *British Journal of Religious Education*. For the Welsh situation see *R.E. News* (Welsh National Centre for Religious Education), 37, 1993.

By early 1994, the situation had become even more confused with the publication of model syllabuses for religious education by the School Curriculum and Assessment Authority (SCAA) and the reported verdict of an unpublished paper on religious education by the Office for Standards in Education (OFSTED). The model syllabuses excited yet more controversy by their recommendation that at least 50 per cent of the time spent on religious education should be given to Christianity – although they also urged that, by the time they left school, all pupils should have studied Judaism, Islam, Hinduism, Buddhism and Sikhism as well. Predictably, both conservative Christian groups and representatives of other religious traditions found these recommendations unsatisfactory – but for broadly opposite reasons. The OFSTED paper, meanwhile, reportedly questioned the government's insistence on a heavy emphasis upon Christianity in religious education, suggesting that it was probably unworkable, at times self-contradictory, and potentially damaging to children's spiritual and cultural development because not enough time was spent on world religions. It was also reported that SCAA had been instructed by government to recommend the 50 per cent allocation of time to Christianity, despite the fact that the government's own legal advisers apparently cautioned against such intervention and emphasized the ambiguity of the 1988 Act and the importance of a general sense of 'balance', rather than fixed proportions of time, in Agreed Syllabuses.[17]

4 Conclusion: there and back again?

In so far as it dealt with religion, the 1988 Education Reform Act was widely presented as an attempt to clarify the notably unspecific clauses concerning religious education and worship in the 1944 Education Act. Whatever other conclusions might be reached about the 1988 Act, however, the one thing that it did not achieve – at least not within the first five years of its existence – was clarity. As we have seen, interpretations of its meaning varied widely. Religious education specialists and professionals were apt to emphasize its continuities with preceding developments. Some Christians saw it as a new opportunity to press the claims for Christianity within the state education system. Many Muslims saw it as at once refocusing existing issues yet also offering new opportunities to voice a distinctively Islamic set of concerns. And successive government circulars

---

[17] For reports of these developments see, again, *The Times Educational Supplement*, 14, 21 and 28 January 1994.

and draft circulars, setting out to clarify the clarifications of the Act itself, managed only to arouse further controversy and create additional ambiguity.

Is the story of religious education from 1944 to 1988 (and beyond) essentially, then, a story of 'there and back again'? It would be convenient if the relationship between the religious clauses of the two Education Acts could be summarized so succinctly. In reality the relationship is more complex. Thus it is the case that the study of a variety of world religions is now formally required in schools, thus consolidating developments in the religious education curriculum from the late 1960s onwards. Similarly, the official disavowal of using religious education as a means of presenting the claims of any particular religion also represents an official consolidation of the priority of 'education' over 'nurture'. But in other ways 'there and back again' is not so wide of the mark. Despite the optimism of some commentators on the 1988 Act, the potential tensions (and contradictions) between the requirement for a daily act of collective worship and the non-confessional teaching of religious education are very similar to those that led to the widespread sense of crisis over 'school worship' in the 1960s and 1970s, and to books such as Hull's *School Worship: an obituary*, and increasingly secularized 'assemblies' celebrating common values. Also, the desire among some politicians and lobbyists to see religious education after the 1988 Act play an integral part in articulating, sustaining and transmitting a particular version of British 'identity' – ill-defined and imprecise in detail, but certainly 'Christian' in form – is also reminiscent of an earlier post-war, predominantly pre-pluralist culture.

In one other way, moreover, the tag 'there and back again' may, indeed, be accurate enough. The 1944 Education Act, as we noted at the beginning of this essay, sought to bring an end to religious controversy and denominational rivalry in English and Welsh education. It was largely successful. And one of the results of that success (though no doubt unlooked for by the framers of the 1944 Act) was the steady – even if never quite complete – liberation of religious education from confessional roles and inter-denominational controversies, and its consequent development as an academic subject in its own right. The 1988 Act, however, has helped to put inter-religious relationships, conflicts and controversies back onto the agenda. In place of the helpfully imprecise terms of the 1944 Act, the 1988 Act sought to define – albeit broadly – what should and should not be taught in school religious education. It used breadth of expression to leave scope and to avoid defining too exclusively; but in opting to define more closely at all it opened a Pandora's Box of contested meanings, potentially offended sensibilities, and endlessly debatable interpretations.

In addition, by empowering and encouraging SACREs to take a more active role in overseeing local provision of religious education, and by establishing a complaints procedure for parents who are dissatisfied with the worship or religious education provided by their child's school, the 1988 Act made it more possible for an essentially litigious and confrontational attitude to emerge and flourish in an area which had previously sought to progress through informal co-operation (Cole, 1990, p.122; Copley, 1989, p.26). The conditions therefore exist for the re-emergence within religious education of religious controversy, inter-religious disputes, and clashes between the religiously zealous and the secularly sensitive. In the longer term it may not turn out that way: but if it does, then the decades from 1944 to 1988 may indeed begin to look like a journey 'there', to religious education at least relatively free of controversy; while the years following the 1988 Act may increasingly go 'back again' to an earlier, but not happier, era in the relationship between religion and education in England and Wales.

Bibliography

ACLAND, R. (1963) *We Teach them Wrong*, Gollancz, London.

(1966) *Curriculum or Life*, Gollancz, London.

ALVES, C. (1991) 'Just a matter of words? The Religious Education Debate in the House of Lords', *British Journal of Religious Education*, 13, pp.168–74.

ASHRAF, S. (1986) 'Foreword' in Halstead.

(1988a) 'The Islamic approach to education and the National Curriculum', *Muslim Education Quarterly*, 5, pp.1–7.

(1988b) 'The conceptual framework of education: the Islamic perspective', *Muslim Education Quarterly*, 5, pp.8–18.

(1992) 'The religious approach to religious education: the methodology of awakening and disciplining the religious sensibility' in Watson (ed.).

BATES (1992) 'Secularity, agape and religious education – a critical appreciation of the work of J.W.D. Smith', *British Journal of Religious Education*, 14, pp.132–44.

BOARD OF EDUCATION (1943) *Educational Reconstruction*, HMSO, London.

BRITISH COUNCIL OF CHURCHES (Religious Education in a Multi Faith Society Consultation Group) (1989) *Worship in Education*, British Council of Churches, London.

BRITISH HUMANIST ASSOCIATION (1975) *Objective, Fair and Balanced: a new law for religion in education*, BHA, London.

CHRISTIANS IN EDUCATION (1988) *Towards a New Sexual Revolution: guidance for governors and parents on sex education in school*, Christians in Education and the Order of Christian Unity, Cambridge.

CITY OF BIRMINGHAM (1975) *Agreed Syllabus of Religious Instruction*, City of Birmingham District Council Education Committee, Birmingham.

COLE, O. (1990) 'The new Education Reform Act and worship in county schools in England and Wales' in King, U. (ed.).

COMMISSION FOR RACIAL EQUALITY (1990) *Schools of Faith: religious schools in a multicultural society*, CRE, London.

COOLING, T. and OLIVER, G. (1989) *Church and School: the contemporary challenge*, Grove Books, Nottingham.

COPLEY, T. (1989) *Worship, Worries and Winners: worship in the secondary school after the 1988 Act*, National Society/Church House Publishing, London.

COUNCIL OF MOSQUES (1986) *Education and the Muslims in the UK: the Muslims and Swann*, The Council of Mosques/U.K. and Eire, London.

COX, E. (1966) *Changing Aims in Religious Education*, Routledge and Kegan Paul, London.

(1977) *What it Means to be an Agnostic*, EARO, Ely.

(1983) *Problems and Possibilities for Religious Education*, Hodder and Stoughton, London.

COX, E. and CAIRNS, J. (1989) *Reforming Religious Education: the religious clauses of the 1988 Education Reform Act*, Kogan Page, London.

CUNNINGHAM, A. (1990) 'Religious studies in the universities – England' in King, U. (ed.).

DARBY, J. et al. (1977) *Education and Community in Northern Ireland: schools apart?*, New University of Ulster, Coleraine.

DAY, D. (1985) 'Religious education forty years on: a permanent identity crisis?', *British Journal of Religious Education*, 7, pp.53–63.

DEPARTMENT OF EDUCATION AND SCIENCE (1989) *Circular 3/89: the Education Reform Act 1988: religious education and collective worship*, DES, London.

DEPARTMENT FOR EDUCATION (1993) *Draft Circular X/94 Religious Education and Collective Worship*, DFE, London.

DURHAM REPORT (1970) *The Fourth R: the Report of the Commission on Religious Education in Schools*, SPCK/The National Society, London.

EARL, W. (1984) 'The 1944 Education Act – forty years on', *British Journal of Religious Education*, 6, pp.88–92.

FITZPATRICK, T. (1988) 'The churches and educational provision in Scotland' in McClelland (ed.).

GATES, B. (1990) 'Religious studies in polytechnics and colleges of higher education' in King, U. (ed.).

GOLDMAN, R.J. (1964) *Religious Thinking from Childhood to Adolescence*, Routledge and Kegan Paul, London.

(1965) *Readiness for Religion*, Routledge and Kegan Paul, London.

GREER, J. (1985) 'Edwin Cox and religious education', *British Journal of Religious Education*, 8, pp.13–19.

(1988) 'The churches and educational provision in Northern Ireland' in McClelland (ed.).

HALSTEAD, M. (1986) *The Case for Muslim Voluntary-Aided Schools: some philosophical reflections*, The Islamic Academy, Cambridge.

HALSTEAD, M. and KHAN-CHEEMA, A. (1987) 'Muslims and worship in maintained schools', *Westminster Studies in Education*, 10, pp.21–35.

HASTINGS, A. (1991) *A History of English Christianity 1920–1990*, SCM, London.

HINNELLS, J. (ed.) (1970) *Comparative Religion in Education: a collection of studies*, Oriel Press, Newcastle-upon-Tyne.

HISKETT, M. (1989) *Schooling for British Muslims: integrated, opted-out or denominational?*, Social Affairs Unit, London.

(1990) 'Religious education in the wake of the Cox Amendment', *The Salisbury Review*, 8, pp.13–16.

HOOKER, R. (1991) 'Introduction' in Hooker, R. and Sargant, J. (eds) *Belonging to Britain: Christian perspectives on a plural society*, CCBI, London.

HOMAN, R. and KING, L. (1993) 'Mishmash and its effects upon learning in the primary school', *British Journal of Religious Education*, 15, pp.8–13.

HORNSBY-SMITH, M. (1987) *Roman Catholics in England: studies in social structure since the Second World War*, Cambridge University Press, Cambridge.

HUGHES, F. (1992) *What Do You Mean – Christian Education?*, The Paternoster Press, Carlisle.

HULL, J. (1975) *School Worship: an obituary*, SCM, London.

(ed.) (1982) *New Directions in Religious Education*, The Falmer Press, Lewes.

(1984) *Studies in Religion and Education*, The Falmer Press, Lewes.

(1989) *The Act Unpacked: the meaning of the 1988 Education Reform Act for religious education*, University of Birmingham and the Christian Education Movement, Birmingham.

IQBAL, M. (1975) *Islamic Education and Single Sex Schools*, Union of Muslim Organisations of U.K. and Eire, London.

ISLAMIC ACADEMY (1991) *Sex Education in the School Curriculum: the religious perspective – an agreed statement*, The Islamic Academy, Cambridge.

ISLAMIC ACADEMY AND ISLAMIC CULTURAL CENTRE (1986) 'Swann Committee Report: an evaluation from the Muslim point of view. An agreed statement', *News of Muslims in Europe*, 36, pp.6–10.

JACKSON, R. (1990) 'Religious studies and developments in religious education in England and Wales' in King, U. (ed.).

KING, J. (1990) *Leading Worship in Schools: an open door for Christians?*, Monarch/Christians in Education, Eastbourne.

KING, U. (ed.) (1990) *Turning Points in Religious Studies: essays in honour of Geoffrey Parrinder*, T&T Clark, Edinburgh.

LIELL, P. (ed.) (1988) *The Law of Education (Ninth Edition): special bulletin, Education Reform Act 1988*, Butterworths, London.

LOUKES, H. (1961) *Teenage Religion*, SCM, London.

(1965) *New Ground in Christian Education*, SCM, London.

MABUD, S. (1988) 'Curriculum designing for natural sciences from an Islamic point of view', *Muslim Education Quarterly*, 5, pp.19–33.

(1992) 'A Muslim response to the Education Reform Act 1988', *British Journal of Religious Education*, 14, pp.88–9.

MATHEWS, H. (1966) *Revolution in Religious Education: a commentary*, The Religious Education Press, Oxford.

McCLELLAND, V. (ed.) (1988) *Christian Education in a Pluralist Society*, Routledge, London.

MICHELL, C. (1984) 'Some themes in Christian education c.1935–60', *British Journal of Religious Education*, 6, pp.82–7.

MILLAR, M. (1971) *Moral and Religious Education in Scottish Schools*, HMSO, Edinburgh.

MURRAY, D. (1983) 'Schools and conflict' in Darby, J. (ed.) *Northern Ireland: the background to the conflict*, Appletree Press, Belfast.

NATIONAL MUSLIM EDUCATION COUNCIL OF UK (1987) *Swann Committee's Report: a Muslim response*, London.

O'KEEFE, B. (1992) 'A look at the Christian Schools Movement' in Watson (ed.).

ORDER OF CHRISTIAN UNITY (1976) *Ways Whereby Christian Education in State Schools Should be Saved*, Order of Christian Unity, London.

PALMER, G. (1992) 'Religious education and the Education Reform Act', *World Faiths Encounter*, 1, pp.25–31.

ROQUES, M. (1989) *Curriculum Unmasked: towards a Christian understanding of education*, Monarch/Christians in Education, Eastbourne.

SARWAR, G. (1983) *Muslims and Education in the UK*, The Muslim Educational Trust, London.

(1989a) *Education Reform Act 1988: compulsory Christian collective worship and Christian Religious Education (RE) in schools: what can Muslims do?*, The Muslim Educational Trust, London.

(1989b) *Sex Education: the Muslim perspective*, The Muslim Educational Trust, London.

(1991) *Proposals for Progress: British Muslims and schools*, The Muslim Educational Trust, London.

SCHOOLS COUNCIL WORKING PAPER 36 (1971) *Religious Education in Secondary Schools*, Evans/Methuen Educational, London.

SMART, N. (1968) *Secular Education and the Logic of Religion*, Faber, London.

SMITH, J.W.D. (1969) *Religious Education in a Secular Setting*, SCM, London.

SWANN, Lord (1985) *Education For All: the Report of an Inquiry into the Education of Children from Ethnic Minority Groups*, HMSO, London.

TAYLOR, J.V. (1976)'Initiation into agnosticism', *Learning for Living*, 15, pp.129–30.

THOMAS, T. (1990) 'Religious studies in the universities – The Open University' in King, U. (ed.).

WALLS, A. (1990) 'Religious studies in the universities – Scotland' in King, U. (ed.).

WATSON, B. (1991) 'Integrity and affirmation: an inclusivist approach to national identity' in Hooker, R. and Sargant, J. (eds) *Belonging to Britain: Christian perspectives on a plural society*, CCBI, London.

(ed.) (1992) *Priorities in Religious Education: a new model for the 1990s and beyond*, The Falmer Press, London.

WEST RIDING OF YORKSHIRE (1966) *Suggestions for Religious Education: West Riding Agreed Syllabus*, County Council of the West Riding of Yorkshire Education Department.

WILLIAMS, C. (1990) 'Religious studies in the universities – Wales' in King, U. (ed.).

WOOD, A. (ed.) (1989) *Religions and Education: Shap Working Party 1969–89*, BFSS National RE Centre, Isleworth.

6

WOMEN AND RELIGION IN POST-WAR BRITAIN

by Kim Knott

New Testament Assembly, Tooting Bec, 1993. Photo: Mike Levers.

Just as our history books deal largely in tales of the struggles of powerful men, their rise and fall, so books describing the development of religions do the same. Such works are concerned generally with religious institutions and with the men who organize them, and those whose religious ideas are their foundation. There are, of course, some well-known religious women whose contributions have not gone unnoticed, but they are small in number. Julian of Norwich is such an example in Christian religious history. Similarly, there are issues relating to women, such as the persecution of witches, which have been given some attention by historians of religion. However, even the recent impact of the women's movement and feminism on academic institutions, courses, research, writing and publishing cannot make up for the centuries of scholarship by and about men's religious activity which fill our libraries and pervade our general knowledge.

Even our awareness in recent decades of this unequal treatment and our debates about its roots in patriarchy, androcentrism and sexism have been slow to change the way we both see our history and write it.[1] However, one change which can be identified in a number of recent books on history and religion is the incorporation of a section or chapter specifically focusing on women. (The essay you are reading now is an example of this.) Such attention to women's roles and experiences is clearly of great value, and represents an important and long overdue acknowledgement of their contribution. Such an occasion may also provide the opportunity to show that women often have different ways of doing things from men.

There are potential problems, however, with this approach to the task of writing women into history. Might it not be yet another means of marginalizing women, of separating them out from the real record of the development of religious institutions? Knowing how best to do justice to the need to address the question of women's contemporary and historical participation in religions is difficult, but at least it is now on the agenda of writers and publishers.

As we are so often reminded in relation to debates about women's roles and opportunities, women make up half the population. In religious terms, they generally represent over half the active membership. It can come as no surprise, then, that despite the silence of religious history on

---

[1] There are many examples of recent works which make a significant contribution to the discussion of women's roles and experiences in recent history, but these are still in the minority. In addition, those who write about institutions, political or religious, have still to allow recent methodological developments, which enable women's voices to be heard more fully, to affect their own work.

their contribution, they have their own point of view. In terms of institutional hierarchies, this is from the bottom up, as women are in a minority – if they are allowed at all – in positions of authority. With the exception of the Sikh religion, Reform, Liberal and Progressive Judaism, the Free Churches and some other Christian churches, and some new religious movements, women are excluded from certain key leadership positions. Despite this limitation, they have had an important and much underrated impact on religious developments.

One example is the way in which the arrival of women from the Indian subcontinent in the 1960s brought about a change to the practice of Hinduism, Sikhism and Islam in Britain, determining the introduction of a range of domestic religious activities (which will be discussed later in this essay) and hastening the establishment of mandirs, gurdwaras and, to a lesser extent, mosques (see Essay 3 in Volume I, and Ballard and Ballard, 1977, pp.35–41; Knott, 1991, p.96; Shaw, 1988, p.49).[2] Women were not to be seen on the management committees of these institutions, nor were they the major religious practitioners appointed to conduct or facilitate worship in them. It was women, however, who felt the desire to replicate the religious and cultural practices of their families and villages, and who stimulated the growth and diversification of these religions and their sectarian subdivisions in Britain by their maintenance of these traditions.

Another important illustration of the role of women in modern religious change concerns the subject of language. Congregants in a number of churches in Britain in recent years have heard biblical readings and prayers rendered in 'inclusive language'. The continued plea by many Christian women to be formally included in the language of liturgy rather than included by default (on the grounds that, for example, 'man' really means 'man, woman and child') led the General Synod in 1985 to establish a Commission on the subject. Its report, *Making Women Visible: Inclusive Language for use with the Alternative Service Book* was published in 1988. This subject will be discussed further later in the essay, but at this point, however, the example raises two issues. One is the more obvious, that here is a change driven by the will of women which will undoubtedly have a lasting impact on Christian liturgies in Britain and on the women and men who participate in them. The second point, however, concerns religious history, the subject the essay opened with. Even supposing, and this begs many questions, that inclusive language becomes the norm in the liturgy of the Church of England – I am limiting the discussion to Anglicanism at this point – how will official religious history remember its incorporation? The

---

[2] The other process which was to have an important consequence for the institutional development of the religions of the Indian subcontinent in Britain was the immigration of East African Asians between 1965 and 1972 (see Volume I, Essays 4 and 5).

Liturgical Commission of the General Synod of the Church of England was comprised of sixteen men and two women for most of the duration of its work (Furlong, 1991, p.80). Official records, then, will suggest that men did much of the work of facilitating language change.

The bureaucratic structures of Britain's religious institutions, whether religious or lay, are comprised largely of men, and the histories of these organizations inevitably convey the perspectives and concern the activities of men. Women's accounts of their work, their views and their feelings have to be sought elsewhere. Fortunately, we are confronting the question of women's religious contribution and experience at a time when feminist critiques have had the effect of drawing attention to the absence of literature on this subject and of stimulating women to fill some of the gaps in our knowledge. There is a growing literature on women's spirituality.[3] While the silent spaces of history are hard to fill, women's present voices can be recorded if we know where to seek them. This means going to the places where women alone or together act in a religious way and think about spiritual matters. Often this is in women's homes, though sometimes it is in public religious spaces.

In order to consider women's location in the religions of Britain and their spiritual journeys, the first section of this essay will look briefly at the roles women perform, their experiences as religious women and their religious expressions. Section 2 will look at a number of issues concerning women, religion and spirituality which have come to the fore in the post-war period. It is there that the impact of feminism on religion will be discussed.

1 Women in the religions of modern Britain

Women's religious roles

When we think of women's roles in the religions it is probably the issue of the ordination of women which comes first to mind because of late twentieth-century debates on the subject (this issue will be examined in section 2). However, women are active at all levels of the religious life. Indeed, as one woman I interviewed said, women are the real builders and sustainers of

---

[3] I introduce the term 'spirituality' here because, although there is still some confusion about what it means, the breadth of its meaning can encompass areas of belief, practice and feeling which fall outside the conventional institutional boundaries which we generally associate with the term 'religion'. For a discussion of the term, see King, 1989, pp.5–7.

religious communities (Knott, 1993).[4] They form the backbone. From their nurturing and prayerful work in the home to their supporting and leadership roles in religious institutions, they sustain the nation's spirituality.

While women contend for a share of public power in some of Britain's religious institutions, their role in what we commonly think of as the private sphere of domestic religiosity remains unchallenged. In the religious communities whose origins lie in the Indian subcontinent, however, the latter is an arena not confined solely to the activities of individual nuclear families. It operates as an alternative public sphere in which power is exercised by women and in which women organize and control the religion and culture of their families and 'communities' (kinship groups, castes, sects or friendship networks) (see *khatmi-Qur'an* below). They also ensure the transmission of this culture from generation to generation. Let us look first, then, at the home and at women's many religious roles within it.

Not all women are able to bear children or wish to bear them. For those who do, pregnancy and childbirth may be experienced as a spiritual process, and the creation of a new human being as a spiritual role. In some religions, such as Hinduism (McDonald, 1987) this may be marked by particular ritual practices. For many women, however, their experiences are highly personal and not mediated by the traditions of a particular religious institution.

The relationship of profound love and service which then grows between the mother and baby may also be interpreted in spiritual terms. Still in the hospital having given birth to Teresa, Leonie Caldecott reflected on the nature of her forthcoming role thus:

> In a few hours the sky will lighten and they will bring her to me, flesh of my flesh, she who is to be my teacher, my guru in a new discipline, a new array of pleasure and pain, struggle and joy. Right now I am a little afraid, am I up to this, these years of carefulness, this new burden?... Death. Birth. The way out is the way in. Gracefully now. Little one I love you. You have taught me the meaning of redemption.
>
> The way that one and one makes three.
>
> (Caldecott, 1987, pp.159–60)

In addition to their capacity as bearers of children, women are frequently their nurturers (Bowker, 1983, pp.188–9, 213). In relation to the continuity

---

[4] In the summer of 1992 I recorded a series of interviews with women from various religions for a cassette to be used as part of the Open University course A231, 'The Growth of Religious Diversity' (Knott, 1993). See p.229 for further information.

of religious traditions, there is hardly a more important role. Women, as mothers, sisters, aunts and grandmothers, tell the stories and enact the rituals of their religious traditions. This has special meaning in Judaism where a child's identity as a Jew is determined by his or her mother's Jewishness. In an interview, one woman told me about the way in which, from the earliest days, she introduced her daughter to the weekly *shabbat* and sang her songs in Hebrew and Yiddish. Another woman, reflecting on a similar process, writes that

> Looking back through the generations at what my mother's mother would have wanted for her, what my mother would have wanted for me – no generation is in any way remotely able to predict what the next generation needs or wants. But I do feel absolutely passionately that I want my daughter to grow up with my love of Judaism. I will try and live and work very hard to make that so for her, and that's a wonderful possibility. It is a great object in one's life, to try and bring up a Jewish child. Not just a Jewish child ethnically, but to have that joy in Judaism, and for that to be a centre of the stories she hears, the food she eats, the experiences she has.
>
> (Jewish Women in London Group, 1989, p.242)

One of the most valuable ways in which children learn about their religious traditions is through imitation. As they participate in the ritual practices undertaken by their parents, particularly their mothers, they learn things which they in turn will pass on. Sometimes they have their own special roles. Penny Logan gives us an example of this in her account of the ritual activities of young Hindu girls who, as *goyanis*, represent the Goddess during the festival of Navaratri (Logan, 1988a, pp.162–3). At other times, they are encouraged to imitate the actions of their elders. This is true for children and their mothers in countless Hindu homes where favourite gods and goddesses are worshipped at the family shrine. Women here are the religious specialists, dutifully looking after the interests of the family and its ancestors by serving the deities, and transmitting important religious and cultural practices to the next generation (Jackson and Nesbitt, 1990; Logan, in press). Nurturing children in the faith of the family and taking ritual responsibility within the home are duties not confined to Hindu women, but undertaken by women in all of Britain's religions.

A further role undertaken in the home concerns the organization and leading of women's religious gatherings. These can have an important function in the life of a religious community, providing women with an opportunity for spiritual expression sometimes lacking in public places of worship. Such a group operates in Oxford's Pakistani community (Shaw, 1988; see also Essay 3 in Volume I and Werbner, 1991). Muslim women gather in one another's homes for khatmi-Qur'an at which those present read the entire Qur'an for the purposes of gaining *sawab* (religious merit). These meetings are generally convened at times of illness, death, house moving, and new business ventures; in fact at any time when Allah's blessing is required. In addition, they provide opportunities for the development of reciprocal relationships constructed on a system of *lena-dena*, the taking and giving of gifts. The religious and cultural purposes of such an occasion are impossible to disentangle. Indeed, it would be meaningless to try to do so.

In addition to their roles in family or group settings, women contribute to the well-being of their religious communities through their individual spiritual contributions. This can take the form of regular prayer, ritual or fasting. In association with this, it is important to mention that single women often feel they have a special role in the life of their religious community. Some of these women are to be found in Religious Orders (in the Catholic and Anglican Christian tradition and in some branches of Buddhism in Britain) where the ascetic and celibate life is clearly defined and accepted (Ayya Candasiri, 1988; Campbell-Jones, 1979; Sister Genevieve, 1988; Ward, 1987). Most, however, are lay women trying to make sense of their religious identity and to convey its importance to others. They witness to the difficulty of fulfilling this role in the context of world views which place great emphasis on family life (Cooper and Morrison, 1991, p.9; Foster, 1992, pp.58–63).

Women's roles extend to cover a range of tasks within the formal religious institutions. These are many, and they range from minor supporting roles to leadership functions. The opportunities available to them vary within the various religions and the sects or divisions to which they belong. In Islam and Judaism the major religious responsibilities occur within the family group and are located in the domestic sphere – although women are, of course, also involved in the leadership of some all-women's groups held in public venues. In mosques and orthodox synagogues, women's attendance is not essential, though provisions are made for them in separate rooms or galleries. They do not have ritual responsibilities. In both Liberal and Progressive, and Reform Judaism, however, they may undertake, with the appropriate training, the same roles as men (Volume I, Essay 2; Brook, 1989).

In Sikhism, women can occupy the same offices as men, reading from the Guru Granth Sahib, singing religious songs , or *kirtan*, cooking for the shared meal, or *langar* (Kaur-Singh, 1990). Women in the majority of Hindu temples do not take formal responsibility for carrying out rituals as this is a role generally restricted to male officiants from the Brahmin castes. An exception to this can be found in the Hare Krishna Movement where people from both sexes can fulfil this role (Knott, 1987). A different religious role, that of spiritual as opposed to ritual leader, is sometimes taken by women. A well-known female guru, Dr Bageeshwari Devi, makes regular tours of Britain's temples and speaks to packed audiences. In an offshoot of Hinduism, the Brahma Kumari or Raja Yoga Movement, women occupy most of the positions of authority and are seen as mediums for the divine message (Bancroft, 1989; Knott, 1986).

In Christian contexts, women's many institutional roles have been well documented, and range from doing the flowers, running the Mothers' Union, working in church offices and running the Sunday school to being a clergy wife, serving at the altar, and acting as deacon, minister or pastor (Dowell and Hurcombe, 1987; Field-Bibb, 1991; Foster, 1992; Furlong, 1991; Maitland, 1983). We will return to the much-debated issue of women's ordination in a later section, where denominational differences will be mentioned. Despite their many roles, numerous women continue to feel unfulfilled in the tasks they are given and under-represented in the hierarchical structure of most churches. Opportunities for women have changed since the nineteenth century, but many women share the feeling expressed so eloquently by Florence Nightingale in a letter to Dean Stanley in 1852:

> I would have given the Church my hand, my heart. She would not have them. She did not know what to do with them. She told me to go back and do crochet in my mother's drawing-room; or if I were tired of that, to marry and look well at the head of my husband's table. You may go to the Sunday School if you like it, she said. But she gave me no training even for that. She gave me neither work to do for her, nor education for it.
>
> (Feminist Library, quoted in Furlong, 1991, p.146)

It is not only younger, more vocal women who feel frustrated by the limitations placed on their roles in the churches. Older women testify to this too in Patricia Hubbert's study (1991, p.61): 'It wasn't fair really. There were always more women in the congregation than there were ever men. Women more or less kept it going and yet men had the preference in everything.'

The final area I wish to mention in relation to women's religious roles is education. Women are involved in teaching about religion at all levels. They teach the languages of communities and their sacred texts in supplementary schools; they teach the stories, the values and the history of their religions in Sunday schools and within voluntary-aided and private religious schools. A few of them are theologians or Religious Studies scholars teaching in higher education institutions or seminaries. It is important to note, however, that, whereas women are much in evidence in some educative roles, they are less so when it comes to the training of religious leaders or the teaching and researching of doctrine or religious texts. We will return to this subject later.

Women's religious experience[5]

Many women and men in post-war Britain who have a religious dimension to their lives at times have experiences which might be called mystical or spiritual (in which, for example, they sense a divine presence, have feelings of great joy, power, bliss or peace, or become absorbed in meditative or contemplative states). What I wish to focus on, however, is those experiences which are gender specific and thus peculiar to women, and those which may not have this quality but which are given a different tone or meaning because they are articulated by women.

The first group of spiritual experiences I wish to illustrate are those which are either unique to women or associated predominantly with them. Perhaps the one which springs first to mind is that of giving birth. Women's childbearing and mothering roles were mentioned in the last section, but let us hear now from a woman reflecting on the powerful experience which accompanies childbirth:

> In giving birth to my first child I had an experience which was to be the beginning of a different understanding of the ground of our spiritual being. I was pushing the baby out and suddenly the hot afternoon, the lonely little room, the white-clad midwives, the bored houseman, the pain, the consciousness of myself as an extremely tired woman in a most undignified posture, disappeared. I became completely centred in the act and I had a vivid inner vision of being at one with the cosmos; I felt very powerful. I felt I was taking part in the enormous act of creation.
>
> (Quaker Women's Group, 1986, pp.38–9)

This participation in the creation of new life, and the relationship with nature it confirms, is not restricted to this experience alone. Women frequently speak for the conservation of the natural world, and reassert the oneness of the material and spiritual realms, shunning notions of duality. A different expression of the wholeness and goodness of women's special experience is given by Una Kroll, a Christian feminist. She describes how, from a childhood steeped in the traditions of the fatherhood of God and the maleness of his representatives, she 're-discovered the womb of God through prayer'.

> My longing for God was so great that I returned to that dark nourishing experience time and again with the easy familiarity of

---

[5] I am referring here not to mystical experience alone, but to the total experience of women as spiritual and religious people. For further discussion of religious experience, see Volume I, Essay 8, 'The religions of the silent majority'.

a child who recognizes her mother in a crowd of people... The effect of the prayer was that I was learning to love myself as God loved me, as a child, as a woman with a womb, as a woman 'created in the image of God' who was 'like' God and bore God's image in the whole of her being, including the whole of her sexuality.

(Kroll, 1987, p.92)

The affirmation by God of women's bodies and experiences is spoken of by many women, and some extend this to an exploration of the motherhood of God (Hebblethwaite, 1984; Knott, 1993). As Kroll suggests, women use their own experiences to teach themselves more about the nature of God. For some, the natural conclusion to this is the experience of the divine as Goddess. Here is one older woman who, by her own account, worships and studies the Goddess as 'a process, a method of consciousness-raising', a means of discovering about herself:

A few years ago, after a traumatic experience, I woke up one morning, saying 'I know where my loyalty and duty and love are owed – to my Mother, the Earth, who births us, feeds us, protects us, and takes us back into herself when we die, to give new life to other life-forms' ... To me, the idea of the God is a false and forced idea, a lie. The idea of the Goddess ... is nearer to the truth ... She is something at the edges of one's vision, in between the salt sea and the sand, the night and the day, something wild which we need to make space in us to live alongside us, but which we can never imprison by too clear a vision.

(quoted in King, 1989, pp.130–1)

Hinduism, to a greater extent than the other religions, offers an opportunity for women to explore their relationship with the Goddess. An account of one woman's experience which illustrates this can be read in *Worlds of Faith* (Bowker, 1983, pp.72, 75, 105, 114–5).[6] As a medium for Mataji, she helps other people with their problems. Here, she describes her earliest experience of the Goddess:

I saw a very nice dream: I followed the dream, and I reached success. In the dream, first I saw a lion: on the lion I saw the one lady just sitting, very beautiful, and she gave her hand into my hand – when I'm nine year old. I've never forgotten that dream up to now.

[6] More information on this woman's role in relation to the Goddess can be found in Knott (forthcoming). A different example is given by an informant in Knott, 1993.

In the bhakti movement in Hinduism where the emphasis is on loving devotion to God or the Goddess, women's traditional role of service and sacrifice (epitomized by the *gopi* women who loved Krishna) provides a model for the aspiration of all devotees, male and female (Knott, 1986). Women from a number of religions refer to the ease with which they and others of their sex develop a relationship with God through an openness in prayer and service. Others refer to the extra dimension given to ordinary domestic experiences by their knowledge that the tasks they carry out are willed by God (Bowker, 1983, p.143; Yuval-Davis, 1992, p.217).

Women also recount the uniquely female aspects of other common experience. The feelings which Asian women have about their part in the transplantation and growth of their religions in Britain, for example, are rooted in their roles and the expectations placed on them. Older women speak of the isolation they felt in coming to Britain and the way in which this has been alleviated by their participation in women's gatherings where they have sung familiar songs, prayed together and shared food, stories and news (Bhachu, 1985, pp.40–1; Knott, 1993; Mercier, 1988, p.32; Michaelson, 1987, pp.41–2; Werbner, 1991, pp.128–60). Young Muslim women speak of the difficulties they experience in relation to how they dress and behave as a result of their parents' conflation of religious teachings and cultural customs (Afshar, 1989, p.219; Knott and Khokher, 1993; Mirza, 1989, pp.23, 27; Sharif, 1985, pp.15–16).

In relation to all religious traditions, there are those women who, despite any problems they may experience of oppression and sexism, wish to stay and fight. For them, the real spiritual benefits outweigh such difficulties. There are others who feel that the only answer is to leave the religion or to stand outside it to witness against its treatment of women. Daphne Hampson graphically describes the feelings associated with this stance in her essay, 'Women, ordination and the Christian Church'. There she writes of demonstrating for women's ordination at a Lambeth Conference:

> It was shattering ... to watch the procession into choral evensong of four hundred Bishops and their advisors, all men, among them my friends, and to know that I was divided from them, irrevocably, by the fact that I was a woman. I felt entirely left on the sidelines – automatically, by definition. It is out of experiences such as these that one finally gets up and leaves – to preserve one's human dignity.
>
> (Hampson, 1986, p.132)

The painful experiences of the 'doubters and dissenters' in the movement 'Women Against Fundamentalism' are also of this nature (Connolly, 1991; Southall Black Sisters, 1989; Women Against Fundamentalism, 1990). In

Refusing Holy Orders (1992) Gita Sahgal and Nira Yuval-Davis record the sense of loss experienced by women who can no longer believe or participate in their religions. A Hindu woman speaks of throwing away her precious shrine after the break-up of an oppressive marriage (p.193); a defiant Jewish woman speaks eloquently of her feelings after severing her links with the community:

> The tree is gone and will not grow again. I don't want to put in a new one. I would rather learn to live with the view of a more open landscape, bare as it might seem, and with the sense of loss – for security, familiarity, for the religious calendar of fasts and festivals and for music most of all – which I don't suppose will ever quite go. Even relative freedom costs.
>
> (Dena Attar, quoted in Sahgal and Yuval-Davis, 1992, p.22)

Women's religious expression

In interviews, letters and essays the women quoted above have conveyed to us their experience of religion. Although women have been largely absent from the histories of religious institutions, they have not been silent. They are not silent now. The question is rather a matter of where and how they can be heard. This short section will look at just this issue.

Women's expression of their spirituality and their views about religion, its beliefs, practices and institutions takes many forms, from formal theological works to simple folk songs and storytelling. Written and oral traditions are important, but so are the visual arts.

We will begin where we left off in the last section, with women angry at their treatment at the hands of religious institutions. Their self-expression, as well as being encapsulated in measured discussions and careful arguments, has been vented in impassioned statements and startling images. Anglican women in 1978, barred from engaging in a formal demonstration of their views, wore T-shirts demanding 'Ordain Women Now'. Women Against Fundamentalism carried banners and shouted slogans in 1989 to make their case in support of Salman Rushie and against those community leaders who they felt to be instrumental in the oppression of Muslim women. The image of the powerful Hindu goddess Kali was used in a controversial poster to encourage women to march against male violence (Southall Black Sisters, 1989, p.33). She was also used by the artist Sutapa Biswas in her painting 'Housewives with steak-knives' to convey the image of Asian women's anger at their multiple oppression by institutions both traditional and western (Leeds City Art Galleries, 1989, p.63).

The pain, rejection and hurt felt by women in their interaction with religions are also expressed poignantly in autobiographical accounts and personal testimonies. Sharan-Jeet Shan (1985) and the Punjabi woman who tells her story in 'The Sacred Thread' (Barton, 1987) are examples of Asian women struggling to make a life for themselves in an alien country in the context of troubled family lives. Religion is important to both, though neither gains the support of the religious community of which they are a part. Personal spiritual struggles are at the fore in Karen Armstrong's account of her early years in a Catholic order (1981) and Michele Guinness's story of her conversion from Judaism to Christianity and her later attempt to make sense of both traditions (1985). Sybil Phoenix, a black Methodist woman from Guyana, tells of her early trying experiences in Britain and her Christian work in south London in *Willing Hands* (1984).

Other forms of expression in which women's own voices are heard are accounts of interviews with women and oral histories. Muslim women's views are quoted extensively in essays by two researchers, Rashda Sharif (1985) and Kauser Mirza (1989). Asian women's experience of religion, though not referred to directly, can also be found in Amrit Wilson's *Finding a Voice* (1978). Women from a number of religions can be found expressing their thoughts and feelings in *Worlds of Faith* (Bowker, 1983) and Jewish women talk about their feminist, political, sexual and religious identities in *Generations of Memories* (Jewish Women in London Group, 1989). In this last book, women learn about their personal histories as members of scattered, post-holocaust communities through the retelling of their own stories and those of their mothers. The technique of oral history which they used helped them both represent the range of Jewish women's experience and understand the construction of their identities. From this attempt it is possible to see that, while the expression of religious thought and feeling is itself important, the forms of expression chosen may also have value.

Fiction, particularly the novel form, has always been a popular medium for women to explore a range of personal thoughts, feelings and ideas about their own societies or those of others. Post-war British women novelists who write about women and religion include Barbara Pym and Susan Howatch (women in post-war Anglicanism), Antonia White and Michele Roberts (women and Catholicism), Sara Maitland and Jeanette Winterson (women's psychological and sexual experience and religion), Alice Thomas Ellis, Rosamund Lehmann, Patricia Angadi and Frances Gapper (women's psychic and spiritual experience) and Sylvia Townsend Warner and Ellen Galford (women and witchcraft).

Other fictional media in which these and other themes relating to women and religion have been explored are plays and short stories. Michelene Wandor, a Jewish writer, has written both. Asian women writers have also adopted the short story form and reflected on the religio-social concerns of their particular ethnic communities. Examples include Ravinder Randhawa, Sibani Raychaudhuri, Lena Dhingra, Rahila Gupta and Rukhsana Ahmad from the Asian Women Writers' Workshop. Some of these women have also written novels or poetry. Another Asian writer working in a number of media is Debjani Chatterjee, a scholar of religions and literature, principal community relations officer and award-winning poet.

In addition to those women who have been professionally successful as writers, there are all those who have engaged with the written form or other artistic media as a way of exploring their personal identities. Ordinary women have written about their religious experience in writing workshops and personal journals, have used this theme in photography and painting, have sung songs in small groups or to their families and have told stories which reflect religious traditions. As we can see, women's expression of spirituality is a private as well as a public matter, and much can be learnt about the nature and vitality of their experience from a study of such material where it is available.

Before moving on to a discussion of recent issues of importance concerning women and religion, let us look finally at a form of expression which has relevance to such issues. Women in recent decades have established groups for a variety of religious or spiritual reasons. These include support groups and lobbying groups, groups for discussion or religious practice, cultural groups, peace and ecology groups. In many ways, all have acted as a forum for women's views and a place for their religious expression. Some have seen part of their task as consciousness-raising. Many have extended the opportunity for expression to newsletters or magazines, set up to bring the issues around which they focus to a wider public. Some of these initiatives will be mentioned further in section 2.

2 Post-war debates on women and religion

In the post-war period, women's participation in and contribution to Britain's institutions has been much discussed. They are now formally protected by equal opportunities legislation and have a right of appeal regarding sexual harassment. These and other causes have been fought by women motivated by a commitment to social equality and liberation from oppression. Women fought for their own causes in the past, but the battles of the 1970s and 80s were located in the discourse of feminism in which patriarchal institutions and traditions were to be transformed, and androcentric and sexist behaviour was to be challenged.[7] The Women's Movement, initially associated with women's liberation wings in leftist

[7] More detailed discussions of the history of the women's movement in Britain and the central tenets of feminism can be found in Wandor (1990); see also King (1989).

political groups but latterly with a broad and informal social movement with which many women identified, had an impact on the agenda of religious as well as other social groups in this period. The issues I will now discuss are those which have been most prominent in recent debates about women's place in the religious traditions and their roles and experiences.

Women and religious thought and language

I wish to look here at the issue of the representation of women in the religious traditions and their participation in the interpretation of these traditions. This means reflecting briefly on women's location and role in scripture, doctrine, liturgy and theology.

In post-war Britain, women from a number of religions have read and evaluated their religious books and teachings with gender issues in mind. Frequently, they have drawn on stories about exemplary or challenging women or have imaginatively reconstructed episodes in which women were the key actors or witnesses. They have also read with a critical eye, ready to confront received wisdom with alternative understandings. The degree of their freedom to interpret and the nature of their interpretations have been conditioned by the particular religious community to which they belong and its ideas about the authority of scripture and who is fit to comment on it. The creation story in the Book of Genesis, for example, has been the subject of much critical comment by both Jewish and Christian women. The writings of Paul in the New Testament have been discussed by Christian women in Black and White-led churches in Britain, by those who are pentecostalists, evangelicals and liberals. Similarly, Muslim women have debated Qur'anic verses on women's legal position, their roles and modesty (Knott, 1993).[8]

One issue which has been of particular importance has been the nature of Ultimate Reality and the language used to describe it. Christian feminist scholars have sought to deconstruct patriarchal notions concerning 'God and His relationship with man' by examining the Hebrew scriptures, the words of Jesus and the writings of the Church Fathers. Some have proposed alternative theological accounts of the human–divine relationship.[9]

This question has also had implications for the language of liturgy. Many women have felt excluded by the male-oriented language used in most Christian services, in scripture, prayers and hymns and, as a result,

---

[8] Discussion about women in religious scriptures can be found in the works of many women scholars including Judith Plaskow, Letty Russell, Phyllis Trible, Elisabeth Schussler Fiorenza, Mary Hayter, Leila Ahmed and Fatima Mernissi.

[9] The work of feminist theologians such as Mary Daly, Rosemary Radford Ruether, Sallie McFague and Janet Soskice are examples of this.

some have taken up the task of finding suitable terms or composing acceptable prose for use in worship (Morley, 1988). Few Christian women have felt entirely happy with the language of 'Goddess' as opposed to God, partly because of unfamiliarity and partly, despite its historical usage, because most would claim that the word 'God' is gender-neutral rather than intrinsically masculine. However, there has been a desire among some to make more effort to reflect women's understanding, concerns and relationships in prayer, song and choice of readings. Notions of God's motherhood, compassion, wisdom and immanence are often stressed (as opposed to the themes of fatherhood, domination and authority) as are stories of Biblical and contemporary women and the themes of peace, care for the planet, and personal relationships. Gender-inclusive language is used, and the whole of creation is given due consideration where male interest would have been the norm in the past. Many churches have not taken these steps, but the fact that some have is evidence of the raising of consciousness about the importance of language for religious communities.

This issue has been important, but in a different context, for some other women in post-war Britain. They are those who identify themselves with wicca and paganism, focusing particularly on the Great Goddess.[10] In their 'thealogy' they look back to a pre-Christian, pre-patriarchal past, many of them believing in an early European matriarchal society. They do not have the problem of interpreting scripture, but rather of creating for themselves a tradition. It is the Goddess who is at the centre of this, and ritual practice and the language of liturgy are focussed on her, her immanence in nature, her benevolence and power (King, 1989, pp.118–60; Komatsu, 1986).

One religion whose participants have not entered the debate about the gender of God, but which ought not to be overlooked here is Hinduism. Female deities such as Parvati, Durga and Kali, as well as male ones, are important in the spirituality of Hindu women and men in Britain. In Leeds, there is a Bengali temple to Kali as well as a temple run by Gujaratis and Punjabis for Krishna. In practice, although most people identify with one deity above others, they generally venerate a number of different deities according to their needs and the occasion.

I will finish this brief account by referring in particular to British women's involvement in Christian theology which, for most of our period, was rather limited (though women were first admitted to theological colleges at the end of the nineteenth century).

[10] 'Wicca' is the name given to the contemporary witchcraft movement. Some women associated with this and other spiritual feminist groups make use of the term 'thealogy' as distinct from 'theology', which they see as inherently patriarchal, to describe their study of the Great Goddess. This term was coined by Naomi Goldenberg (1979).

In the 1980s and 1990s this has changed with, for example, the establishment of the European Society of Women for Theological Research (in which British women have been active), WIT (Women in Theology), a seminar on 'Feminism and Theology' in the meetings of the Society for the Study of Theology, and feminist theological initiatives in various denominations. In addition, a number of British women scholars have published work on the subject. Those represented in *Women's Voices* (Elwes, 1992) include Janet Soskice, Sarah Coakley, Mary Grey, Daphne Hampson and Ursula King.[11] Most writers have approached the theological task from a position, albeit feminist, firmly within Christianity. However, Daphne Hampson, like Mary Daly in the United States, describes herself as 'post-Christian' and questions whether a person can be truly both feminist and Christian considering the rootedness of sexism in the texts, institutions and practices of the religion (Hampson and Radford Ruether, 1986).

Women and religious leadership

We looked at the various roles of women in Britain's religions in an earlier section. Here I wish to concentrate on recent debates which consider whether women can and should be rabbis and priests. It is not simply the case that in Judaism and Christianity there are differences of opinion on this matter, but that the issue itself is of varying importance in different branches of both.

In Judaism, ultra-Orthodoxy refutes the idea of women's leadership of men, but accepts that women can be educated in the Torah in women's *yeshivot* or seminaries (of which there are now two in Britain). Orthodox Judaism does not allow women to become rabbis either. It operates with the idea that, in Judaism, women are equal but different. Their authority lies in a different sphere to that of men – the home – and in the synagogue they are of secondary importance. The rabbi, cantor and those who make up the minyan are all men, and this seems unlikely to change. However, women in the Reform and Liberal and Progressive traditions have been training for the rabbinate at Leo Baeck College since the mid 1970s. By 1989, ten women had been ordained. Julia Neuberger, a British female rabbi, supported her Anglican sisters with the following statement made in an article in *The Times*:

> Let it be understood that women will no longer be silent. We wish to minister, alongside men, to the needs of Jews and Christians irrespective of sex. In the non-conformist churches it has happened for years. In progressive Judaism we have been

[11]   See also Grey (1989); Hampson (1990); King (1991); Loades (1987 and 1990).

around for 15 years. The earth has not opened up nor the heavens caved in. Our congregations have not diminished nor have those in our care perished. Perhaps we have something of value to offer, which the Church of England would do well to use.

(Julia Neuberger in *The Times*, 8 March 1987)

As Neuberger indicates, some Christian denominations have countenanced women's full participation in the ministry for decades. The Unitarians ordained a woman in Britain as early as 1904. Of the mainline groups, the Baptists introduced women's ordained ministry in 1922 (though women were not fully recognized by the Church until 1975) and, after considerable debate, the Methodists followed in 1974 (Field-Bibb, 1991; Langley, 1989). The United Reformed Church had women ministers since its inception in 1972. Some Black-led churches too have women pastors (Foster, 1992). Women were fully ordained in the Presbyterian Church of Scotland as early as 1969; the Episcopal Church aimed to have women priests by 1995. Women were ordained deacons in the Church of Wales from 1980, and in the Church of Ireland from 1987. It is in these churches, and in the Church of England (though this will change once parliament has ratified the General Synod's decision of 1992), the Roman Catholic Church and the Orthodox Church, that women could not be priests with the authority to preside at the eucharist.

The arguments concerning women's ordination have centred on the issues of scriptural authority, the ministry of Christ and Christ's maleness, the origins of the one Catholic and Apostolic church, and Christian ecumenism (Field-Bibb, 1991; Furlong, 1984; Langley, 1989; Peberdy, 1988). Those against women's ordination have in the past drawn on passages from Paul's letters to the Corinthians and to Timothy to support a view that women's and men's roles should be different, thus inferring that the former should not be ordained priests. They have referred to the maleness of Christ and the apostles, and have drawn from this an understanding that Christ's representatives, and those in the lineage of his apostles, should also be male. The unbroken tradition of the Church is also cited as a reason to resist change, particularly by Catholic and Orthodox critics. In the Church of England the hope that a dialogue with Rome might issue forth in the renewal of firm ties was seen by some as seriously threatened by talk of women's ordination. Some male clergy said they would leave the Church if women were allowed to take the final step to priesthood.

On the opposing side, those for the ordination of women have cited the issues of women's roles in the earliest Christian communities, the irrelevance of gender in the nature of God or Christ, God's plan for a changing world, the need for the Church to be heard in a secular context, equality of opportunity and, in the context of Church of England debates, unity with other denominations in Britain.

In an Anglican context, the debate has been a bitter one since the campaigning of Maude Royden and others in the second decade of the twentieth century. It has been kept on the agenda of Lambeth Conferences by moves elsewhere in the Anglican Communion to ordain women priests (for example Hong Kong, 1944, 1971; USA, 1974; Canada, 1975; New Zealand, 1976). It was after the General Synod in 1978 voted against ordaining women that MOW, the Movement for the Ordination of Women was founded (1979). The campaigning of its members helped to keep the issue on the Church's agenda. In 1985, the General Synod agreed that women should be allowed to become deacons. Before the ratification of this by parliament two years later, another campaigning movement had come into being. Women Against the Ordination of Women was started in 1986 by a group of women who felt that the traditional sacramental nature of the Church was under threat. Bitter arguments continued throughout the 1980s and early nineties which were fuelled by the news in 1989 that the Episcopalian Church in the United States was to consecrate its first woman bishop, Barbara Harris.

A more detailed account of the process of the debates in the post-war period can be found in Monica Furlong's *A Dangerous Delight* (pp.89–128). Published in 1991, it stops short of the climax of the story, however. On 11 November 1992, General Synod voted in favour of women's ordination. The process towards ratification was expected to take about eighteen months with the first women hoping to be ordained priests in 1994.

Segregation and separation

An old debate which has resurfaced in recent years is that of the separation of women and men. Those with a concern to show that women can act and compete on equal terms with men (for example in leadership roles) are not infrequently opposed by those who articulate the value to women of men and women doing things separately. While the former, in the early days of the women's movement, was held to be the more radical stance, there has been a gradual shift towards a call for greater division between the sexes with arch-traditionalists siding with new radical separatists (though rarely sharing the same platform). In relation to Britain's religions, issues where this debate has surfaced include celibacy and the religious life, segregation in worship, *purdah* and modesty in dress, the provision of safe houses for women and separate schools. I wish now to look briefly at the first three of these. (See next section for a discussion of the last of these.)

The period from the 1960s onwards has been referred to as one of sexual revolution. However, despite changes in attitude towards sexuality, the validity of celibacy has continued to be argued, not least of all in the context of more recent discussions about AIDS. Several of Britain's religions have no formal place for a celibate way of life (Islam, Judaism and

Sikhism) but Christianity, Buddhism and Hinduism have established traditions for enabling some of their members to make this choice. In David Lodge's novel *How Far Can You Go?*, in which the sexual revolution of the sixties is depicted, Ruth, a Roman Catholic nun, finds fulfilment in the celibate life. However, Karen Armstrong, in *Through the Narrow Gate* (1981) finds the experience stifling (see also Sarah Maitland's novel, *Virgin Territory*). They represent the many Catholic and Anglican women in Britain in Religious Orders of whom some are contemplative and the majority active nuns involved in teaching and social work (Campbell-Jones, 1979; Langley, 1989; Maitland, 1983). A small but growing number of women are also being ordained in Buddhist orders in Britain (Candasiri, 1988; Knott, 1993). A quasi-Hindu movement, the Brahma Kumaris, is led by celibate, though not ordained women.

Celibacy is not an easy path to follow, but for those who actively choose it the benefits can be great (Ward, 1987). Lavinia Byrne argues for its symbolic significance:

> I believe it offers us an interesting way of interpreting images of seclusion and withdrawal ... Where the veil, the cloister and silence are freely chosen, they can guarantee a degree of apartness which is highly desirable ... Women are entitled to space both in the domestic context and in the public domain. Where some women are free to make vows of chastity, we are reminded that all women should be free to refuse men access to them.
>
> (Byrne, 1990, p.106)

Her argument can be transplanted to the other religious contexts I wish to discuss. For women for whom a separate space for worship is important and for those Muslim women who choose the *hijab* or headscarf, the 'apartness' is of value and the opportunity to withdraw from encounters with men liberating.

Two women I interviewed spoke of the desirability of men and women worshipping separately (Knott, 1993). A Hindu woman saw such a situation as protective of women and liberating for them; a Jewish woman said that it enabled those who wanted to pray to do so without the distraction caused by sexual difference, and that for women to pray together was itself spiritually uplifting (see also the section on 'The spirituality of women' below). An alternative case might be made by many Christian women or women in liberal Judaism for whom the opportunity of worship in family groups is valued.

Muslim women, when in a mosque, also pray separately from men, and it is in relation to them that another important issue related to gender separation has relevance, that of seclusion or purdah. The principle which lies behind this is modesty of appearance, particularly in the marital home in the presence of men other than one's husband or his younger male kin. 'Purdah' means 'curtain', that which separates the world of women from that of men. It relates also to the veiling of women in public and ranges from a *burqa*, or all-encompassing outer garment to the light chiffon scarf, *dupatta*, worn by some younger Muslim women.

Debates about Muslim women covering their heads are similar to those mentioned above. The Qur'anic prescription is modesty in dress and this has been variously interpreted (see Volume I, Essay 3). In some families there might be pressure on girls over the age of puberty to cover their heads in public, but other families might see this as needlessly strict. A Muslim woman described to me how, once she had donned a *hijab* or headscarf, her parents felt threatened by her zeal. Young Muslim women argue the case among themselves, with some wishing to identify with Muslim sisters worldwide by wearing the *hijab* and explaining its purpose in terms of liberation from sexual attention and a stand against western codes of morality. Some see it as representing the patriarchal oppression of women. Others see it as an unnecessary symbol of piety.

Women, ethnicity and religion

The hijab is one issue which brings to the fore an ethnic as well as a religious agenda. A dupatta, slung loosely over the shoulders covering a *salwar kamiz* is part of traditional north Indian dress, and the expectation of some parents that their daughters will wear it is a cultural as much as a religious one. There are other issues too where the relationship between religious and ethnic identity becomes complex.

The ambiguities of this are certainly perceived by younger women who, having been brought up in Britain, an alien cultural milieu, are more attuned to the differences between traditional ethnic customs and religious practices. In the case of Islam, those who have read the Qur'an, in Arabic, Urdu or English, often make a point of distinguishing cultural tradition from religious prescription, particularly in relation to the activities and demands of their parents (Afshar, 1989; Ali, 1992; Knott and Khokher, 1993; Mirza; 1989; Sharif, 1985).

Young Hindu and Sikh women sometimes make a similar point about caste-related practices including caste marriages. Sikhs point to the teachings of Guru Nanak to question the religious relevance of this. Dowry is another issue where religious and ethnic traditions have sometimes been confused. Women in some Hindu sects have called for the outlawing of the demand for dowry at marriage, a practice which they see as having nothing to do with being a good Hindu, but more to do with social climbing and materialism.

The issue of language is important in both an ethnic and a religious context. The distinct nature of an ethnic community can be properly maintained only if its spoken language continues to be taught to children and used by them as they grow up. Generally, as a minority community produces its second and third generations its original language becomes less central to family life and the boundary between the community and those outside it changes. Some young British Asians, for example, have a good grasp of Gujarati or Punjabi, Hindi, Bengali or Urdu; others do not. Many places of worship offer classes in the appropriate vernacular language, some also in a sacred language (for example Qur'anic Arabic). As a result of these efforts and those of the families themselves (as only a minority of schools with minority community pupils offer community languages) many young people feel at ease with both their mother tongue and the language of religious worship. Others do not and they sometimes feel at a disadvantage when they visit their local temple, gurdwara, mosque or church. What is going on? What does it all mean? How is it relevant to them? How could they explain it if asked by an interested and well-meaning teacher? Some groups have introduced an element of English into their work with young people, but the practices of others are so deeply rooted in a sacred language that such a transition is considered by many to be undesirable.

Language is an important element in the education of a child in the culture and religion of its parents. Reinforcement of traditional stories, ritual practices and moral values is also a part of the process of nurture that most families from minority communities undertake in the home. The main debate about religion and education in recent years has not concerned itself with this type of provision, but with the question of separate religious or 'denominational' schools. And, in relation to this, it is the call for separate schools for Muslim girls that has been made most often. Not all Muslim parents support the idea, and many young women are against it seeing it as a potentially oppressive institution shielding girls from the realities of life in Britain. Those who favour them are concerned about those issues mentioned in the last section relating to the separation of young women for the sake of their modesty and moral virtue. As Niggat Mirza, head of an independent Muslim girls' school in Bradford, pointed out in an interview, young women's education in all subjects can benefit from their working in a single sex environment (Knott, 1993; see also Khanum, 1992): 'The greater self-confidence they are able to develop will be of enormous value to them in the future in interpreting Islam to outsiders and in enabling them to contribute alongside men to its development in Britain' (Niggat Mirza, in interview with the author).

Sexuality and the family

We have touched on certain aspects related to sexuality in the previous two sections. To celibacy and the issue of gender separation, we might add issues relating to homosexuality and heterosexuality, sexual abuse, abortion, contraception, divorce, motherhood and domestic violence. All of these have been important in debates about religion and gender in Britain in the post-war period. The Christian churches have debated passionately the question of gay and lesbian relationships. Some Christians conclude that sexual identity is biologically derived and others see it as a type of behaviour which can, with help and determination, be changed. In relation to this and the other issues listed above women have struggled to do justice to both the traditional teachings of their religions and the feeling that they are in some sense the owners of their own bodies.

Women in different religions, and in different branches of the same religion, have a variety of ideas about what is good and right for them in relation to the issues of sexuality and the family. In Judaism, for example, there is great emphasis placed on the wholesome nature of the sexual relationship between wife and husband. Nevertheless, many Jewish feminists have argued for other types of relationship to be recognized and valued. This is true in Britain's other religious communities. In the case of the Jewish community, however, many would say that Judaism in the post-holocaust world requires Jewish women's active participation in pro-creation and religious nurture to ensure its future survival (Knott, 1993).

In Hinduism, though women and men engage in family life, there is a strong tradition of renunciation of the material world in one's later years. Some branches of modern Hinduism stress the idea that we are not our bodies, but are that spiritual spark which is in all of us. Many Hindus aspire to achieve a sense of detachment from bodily concerns and the feelings associated with them while accepting that, until the body dies, they must act in accordance with it. One area in which Hindu women are marked out for their female bodies is menstruation. During this part of their monthly cycle, by tradition, they should refrain from preparing food, cooking and participating in religious worship, thus being isolated from normal relationships and activities (Gupta Gombrich, 1990). Although this practice is rooted in notions of ritual impurity, it is often explained as a means of protecting women at a difficult time. What religions teach about the body and sexual and moral issues is often contradicted by the behaviour of their adherents, however. Many women cook during menstruation or visit the temple; many men contravene their roles as protectors. There are Hindu women as well as those from other minority religious communities who have sought help from Asian women's aid agencies because of their experience of domestic violence.

Women from all communities and religions are the potential victims of sexual harassment and abuse, and physical violence at the hands of men. Control of women's bodies extends beyond these painful subjects, however.

Contraception and abortion are other issues which have been at the centre of post-war religious debates. Traditional Roman Catholic views on these are well-known (and are expressed, along with dissenting views, in the characters of David Lodge's novel *How Far Can You Go?*). While some other groups are less strict in their teaching on contraception, abortion is viewed in most as a contravention of nature and the will of God. The religious traditions may be unequivocal on this, but for some women the issue is less clear-cut. It is one that each individual must argue out for herself, especially if she is faced with the possibility of having an abortion. There is her health and psychological well-being to consider and that of her family if she has one, the physical and social conditions of the baby if he or she were to be born, the views of those around her, and the teachings of her religion on human life, family relationships, the status of the embryo and abortion itself.

In such a short discussion, it has been impossible to do justice to the variety and fervour of the views held by religious people on moral issues. I have just touched on several of those which have related most particularly to women.

Women and the planet

As we saw in section 1, women often feel very close to nature and its creative energy. It is partly for this reason that they feel drawn to work for those concerns which will help save the planet and humankind, particularly peace and ecology.

The 1970s and 1980s saw the revival of the debates about the proliferation of nuclear weapons (first started in the 1950s with the establishment of the Campaign for Nuclear Disarmament, CND). At this time there was a real fear among very many people that the arms race being conducted by the 'superpowers' would end in global destruction. Many peace initiatives were begun to witness against the build-up and its likely consequences. As Fiona Cooper pointed out in 1983,

> There have always been women working for peace, holding bazaars, making tea after meetings, and generally being supportive; but today an enormous and growing number of women are taking the initiative in peace work. Greenham Common Women's Peace Camp, started in September 1981 to oppose the installation of cruise missiles, has inspired camps outside military bases and nuclear installations in Scotland, all over Europe and recently in the USA. There is a proliferation of women's peace organizations: the Women's Peace Alliance, Women Oppose the Nuclear Threat, Mothers for Peace, The Women's International League for Peace and Freedom, Women for Life on Earth, The

Women's Pentagon Action – the list is much longer and growing daily.

(Cooper, 1983, p.132)

The Greenham women and those who supported them were working in a substantial tradition including the writers Vera Brittain and Dora Russell, Women's Caravan of Peace which toured Europe in 1958, and the movement founded in 1915, Women's International League for Peace and Freedom. Although the Greenham women's focus was nuclear arms, their understanding of the issues was rooted in a desire both for an end to violence, suffering and injustice and a future with 'bread, and roses and dancing' (Cooper, 1983, p.134) a hope of survival with joy. Not many of these women were formally religious, but their Movement was clearly a spiritual one, combining a consciousness of global and individual suffering, a hope for the future, the means for bringing this about (using non-violent resistance, direct action, rituals and so on), a feeling of group identity and energy, the possibility of self-transcendence, and the use of powerful symbols. These were located not only in the context of a critique of nuclear weapons, but in a feminist discourse. It was important that women together were acting in this way, that their consciousness as women was raised by their participation, that the rituals and symbols they used were rooted in a woman's perspective on nature and human relationships. A representation of the Goddess headed some of the protest marches; the tree of life, the rainbow and the web symbolized strength, difference, hope, and women joined together (Cooper, 1983; Jones, 1983).[12]

These images of nature help us to see the link between this campaign and the wider issue of the survival of nature. Despite its focus on military hardware, part of the eco-feminist strategy for life on earth continues to work for the preservation of the land, its trees, wildlife and natural ecology (Caldecott and Leyland, 1983). Women have actively participated in Christian initiatives for 'Justice, Peace and the Integrity of Creation'; they have spoken out on the importance of these issues in other religions. Ursula King refers to these as 'voices of prophecy and integration' calling for a new future in which all beings are valued and the interconnectedness of all life is affirmed (King, 1989, p.220).

---

[12] A women's Christian witness was also a part of the peace initiative focussed on Greenham. Angela West described the regular vigil and worship at Blue Gate and its theological significance in an article in 1987, and the Quaker Women's Group described their involvement in *Bringing the Invisible into the Light* (1986). See also Dowell and Hurcombe, 1987, p.xxiii.

The spirituality of women

The discussion about women's work for the planet reveals some of the beliefs and values which are commonly associated with feminist spirituality. In this last section, I wish briefly to consider the debate about spirituality and its relationship to gender. Is the spirituality of men and women different? If it is, is this explained by biological or social and cultural differences? What forms has feminist spirituality taken and what debates have occurred in this context?

In its early days, the women's movement was concerned primarily with political activity, changing women's conditions at work, and with the law of the land. However, even from the beginning there was a sense in which focusing on women's concerns led to the raising of their consciousness of both oppression and the possibility of liberation. A close examination of the history of patriarchy and the operation of sexism led women to consider their alternatives. Could women do things better if given the chance? Were there qualities and strengths inherent in women which could become the basis for an alternative society? Ursula King discusses these resources, describing them as 'the biological, emotional and psychic attributes and abilities' of women (King, 1989, pp.92–4). In general, men's characteristics differ. Michele Roberts, who sees these as differing forms of potential energy rather than as biological attributes, writes 'The feminine way tends towards receiving, opening, waxing and waning, relating, uniting. The masculine way tends towards dividing, ordering, separating, naming' (Roberts, 1983, p.65).

Whether these are inherent differences, different forms of energy or cultural traits developed in a gendered society, there is no doubt that their recognition and influence have been at the heart of discussions on feminist history, philosophy, theology and spirituality. To consider only the latter further, it is essential to recognize that for some women their spirituality is inextricably bound up with their womanliness. We saw this expressed in relation to motherhood in section 1. This confirms that the issue here is women's bodies, their nature, rhythms and roles. Another illustration of this is the language used in Wicca movements and by other spiritual women of the power of women in the three stages of maiden, mother and crone. This is further linked to the phases of the moon and the Celtic calendar's solstices and equinoxes with which particular rituals are associated (King, 1989; Komatsu, 1986).[13]

Focus on the Great Goddess is for some feminists an extension of their desire to define their own identity and spirituality. Amongst this number,

[13]   The main writers associated with these views are American: Naomi Goldenberg, Carol Christ, Starhawk, Zsuzsanna Budapest, Merlin Stone.

there are those for whom she is principally a vehicle for consciousness-raising and self-understanding. Imagining Her enables one to know more about oneself, one's strengths and one's connectedness with nature. For others She is real, powerful, and to be worshipped: She is Ultimate Reality. Spiritual feminists differ on this point. They also differ on the question of existence in pre-history of matriarchal societies. Did women rule under the eye of the Great Goddess? For some this is an essential part of their view of history; for others, thinking it, irrespective of its existence in fact, helps women to rethink the present and the future.

There are other women for whom the Great Mother Goddess is no better an idea than that of the Great Father God. She moves us no farther forward, simply transposing one inadequate and biased view of reality for another. For women to depend on Her is for them to fail to focus on the real conditions of their lives and to resist the need to take responsibility for themselves.

3 Conclusion

For women whose spirituality is gender-related (even, for some, bodily determined) meeting together for worship and discussion is of great importance. Women do this in formal all-women's groups and informal friendship or kinship circles. Women of all religious traditions and none meet in this way. In addition, in new ventures, women from different religions have met in encounter and dialogue to discuss common interests and differences, and to work together against racism and misunderstanding and for peace and justice (*Discernment*, 1992; Interfaith Network, 1992). There is a feeling in such settings that women together can go far.

All too briefly, I have attempted here to examine women's participation in Britain's religions, and those debates which have revolved around this. I have focused mainly on the roles and experiences of women who see themselves as belonging to particular religious traditions and institutions, but have mentioned also those more critical women who stand outside them, often witnessing against them.[14]

And what of the future? This will depend on Britain's religions being able to speak to women's concerns, to enable their satisfactory partici-

[14] There are several small groups I have not mentioned at all, such as the Jains and Parsees, because of shortage of space. Information about them would only add to our knowledge of the character of religion and spirituality in post-war Britain.

pation, and to make room for their spirituality. The purpose of their rituals and beliefs, their meaning, and the language in which they are expressed are all important factors. As women have shown in recent decades, the possibility of meeting without men and standing together outside will always be open to them.

It is likely that women will continue to comprise a greater proportion than men of the nation's religious adherents. The real challenges will be trying to ensure that their contribution does not go unnoticed and unrecorded.

Bibliography

AFSHAR, H. (1989) 'Gender roles and the "moral economy of kin" among Pakistani women in West Yorkshire', *New Community*, vol.15, no.2, pp.211–23.

ALI, Y. (1992) 'Muslim women and the politics of ethnicity and culture in Northern England', in Sahgal and Yuval-Davis (eds).

ARMSTRONG, K. (1981) *Through the Narrow Gate*, Pan, London.

BALLARD, R. and BALLARD, C. (1977) 'The Sikhs: the development of south Asian settlements in Britain', in Watson, J. (ed.) *Between Two Cultures: migrants and minorities in Britain*, Basil Blackwell, Oxford.

BANCROFT, A. (1989) *Weavers of Wisdom: women mystics of the twentieth century*, Arkana, London.

BARTON, R. (1987) *The Scarlet Thread: an Indian woman speaks*, Virago, London.

BENNETT, G. (1987) *Traditions of Belief: women, folklore and the supernatural today*, Penguin, Harmondsworth.

BHACHU, P. (1985) *Twice Migrants: East African Sikh settlers in Britain*, Tavistock, London.

BOWKER, J. (1983) *Worlds of Faith: religious belief and practice in Britain today*, BBC / Ariel Books, London.

BROOK, S. (1989) *The Club: the Jews of modern Britain*, Constable, London.

BYRNE, L. (1990) 'Apart from or a part of: the place of celibacy', in Joseph (ed.)

CALDECOTT, L. (1987) 'Inner anatomy of a birth', in Hurcombe (ed.).

CALDECOTT, L. and LEYLAND, S. (eds) (1983) *Reclaim the Earth: women speak out for life on Earth*, The Women's Press, London.

CAMPBELL-JONES, S. (1979) *In Habit: an anthropological study of working nuns*, Faber and Faber, London.

CANDASIRI, A. (1988) 'Going forth: the order of nuns at Amaravati Buddhist Centre', in Shap Working Party.

CONNOLLY, C. (1991) 'Washing Our Linen: one year of Women Against Fundamentalism', *Feminist Review*, 37, pp.68–77.

COOPER, F. (1983) 'Women in the Peace Movement', in Garcia and Maitland (eds).

COOPER, H. and MORRISON, P. (1991) *A Sense of Belonging: dilemmas of British Jewish identity*, Weidenfeld and Nicolson/Channel 4, London.

Discernment (1992) vol.5, no.3 (a special topic on 'Women in Encounter').

DOWELL, S. and HURCOMBE, L. (1987) *Dispossessed Daughters of Eve: faith and feminism*, 2nd edition, SPCK, London.

DRURY, B. (1991) 'Sikh girls and the maintenance of an ethnic culture', *New Community*, vol.17, no.3, pp.387–400.

ELWES, T. (ed.) (1992) *Women's Voices*, Marshall Pickering, London.

FIELD-BIBB, J. (1991) *Women Towards Priesthood: ministerial politics and feminist praxis*, Cambridge University Press, Cambridge.

FOSTER, E. (1992) 'Women and the inverted pyramid of the Black Churches in Britain', in Sahgal and Yuval-Davis (eds).

FURLONG, M. (ed.) (1984) *Feminine in the Church*, SPCK, London.

(ed.) (1988) *Mirror to the Church: reflections on sexism*, SPCK, London.

(1991) *A Dangerous Delight: women and power in the Church*, SPCK, London.

GARCIA, J. and MAITLAND, S. (1983) *Walking on the Water: women talk about spirituality*, Virago, London.

GOLDENBERG, N. (1979) *Changing of the Gods: feminism and the end of traditional religions*, Beacon Press, Boston.

GREY, M. (1989) *Redeeming the Dream: feminism, redemption and Christian tradition*, SPCK, London.

GUINNESS, M. (1985) *Child of the Covenant*, Hodder and Stoughton, London.

GUPTA GOMBRICH, S. (1990) 'Divine mother or cosmic destroyer: the paradox at the heart of the ritual life of Hindu women', in Joseph (ed.).

HAMPSON, D. (1986) 'Women, ordination and the Christian Church', in Eck, D. and Jain, D. (eds) *Speaking of Faith*, The Women's Press, London.

(1990) *Theology and Feminism*, Basil Blackwell, Oxford.

HAMPSON, D. and RADFORD RUETHER, R. (1986) 'Is there a place for feminists in the Christian Church?', *New Blackfriars*, March, pp.7–24.

HEBBLETHWAITE, M. (1984) *Motherhood and God*, Geoffrey Chapman, London.

HUBBERT, P. (1991) 'The Spirituality of Elderly Women, Landbeach, 1990', MA thesis, University of Leeds.

HURCOMBE, L. (ed.) (1987) *Sex and God: some varieties of women's religious experience*, Routledge and Kegan Paul, London.

INTERFAITH NETWORK (UK) (1992) 'What are women of faith saying? Report of a day conference', Interfaith Network, London.

JACKSON, R. and NESBITT, E. (1990) *Listening to Hindus*, Unwin Hyman, London.

JEWISH WOMEN IN LONDON GROUP (1989) *Generations of Memories: voices of Jewish women*, The Women's Press, London.

JONES, L. (ed.) (1983) *Keeping the Peace*, The Women's Press, London.

JOSEPH, A. (ed.) (1990) *Through the Devil's Gateway: women, religion and taboo*, SPCK/Channel 4, London.

KABBANI, R. (1989) *Letter to Christendom*, Virago, London.

KAUR-SINGH, K. (1990) 'Sikh women', *Sikh Messenger*, Spring/Summer, pp.20–5.

KHANUM, S. (1992) 'Education and the Muslim girl', in Sahgal and Yuval-Davis (eds).

KING, U. (1989) *Women and Spirituality,* London, Macmillan (second edition, 1993).

(ed.) (1991) *Liberating Women: new theological directions,* Conference Reader, European Society of Women for Theological Research, University of Bristol.

KNOTT, K. (1986) *Hinduism in Leeds,* Community Religions Project Monograph, Department of Theology and Religious Studies, University of Leeds.

(1987) 'Men and women, or devotees? Krishna Consciousness and the role of women', in King, U. (ed.) *Women in the World's Religions, Past and Present,* Paragon House, New York.

(1991) 'Bound to change? The religions of South Asians in Britain', in Vertovec, S. (ed.) *Oxford University Papers on India Vol. 2, Part 2: Aspects of the South Asian Diaspora,* Oxford University Press, Delhi, pp.86–111.

(1993) *Women and Religion* (audio-cassette of interviews), The Open University/BBC, Milton Keynes.

(forthcoming) 'The Mochis of Leeds: from leather stockings to surgical boots and beyond', in Ballard, R. (ed.) *Desh Pardesh,* Hurst, London.

KNOTT, K. and KHOKHER, S. (1993) 'The relationship between religion and ethnicity in the experience of young Muslim women in Bradford', *New Community,* vol.19, no.4.

KOMATSU, K. (1986) 'An empirical study of matriarchy groups in contemporary Britain and their relationship to New Religious Movements', MA thesis, University of Leeds.

KROLL, U. (1987) 'A womb-centred life', in Hurcombe (ed.).

LANGLEY, M. (1989) 'Attitudes to women in the British Churches', in Badham, P. (ed.) *Religion, State and Society in Modern Britain,* Edwin Mellen Press, Lampeter.

LEEDS CITY ART GALLERIES (1989) *Images of Women,* Leeds.

LOADES, A. (1987) *Searching for Lost Coins: explorations in Christianity and feminism,* SPCK, London.

(ed.) (1990) *Feminist Theology: a reader,* SPCK/W/JKP, London.

LOGAN, P. (1988a) 'Practising religion: British Hindu children and the Navaratri festival', *British Journal of Religious Education,* 10, pp.160–9.

(1988b) 'The heart of Hinduism: Hindu women and the home', in Shap Working Party.

(in press) 'The heart of Hinduism: domestic Hinduism in Britain', *Community Religions Project Research Papers* (new series), University of Leeds.

MAITLAND, S. (1983) *A Map of the New Country: women and Christianity,* Routledge and Kegan Paul, London.

McDONALD, M. (1987) 'Rituals of motherhood among Gujarati women in East London', in Burghart, R. (ed.) *Hinduism in Great Britain: the perpetuation of religion in an alien cultural milieu,* Tavistock, London.

MERCIER, C. (1988) 'Women in the Hindu community', in Shap Working Party.

MICHAELSON, M. (1987) 'Domestic Hinduism in a Gujarati trading caste', in Burghart, R. (ed.) *Hinduism in Great Britain: the perpetuation of religion in an alien cultural milieu,* Tavistock, London.

MIRZA, K. (1989) 'The silent cry: second generation Bradford Muslim women speak', *Muslims in Europe Research Papers,* 43, Centre for the Study of Islam and Christian–Muslim Relations, Birmingham.

MORLEY, J. (1988) 'Liturgy and danger' in Furlong (ed.).

NEUBERGER, J. (1987) 'Needing the ministry of women', *The Times*, 28 March.

PANDYA, R. (1988) 'The role of an orthodox Hindu woman in a Hindu family in England', in Shap Working Party.

PEBERDY, A. (ed.) (1988) *Women Priests?*, Marshall Pickering, London.

PHOENIX, S. (1984) *Willing Hands*, The Bible Reading Fellowships, London.

QUAKER WOMEN'S GROUP (1986) *Bringing the Invisible into the Light*, Quaker Home Service, London.

ROBERTS, M. (1983) 'The woman who wanted to be a hero', in Garcia and Maitland (eds).

SAHGAL, G. and YUVAL-DAVIS, N. (eds) (1992) *Refusing Holy Orders: women and fundamentalism in Britain*, Virago, London.

SHAN, S. (1985) *In My Own Name*, London, The Women's Press.

SHAP WORKING PARTY (1988) *Women in Religion: world religions in education*, Commission for Racial Equality, London.

SHARIF, R. (1985) 'Interviews with young Muslim women of Pakistani origin', *Muslims in Europe Research Papers*, 27, Centre for the Study of Islam and Christian–Muslim Relations, Birmingham.

SHAW, A. (1988) *A Pakistani Community in England*, Basil Blackwell, Oxford.

SISTER GENEVIEVE (1988) 'A nun in the last years of the twentieth century', in Shap Working Party.

SOUTHALL BLACK SISTERS (1989) *Against The Grain: a celebration of survival and struggle*, Southall Black Sisters, London.

WANDOR, M. (1990) *Once A Feminist: stories of a generation*, Virago, London.

WARD, H. (1987) 'The lion in the marble: choosing celibacy as a nun', in Hurcombe (ed.).

WERBNER, P. (1991) *The Migration Process*, Berg, London.

WEST, A. (1987) 'The Greenham Vigil: a women's theological initiative for peace', *New Blackfriars*, January, pp.125–37.

WILSON, A. (1978) *Finding a Voice: Asian women in Britain*, Virago, London.

WOMEN AGAINST FUNDAMENTALISM (1990) *Newsletter*, 1.

YUVAL-DAVIS, N. (1992) 'Jewish fundamentalism and women's empowerment', in Sahgal and Yuval-Davis (eds).

7

BETWEEN LAW AND LICENCE: CHRISTIANITY, MORALITY AND 'PERMISSIVENESS'

by Gerald Parsons

Sir Bernard Braine MP addresssing a Festival of Light rally, Trafalgar Square, London, 25 September 1976. Photo: Keystone/Hulton-Deutsch.

'Sexual intercourse', according to some famous lines by the poet Philip Larkin, 'began/ In nineteen sixty-three ... Between the end of the Chatterley ban/ And the Beatles first LP' (Larkin, 1988, p.167). Thirty years later – as the essays in this volume and its companion were being written – the sixties were back in vogue. For some they were back as nostalgia, expressed through increasing numbers of journalistic or televisual retrospectives looking back to the 'swinging decade', when post-war austerity finally gave way to sixties affluence, when education and opportunity both seemed set to expand indefinitely, when the stuffy establishment restraints of the fifties gave way to liberation and the liberalization of personal morality, when for a moment British pop music could take the American charts by storm, and England won the World Cup. For others, the sixties were back as a scapegoat, as a convenient explanation and whipping boy for all the discontents, declines and dilemmas of the ensuing decades, as the origin of the 'permissiveness' that led inexorably to moral decline, to the collapse of 'family values', to soaring crime, abortion and divorce rates, and to moral chaos.

Both the uncritical nostalgia and the equally uncritical scapegoating were, of course, caricatures. The reality of the sixties was more complex, more ambiguous, and just more downright muddled than such selective memories and interpretations will allow. What they share, however, is the instinct that the decade was a crucial one: a turning point or watershed; a moment when, one way or another, something fundamental changed. And, equally certainly, personal and sexual morality was one of the major areas in which such change occurred.

The novelist David Lodge saw the sixties in this way in *How Far Can You Go?*, his compelling and revealing portrayal of the changing nature of the lives of a group of English Catholics from the early 1950s to the mid 1970s. As argued in the introduction to this volume, *How Far Can You Go?* is about far more than sexual morality. It is fundamentally about 'how far you can go' in changing, dismantling and reinterpreting a whole religious system before 'something vital is left out'. But sexual morality was, inescapably, at the centre of a broader crisis in Roman Catholicism, and also, therefore, central to Lodge's narrative. And it is the sixties that provide the crucial turning point for Lodge and his characters, the hinge upon which the whole narrative turns. The central chapter is the shortest in the novel. It begins with the sentence, 'At some point in the nineteen-sixties, Hell disappeared'. It ends with most of the key characters gathered in a pub, sipping their drinks, discussing why it took them all so long to rebel against their church's ban on artificial contraception, agreeing that in the end it was fear of hell that had held them back, and realizing 'if they had not realized it before, that Hell, the Hell of their childhood, had disappeared for good' (Lodge, 1980, pp.113 and 126–7).

In this essay we will examine a number of aspects of the interaction between religion – and in particular the Christian churches – and changing attitudes towards issues of personal and sexual morality in Britain in the period from 1945 to the early 1990s. Firstly, we will note briefly the extent of the changes that occurred within British society concerning sexuality and sexual morality. Secondly, we will examine the way in which the churches engaged in debate over these issues. And thirdly, we will seek to identify the underlying issues within the churches' debates and responses to these questions, and to offer a concluding assessment of the range of issues related to questions of sexual morality which remain on the agenda of religious debate in the early 1990s. In addressing these questions, we will return to Lodge's novel as a convenient and effective means of focusing the issues involved, while also ranging more widely over a variety of other evidence.

I How it was and how it became

A widespread interest in the nature and expression of human sexuality was not a sudden invention or innovation of the 1960s: and neither were sexual activity before or outside the bounds of marriage, the existence of homosexuality and its physical expression, nor the *de facto* occurrence of abortion. It is as well to remember these manifestly obvious facts, for the danger of many of the more polemical accounts of the 'sexual revolution' of the 1960s – by both its supporters and its opponents – is that they are apt to imply, by omission, that such matters were somehow 'discoveries' of the 1960s. They were not, and to suppose that they were is singularly to miss the point. Previously they may have been for the most part hidden, morally and socially censured, and subject to official condemnation – and in the cases of abortion and homosexual activity subject also to criminal prosecution – but they were not, therefore, absent.

For example, in a study of the English character conducted in the early 1950s, it was found that of the married people surveyed, half of the sample said that they had had no other sexual partner apart from their spouse, either before or after marriage. Such evidence, along with similar responses to other questions, led the author of the study to conclude that the English were considerably more conventional and chaste in their sexual habits than many other nationalities (Weeks, 1989, p.239). In the present context, however, the point to note is that the survey also indicated that half of the married population had had a sexual partner other than their spouse – either before or after marriage. One should not make too much of any single statistic, but the example serves to illustrate the falsity of any assumption that, before the 1960s, chastity and marital fidelity were everywhere predominant among the British population. Similarly, it has been noted that the period after the Second World War saw a significant reassessment of the role of sex and sexuality within marriage – including recognition of the importance of mutual sexual fulfilment within such a relationship (Haste, 1992, p.145; Weeks, 1989, pp.237–8) – and also that, in the later 1950s, there was an increasing public interest in sex and its discussion and portrayal in, for example, books, plays, films, and the press (Booker, 1992, pp.40–1). And it should not be forgotten that, despite the widespread contemporary moral panic over homosexuality and the profound antagonism – often amounting to persecution – of homosexuals, yet it was in 1957 that the Wolfenden Report recommended the decriminalization of homosexual acts in private (Weeks, 1989, pp.239–43).

At the same time, however, the essentially conservative nature of the period from 1945 to the end of the 1950s should not be underestimated. Thus, the increased recognition of the importance of sex and sexuality was located firmly within the institution of marriage. Pre-marital sex – whatever might actually be happening in many cases – remained controversial and subject to official censure. Indeed, monogamous marriage and family life were fundamental elements in the philosophy of the post-war welfare state. And if some of the thinking of official bodies during these years was innovatory in recognizing the importance of *mutual* sexual fulfilment in marriage, yet the general assumptions concerning women's nature and role in society remained firmly conventional: motherhood and home-making were their 'natural' and officially approved functions. The increased stress on sexuality and its importance was thus designed, quite specifically, to cement the family and the institution of monogamous marriage (Haste, 1992, pp.143–7 and 152–3; Weeks, 1989, pp.235–9). A similar ambivalence – and potential paradox – can be discerned in the attitude of the British Board of Film Censors. Thus, while films made in the late 1950s – such as *Room at the Top* and *Saturday Night and Sunday Morning* – actually managed to avoid undue or excessive censorship, consideration of the stated concerns of the censors, particularly in the matter of 'language', reveals what has been described as the 'prevailing prissiness' of such official bodies, even at the end of the 1950s (Marwick, 1984, especially pp.131–3).

In matters of sexual morality, therefore, the period from the end of the Second World War until the beginning of the 1960s was one of uneasy balance. On the one hand, the continuing influence of much restraining and controlling legislation and values inherited from earlier decades – and in particular from the high-noon of Victorian moralism – was still substantial. It is thus not surprising that the subsequent dismantling of much of this legislation has been described as 'the end of Victorianism', or that the crucial role of evangelicalism in the initial construction and subsequent maintenance of this legacy of 'Victorian' control over personal morality should also have been emphasized (Marwick, 1990, ch.9). Yet, on the other hand, by the end of the 1950s there was also already increased recognition of the importance of sex and sexuality (albeit within the sanctioned area of marriage and the family); the emergence of pressure for change and reform in some of the laws governing the regulation of sexual practices; an increasing public interest in sex and its discussion and portrayal; and a growing sense of the inconsistencies and hypocrisies which lurked within many British attitudes to sex and sexual morality.

Those inconsistencies and hypocrisies were revealed with particular clarity by the Lady Chatterley trial in 1960, in which Penguin Books were acquitted of contravening the Obscene Publications Act by publishing an unexpurgated version of D.H. Lawrence's novel, *Lady Chatterley's Lover*. The trial is famous for revealing the already dated intermingling of assumptions among conservative members of the establishment about the relationships between sex, class and gender – not least at the moment when the prosecution counsel asked members of the jury to consider whether this was the kind of book they would wish their wife or servant to read. The public's response to the acquittal was to purchase some two million copies of the book within a year.[1]

The Chatterley trial suggested a society ripe for change in matters of sexual morality – and by the end of the 1960s a remarkable change had, indeed, taken place. The mid to late 1960s, it has been suggested, constituted a 'permissive moment', a point at which, as a result of the concurrence of a whole range of social, economic, moral, cultural and political factors, it became possible to reform much of the legacy of restrictive and restraining legislation relating to personal and sexual morality inherited from the Victorian era. A central element in the process of reform was a shift, in a number of areas, but particularly in matters of sexual morality, away from overt public and social control of personal and sexual morality, and towards a more liberal approach, which relocated far more of the decision making in such matters to the private sphere. What took place, it is argued, was nothing less than a legislative restructuring of the moral regulation of society, at the heart of which was a series of reforms relating to sexual behaviour. Collectively, these constituted 'the most significant package of legislative changes in morality for over half a century' (Weeks, 1989, pp.249–52).

The catalogue of changes involved was, indeed, substantial. Perhaps the most striking changes were those relating to abortion, homosexuality

---

[1] For an edited transcript of the Chatterley trial together with a discussion of its significance, including the overt sexism and class consciousness which it revealed, see Rolph, 1990.

and divorce. Thus, the Abortion Act (1967) made abortion legal provided that two doctors agreed that the operation was justifiable on medical or psychological grounds; the Sexual Offences Act (1967) decriminalized homosexual acts between consenting adults in private – thereby also removing a powerful and pernicious potential for blackmail; and the Divorce Reform Act (1969) abolished the concept of 'matrimonial offence' as the sole grounds for divorce, replacing it with the concept of 'irretrievable breakdown'. But to these three key reforms must be added a whole variety of other reforms and trends which, collectively, both represented and symbolized a remarkable relaxation and 'opening up' of the range of British attitudes to personal morality in general and sexual morality in particular.

Thus, the acquittal of Penguin Books at the Lady Chatterley trial was followed by an immense expansion in the range of sexually explicit material which could be published (James, 1993, p.56) – a development self-consciously echoed in the text of Lodge's *How Far Can You Go?*, itself simultaneously a portrayal and a manifestation of the greater freedom of expression made possible by the Chatterley verdict (Lodge, 1980, p.76). Similarly, the abolition of theatre censorship in 1968 allowed the performance of a variety of explicit and avant-garde plays, while the steady relaxation (though not abolition) of cinema censorship during the 1960s extended the range of expression available to film-makers and cinema goers. The role of television, meanwhile, was equally significant. Under the liberalizing leadership of Hugh Greene (Director General of the BBC from 1960 to 1969), the BBC dramatically expanded the range of topics with which it engaged, the explicitness of their treatment, and the extent to which, in drama and comedy in particular, conventional and traditional assumptions and conventions could be challenged, criticized or satirized. Significantly, it was to be television – and in particular the BBC under Hugh Greene – that first stimulated a concerted religious backlash against the 'permissive moment' and impact of the 1960s.

Contraception was yet another important area in which official reform combined with both technological innovation and changing *mores* to bring about a fundamental transformation of attitudes. The oral contraceptive pill began to be widely available in the 1960s. This in itself did not lead to a sudden or marked increase in 'permissive' behaviour, but it did prompt an explosion of debate and discussion about contraception in general, as well as extend the range of options available and offer the potential for much greater control in such matters, especially for women. This in turn further stimulated a new openness in discussing the morality and significance of a whole range of sexual activity. Contraceptive advice, moreover, began to become available for unmarried women – initially, from 1964, under the auspices of the Brook Advisory Centres and the Family Planning

Association, and subsequently under the National Health Service (Haste, 1992, pp.205–6; Marwick, 1990, pp.149–50; Weeks, 1989, p.260).

However, such developments did not go unchallenged. The principal organized resistance to the 'permissive' reforms and increasingly liberal attitudes towards sexual morality which resulted from the 1960s came from conservatively inclined Christians. Thus, in 1964 Mary Whitehouse founded the Clean Up TV Campaign, which rapidly turned into the National Viewers and Listeners Association (NVLA). Strongly and conservatively Christian in ethos, the organization set out to resist what it perceived to be the morally undermining and secularizing influence of an increasingly liberal, permissive and secular humanist broadcasting establishment – especially in the BBC during Hugh Greene's years as Director General (Tracey and Morrison, 1979, chs 4–8; Weeks, 1989, pp.279–80). Later in the 1960s came the formation of the Society for the Protection of the Unborn Child (SPUC), an organization founded to oppose and seek the repeal of the 1967 Abortion Act. As the 1960s gave way to the 1970s, meanwhile, the Roman Catholic peer Lord Longford conducted a campaigning investigation into pornography, while a group of staunchly evangelical Christians organized the Nationwide Festival of Light to combat 'moral pollution' and 'moral decline' in British life (Capon, 1972; Perman, 1977, ch.11; Thompson, 1992; Wallis, 1979, chs 7–9; Weeks, 1989, pp.277–81).

Significantly, such groups and campaigns crossed traditional theological and denominational boundaries. Thus, although SPUC had a disproportionately high number of Roman Catholic supporters, while the Festival of Light was predominantly evangelical, yet both movements involved a *de facto* alliance of conservative Christians from both the catholic and evangelical theological traditions. Also, as a number of commentators have noted, these various campaigns shared a number of underlying concerns, focused in particular upon the young and the family. Thus education – and especially the question of sex education in schools – was a major concern, while opposition to the allegedly secularizing and morally polluting influence of television was directly related to the fact that television 'invaded' the home and thus threatened the very heart of the family, itself conceived as the basis of traditional Christian nurture and moral values (Perman, 1977, pp.177–9; Tracey and Morrison, 1979, ch.6 and pp.184–5 and 197–9; Weeks, 1989, pp.254–6 and 281). Similarly, it has been noted that the emergence of such groups at this point may plausibly be interpreted as a conscious reaction, and reassertion of their values, by the contemporary heirs of the Victorian evangelicals who had so successfully stamped their morality upon British moral and cultural life. Joined now by morally conservative Roman Catholics, such contemporary evangelicals, it is argued, recognized the changes of the 1960s as a liberalizing and secularizing dismantling of the old religiously based morality and duly set about regrouping, resisting and, in due course, fighting back (Thompson, 1992, p.85; Tracey and Morrison, 1979, chs 1 and 10; Weeks, 1989, pp.277–82).

During the 1970s the opposition of morally conservative Christians to the changed and still changing attitude to sexual and personal morality continued to gather strength. The Nationwide Festival of Light eventually gave rise to two further movements, Christian Action Research and Education (CARE) Trust, and CARE Campaigns – the former for research and gathering and disseminating information, the latter for organizing and co-ordinating pressure-group activity and lobbying. Other groups and movements which emerged in this period included the Order of Christian Unity and various local Community Standards Associations (Perman, 1977, pp.170 and 183; Thompson, 1992, pp.72–7). The increasingly diverse subculture of pressure groups which thus emerged was then further strengthened by its informal yet effective linkage with the similarly burgeoning network of evangelical and charismatic groups and organizations which also assumed growing prominence during this same period (Thompson, 1992, pp.69–71).

But such opposition did not result in the slowing down – still less the fundamental reversal – of change and diversification in British attitudes to matters of sexual morality. On the contrary, the 1970s brought two further important strands of opinion into the centre of debates over personal and sexual morality and practice. Thus the rise of the Women's Movement and the steady development of a feminist critique of sexuality, sexual relationships and sexual morality, posed further insistent challenges to both 'traditional' attitudes and assumptions and new 'permissive' ones as well. The insistence upon the equality of women and their right to articulate and define their own identities and roles included the right to articulate, define and express their own sexuality and to assert control over their own bodies. The critiques that flowed from such developments drew attention to the still patriarchal and oppressive presumptions within much of even the most apparently 'permissive' sexual questioning and practice of the 1960s. This did not imply a rejection of the 'permissive' impulse as such, however, but rather the need for an extension of notions of sexual 'liberation' to include the questioning of traditional assumptions concerning clearly defined gender roles, conventional definitions of women's natures essentially in terms of motherhood and home making, and the simultaneous repression and oppression of female sexuality by the imposition of sexual stereotypes and presuppositions derived from avowedly patriarchal assumptions and world views (Haste, 1992, pp.207–12).

The feminist emphasis upon the right of women to define their own roles and to choose their own expressions of their sexuality also included the right of choice and self-expression in the matter of basic sexual orientation. The issue of lesbian rights thus became a key issue within feminism in general – and so linked feminism with the other important additional strand within debates over sexual morality during the 1970s, namely the emergence of the Gay Liberation Movement, and the campaign for the equality and acceptance of homosexuals and homosexuality as a legitimate sexual orientation and option. The Sexual Offences Act of 1967 had decriminalized homosexual practice but continued to view it negatively, as a fundamental abnormality – a 'disability', from which punitive sanctions should now be removed but which remained, nevertheless, an essentially 'disordered' expression of sexuality. In the 1970s, however, the agenda was extended to include the articulation and open expression of both the fundamental legitimacy and the specifically positive potential of a homosexual orientation and identity.

Such developments again prompted fierce opposition – not least from the morally conservative Christian groups noted above. Indeed, the underlying basis of the resurgence of moral conservatism in general in the 1970s has been described as 'a revival of an evangelical moralism, fired by an apprehension of basic changes, but made despairing by ... legislative reforms' (Weeks, 1989, p.273). And in 1977, it was the campaigning opposition of the evangelical Mary Whitehouse that produced a crucial and defining moment in the continuing conflict between morally conservative Christians and the liberalizing and secularizing trend of developments in sexual morality since the 1960s. In that year she initiated a successful prosecution of the magazine *Gay News* for its publication of a poem, 'The love that dares not speak its name', in which the centurion at the crucifixion was portrayed as expressing homosexual fantasies about the crucified Christ. What was particularly significant about the prosecution was that it was brought under the blasphemy law. One could hardly ask for a more effective symbol of the interwovenness of religious and sexual concerns in the reaction of morally conservative Christians to the 'permissive' legacy of the 1960s. It was also an incident that further polarized opinion (Tracey and Morrison, 1979, pp.3–21; Weeks, 1989, p.280).

The 1980s duly brought continued debate, sharpened from the mid 1980s onwards by the appearance of the HIV virus, which greatly intensified an already significant backlash against sexual liberalism and diversity in general, and homosexuality in particular (Davenport-Hines, 1990, ch.9; Haste, 1992, ch.11; Weeks, 1989, pp.300–3). Morally conservative Christians were prominent in this process, and displayed a range of specific responses which ran from compassionate care of those who have AIDS, combined with continuing belief that their sexual practices were at root sinful and immoral, to fierce condemnations of moral depravity, the suggestion that AIDS was a punishment sent by God, or an insistence that homosexuality was an affliction from which individuals needed to be either 'cured' or 'delivered', and from which society needed to be protected (Bradley, 1992, pp.145–6; Crowther, 1991, pp.6–14; McCloughry and Bebawi, 1987; Patey, 1988, pp.90–9). It was not only AIDS and homosexuality which continued to excite debate, however: abortion also continued to be a major area of confrontation, as did sex education in schools, the provision of contraceptive advice to those under the age of consent, and the monitoring and control of videos and television (Stanford, 1993, pp.169, 177–80 and 183–6; Thompson, 1992, pp.77–9 and 84–9; Weeks, 1989, p.297). Moreover, the various groups that campaigned on these issues continued to bridge traditional theological and denominational boundaries: the *de facto* alliance of morally conservative Christians from both the Roman Catholic and evangelical theological traditions was, if anything, even stronger by the beginning of the 1990s than it had been at the beginning of the 1970s (Bradley, 1992, pp.147–50).

Indeed, by the early 1990s, critical observers of the network of Christian groups committed to shifting public policy on matters of sexual morality in conservative and restrictive directions were beginning to speak of the attempt, among such groups, to construct a potential or would-be 'moral majority' or 'new moral right' (Maitland, 1992; Stanford, 1993, ch.9; Thompson, 1992).The extent to which such suggestions were valid remained a matter of debate. Many of those thus characterized protested that such terms misrepresented their intentions and over-simplified their political positions.[2] Meanwhile, other observers pointed to the limits of the actual power of such groups, citing the fact that they were, in reality, very far from constituting a majority (moral or otherwise), and that, despite the solidly Conservative period of government from 1979 onwards, there had not been a fundamental reversal of the liberalizing legislation of the late 1960s. Thus, anti-abortion campaigners had met with only limited success, while government campaigns to combat AIDS had focused upon 'safer sex' and the means of achieving this end rather than emphasizing 'traditional' Christian concepts of chastity and celibacy.

There was, indeed, a certain irony in the fact that successive politically conservative governments could be charged by even more morally conservative Christians with having helped, through the anti-AIDS campaigns, to create a 'condom culture'. But such paradoxes helped to point up the essentially complex and confused nature of debate on personal and sexual morality in Britain by the late 1980s and early 1990s.

---

[2] For a further discussion of the debate over whether or not such groups are appropriately described as a potential 'moral majority' or 'new moral right', see the concluding section of essay 4 in this volume.

Though criticized by some morally conservative Christians for failing to reverse the 'permissive' legacy of the 1960s, the Conservative governments of the 1980s and early 1990s nevertheless routinely castigated the 'permissive' ethos of the sixties, and blamed it for the social, economic and political declines and problems of subsequent decades. Similarly, they extolled the virtues of so-called 'Victorian', 'traditional' and 'family' values.

In such a context – as moral liberals and radicals sought to defend and consolidate the reforming legacy of the 1960s, and moral conservatives sought to curtail and reverse it – sexuality and issues of sexual morality had, by the early 1990s, returned to the political stage in a way not seen since the late 1960s. By the early 1990s, however, what was most striking was the marked 'absence of an agreed moral framework'. Questions crowded insistently: in recent decades had sex and sexuality essentially been demystified, liberated and set free, or merely commercialized, debased and trivialized? Did adherence to fundamental values of love and faithfulness in reality demand the retention of a more or less conventional monogamous sexual morality? Or were more varied and less formal arrangements equally – or even more – compatible with genuine love and commitment? (Weeks, 1989, p.288). A decade and a half on from the point at which David Lodge had finished writing his novel, the relevance and topicality of the question 'how far can you go?' remained as pressing as ever.

2   Deeds and rules in Christian ethics

The protests of the NVLA, SPUC, CARE and similar morally conservative groups were by no means the only Christian responses and contributions to debates over changing attitudes towards personal and sexual morality from the late 1950s and early 1960s onwards. Far from being limited to conservative protests and calls for the upholding of, or return to, 'traditional' moral values, the Christian contribution to such debates also included a profound and long-running attempt to reassess and reinterpret conventional understandings and assumptions about 'Christian morality' and its implications for particular questions of personal and sexual morality. Indeed, it has been argued that one of the most significant factors in the more general shift in attitudes to personal and sexual morality was precisely the breakdown of an 'absolutist position' within the Christian churches (Weeks, 1989, p.261).

The beginnings of such reassessment within the churches can be discerned clearly in the 1950s. Two examples in particular illustrate the point. In 1953 the Church of England Moral Welfare Council asked the Home Secretary formally to initiate an official enquiry into the issue of homosexuality and the law relating to it. In due course, the Church of England, as well as other churches, submitted formal evidence to the resulting Wolfenden Committee, which reported in 1957. The principal burden of the Church of England's evidence was that, although homosexual acts remained morally unacceptable in Christian terms, yet the law of the land should be reformed so that such acts were no longer criminal. The Church of England thus argued for the extension to homosexual acts of the distinction between 'sin' and 'crime' which was already applied, for example, in the matter of adultery. Other churches and church leaders argued similarly for reform of the criminal law without conceding the moral legitimacy of homosexual activity (Coleman, 1989, pp.115–33).

In 1958, meanwhile, the Lambeth Conference of Anglican bishops received a report entitled *The Family in Contemporary Society*. Re-read in the early 1990s, the report would probably strike most readers either as unremarkable or, if remarkable at all, then so only for the conservatism of its position. The discussion of contraception, for example, although it concluded that artificial contraception was potentially morally positive in its effects, was tentative, cautious, and by no means unambiguous or without substantial qualification – despite the fact that the context was strictly that of the use of artificial contraception within marriage. (The report is thus a salutary reminder that, in the late 1950s, the Roman Catholic ban on contraception was distinctive in its severity, but by no means wholly removed or distinct from the general tenor of formal Christian discussion and teaching on contraception, sexuality and the place of sex within human relationships, including that of Christian marriage.)

In its own day, however, the report was genuinely innovative and even something of a landmark in Christian discussion of sexual morality. Thus, writing over a decade later from the vantage point of the early 1970s, Ian Ramsey, then Bishop of Durham and one of the Church of England's leading contemporary moral and ethical thinkers, could look back and see in the 1957 report on the family 'the beginning of a new era in Christian moral thinking'. It was so, in Ramsey's view, because of its underlying approach to moral problems: the report drew on the expertise of specialists in a wide range of fields and thereby acknowledged that, 'Christian moral decisions can only be made reliably when full justice is done to the empirical situation in which a moral judgement is made.' Moral theology, therefore, could no longer be thought of as simply 'dispensing answers' or applying them in a 'rule of thumb' fashion (Ramsey, 1970, p.221).

The 1950s, then, had already witnessed significant, if cautious, explorations and initiatives in Christian moral thinking. As in so many other areas, however, it was to be the 1960s that brought such alternatives to prominence and to the centre of debate. Indeed, in the 1960s, questioning of received and conventional Christian approaches to moral decision making – including, in particular, matters of sexual morality – became a major issue within the British churches. And as with the Christian radicalism of the decade in general, it was Bishop John Robinson who first effectively focused many of the issues for the Christian laity and the public at large – and in the process, it should be noted, also provided an important catalyst for the moral conservatism of Mary Whitehouse and many of her supporters (Tracey and Morrison, 1979, pp.29, 181 and 197).

Robinson had clearly signalled his position as a radical in matters of Christian ethics by his appearance as a witness for the defence in the Lady Chatterley trial, arguing, for example, that it was Lawrence's intention to 'portray the sex relationship as something essentially sacred', and that the overall effect of the book was 'against rather than for promiscuity' (quoted in Rolph, 1990, pp.70–1). Subsequently, in 1963, Robinson included a chapter on 'The New Morality' in *Honest to God*. Here he set out a contrast between a traditional Christian morality based on absolute standards and rules (according to which certain acts were always and by definition wrong) and a more contemporary understanding of Christian ethics, which held that the basis of Christian morality was not adherence to absolute rules, but rather the duty always to respond with love and compassion in every situation – or as one of the subheadings put it: 'Nothing prescribed – except love' (Preston, 1988; Robinson, 1963, ch.6). Later in 1963, Robinson developed this argument in a series of lectures in Liverpool Cathedral on 'Christian Morals Today', and in due course included these in an even fuller consideration of contemporary Christian ethics entitled *Christian Freedom in a Permissive Society* (Robinson, 1970).

Robinson's position was easily caricatured as a licence to do as you please, and as a denial that rules – even rules interpreted as general principles rather than strict regulations – had any place in liberal or radical Christian ethics. That was emphatically not Robinson's position, as even a brief reference to the preface of *Christian Freedom in a Permissive Society* makes clear. There Robinson suggested a contrast between the concept of 'permissiveness' and that of 'Christian freedom'. 'Permissiveness', he argued, suggested 'freedom from interference or control, doing your own thing, love, laxity, licence, promiscuity', or in terms of verbs, 'swinging, sliding, eroding, condoning'. Christian freedom, by contrast, he argued, was characterized by the demands of truth, grace, love, service, responsibility, wholeness, authenticity, authority, maturity, coming-of-age and self-possession (Robinson, 1970, p.x). Put thus, the critical tension and profound demands within Robinson's position are clear – but the apparent polarization of the demands of 'law' and 'love' in terms of a sharp antithesis, in much of his writing, made dismissive caricature all too easy (Preston, 1988, p.172).

Robinson was not the source of, nor even the principal force behind, the debate over the 'new morality'. On the contrary, as with much of the rest of his theological radicalism, he was simply – but importantly – the means by which contemporary theological ideas of a radical kind were translated effectively into popular form. In this case, the principal debate in the background was that surrounding the advocacy of 'Situation Ethics' by the American Protestant theologian, Joseph Fletcher. Fletcher's book of that title was published in Britain in 1966, thus further fuelling the debate. That Robinson was essentially a particularly effective representative of a much more broadly based concern for the reassessment of Christian morality – and in particular sexual morality and a range of related issues – within the Christian churches in the 1960s is clearly demonstrated by a number of other publications, reports and developments during that decade.

Thus, for example, in 1963 an unofficial group from the Society of Friends produced an influential report entitled *The Quaker View of Sex*. This report emphasized the centrality and priority of love and its demands and requirements as the basis of sexual morality within human relationships, rather than dependence upon rules derived from tradition, authority or revelation. Later, in 1966, a working party of the British Council of Churches published a report, *Sex and Morality,* which emphasized the range and variety of different Christian approaches to issues of sexual morality, including both those that appealed to the priority of rules as such, and those that regarded 'moral rules' as general principles to be applied flexibly in particular situations. Significantly, the fact that neither report unequivocally ruled out sexual intercourse outside marriage prompted criticism and aroused particularly heated debate.

There were also other examples of the wider Christian debate on issues of personal and sexual morality during these years. Thus, in 1966, Ian Ramsey edited an influential anthology of papers entitled *Christian Ethics and Contemporary Philosophy.* In the introduction to this book, Ramsey affirmed that it was clear that 'Christian morality is no morality of rules, no morality of mere obedience to commands' – a judgement prompted, specifically and significantly, by the inclusion in the anthology of an extract from the report on the family in contemporary society presented to the 1958 Lambeth Conference. Similarly, the 1960s also saw the beginning of what was to become, over the next twenty-five years, a steadily increasing stream of official reports, surveys and responses by various churches on a whole range of matters of personal and sexual morality.

Moreover, during the mid and late 1960s, reassessments of the nature and bases of Christian sexual morality within the Protestant churches were being conducted against the background of the ongoing and passionate Roman Catholic debate over birth control. This culminated, in 1968, in the controversy over the papal encyclical, *Humanae Vitae* and its reiteration of the ban on artificial contraception. Not only did that controversy inevitably stimulate more Christian debate and discussion of sexual morality in general, but it provided a compelling example of both clergy and laity wrestling with the pastoral implications and demands of the Catholic Church's official teaching in this particular matter. In practice many clergy, in the privacy and pastoral context of the confessional – and even more of the laity in the privacy of their own lives and relationships – decided to defy the official teaching of their church in the light of their personal situations and the moral judgement of their informed consciences. Increasing numbers of individual Catholics refused to accept a straightforward application of fixed 'rules' to the regulation of this particular aspect of their sexuality. Therefore, at one level, the whole controversy represented a vast and very public demonstration of the actual practice – in numerous individual Catholic lives and relationships – of the more situational, contextual style of Christian ethics which many Christian theologians were coming to recommend in theory.

It is also essential to bear in mind that, during the mid and late 1960s, all of these debates, both Catholic and Protestant, were conducted in the context of a general questioning of traditional attitudes to sexual morality in British society, and a growing support for legislative changes. These were embodied, above all, in the 'permissive moment' of 1967 with its reform of the law relating to abortion and homosexuality, to the end of theatre censorship in 1968, and to the reform of the divorce law and extension of provision of contraceptive advice in 1969. Therefore, in the context of this essay, it is important to note that the Christian churches were by no means simply or straightforwardly opposed to these pieces of legislation. Although individual Christians and Christian pressure groups were adamantly opposed to the various moral reforms, at an official level the churches were apt, rather, to adopt a position of extreme caution, characteristically reiterating Christian *ideals* in the issues involved, while conceding the rightness of legislation to reform the law of the land in a legally more 'permissive' direction. At root, it was the same distinction which had been made in the churches' response to the Wolfenden Committee and Report, but now applied over a much wider number of issues.

Thus the Church of England report on divorce, *Putting Asunder*, published in 1966, presented a particularly notable reapplication of the distinction between what was regarded as both socially and morally appropriate in terms of the law of the land (easier access to divorce and the removal of the pejorative and essentially conflictual concept of 'matrimonial offence'), and the ideal of life-long Christian marriage demanded by the church of its members. The issue of abortion posed even more formidable difficulties. Again, a Church of England report, *Abortion: an ethical discussion*, published in 1966, argued that in certain circumstances abortion could be justified – and once again Christian acceptance (and even qualified support) of the case for reform in this direction was influenced by recognition of the social and moral evil of backstreet abortions and their frequently awful consequences. In this instance, however, the decision by most of the churches not to oppose the Abortion Act was also much qualified by firm reiteration of the general principle of the inviolability of the foetus and marked opposition to the range of grounds on which abortion might be carried out (Brake, 1984, pp.561–4; Perman, 1977, pp.180–6).[3] The delicate balance in 'official' Christian responses to the 'permissive' legislation of the late 1960s was encapsulated in the contributions of Michael Ramsey to debates in the House of Lords during this period. As Archbishop of Canterbury during these years, Ramsey saw it as his duty to participate fully in these debates. His position – for which he received no little criticism and abuse – was characteristically to support reforming legislation for the specific benefits which might thus be secured and the specific evils which might be prevented, while witnessing to a variety of more austere and severe Christian *ideals*, above and beyond the demands of the law of the land (Chadwick, 1990, pp.145–56).

By the end of the 1960s, therefore, Christian attitudes to personal and sexual morality had become contested ground, not merely between Christians and the prevailing ethos of 'the permissive moment', but also within the churches and between Christians who interpreted the implications of their faith and its inheritance of beliefs in markedly different ways. While for some the appropriate response was opposition to the 'permissive' ethos and reassertion of 'traditional' Christian values and principles, for others the Christian tradition itself called for a reassessment of 'traditional' values and rules and the development of a more flexible, innovative response to the various issues in personal and sexual morality to which the contemporary situation gave rise.

Moreover, the expression of a more 'liberal' Christian approach to

---

[3] Not surprisingly, the particular issue of abortion consistently produced some of the fiercest debate and controversy within the churches over questions of personal morality. For two brief but informative surveys of the issues involved and some of the major stages in the debates, see the Church of Scotland Board of Social Responsibility publication, *Abortion in Debate* (1987) and the Church of England Board of Social Responsibility report, *Abortion and the Church: what are the issues?* (1993). For a sharp and perceptive critique of the often polemical and question-begging nature of the 'pro-life' and 'pro-choice' campaigns in this area, and the distorting influence of such slogans on debate, see Oppenheimer, 1992.

ethics and moral theology was by no means merely the concern of theological specialists, clergy and church leaders. On the contrary, it also received 'popular' expression. Thus, for example, in 1974 Monica Furlong published a series of short articles in the *Church Times*, subsequently republishing them in book form a year later as *Christian Uncertainties* – the title signalling the author's underlying approach to the business of Christian ethics and moral decision making. In these short meditations, Furlong addressed such issues as abortion, the church's attitude to women, sex before marriage, divorce and homosexuality. While acknowledging that 'radical' answers to these (and other) issues could themselves be unhelpful and heartless, she expressed her profound disquiet with the assumption that there could be clear or definitive 'Christian answers' to such moral dilemmas. Such answers, she suggested, while apparently based upon an appeal to authority, in fact displayed a desire to avoid the agonies, doubts, guilts and inner conflicts which resulted from struggling with conflicting evidence and mixed emotions. In place of such struggle, she argued, the appeal to 'Christian answers' – when conceived in terms of 'certainties' based on external authorities – offered an escape into reassuring simplicities. Furlong was also troubled by the fact that such 'Christian answers' nearly always turned out to be 'tough (not to say brutal) answers, giving blanket commands to do what turns out to be the impossible'. Her own experience of life, she added, did not lead her to think that this was 'the way of love', a way which, as she understood it, tried 'to set pre-judgements on one side and see what is the most loving solution for the greatest number of people' (Furlong, 1975, pp.105–7 and also pp.108–28).

The later 1970s and the 1980s brought neither an end nor even a respite to the debates over personal and sexual morality within the Christian churches. On the contrary, as with the more general debates over these issues within British society as a whole, so also among Christians and within the churches, the debates were both broadened in scope, and sharpened in intensity by the emergence and increasing prominence of issues relating to homosexuality and feminism. Nor, moreover, were these issues simply pressed upon the churches from without. Indeed, what made the debates within the churches on these issues so urgent was the fact that the questions posed, and the critiques of 'traditional' Christian teaching which resulted, came from *within* the Christian community itself, from gay and lesbian Christians (and others who supported them and their approach) and from Christian feminists.

The Gay Christian Movement (GCM) was founded in 1975 to provide an ecumenical organization for homosexual Christians from various denominational backgrounds, and to replace a number of smaller groups and societies. A decade later, the movement changed its name to the more inclusive Lesbian and Gay Christian Movement (LGCM). These organizations aimed to provide a source of fellowship and mutual support for gay Christians; to present the case for the acceptance of both gay Christians and their sexuality within the wider Christian community; and to challenge the churches to rethink their attitudes to both homosexuality in particular, and sexuality in general. The movement therefore combined campaigning for recognition and acceptance of the rights and sensibilities of gay Christians with affirmation of the goodness and 'God-givenness' of the sexualities involved, and celebration of the positive contribution that it believed such Christians could make to the life of the churches as a whole (Coleman, 1989, pp.140–2). Such aims were expressed in a collection of essays entitled *Towards a Theology of Gay Liberation*, published in 1977, the same year that *Gay News* was successfully prosecuted for blasphemy – a coincidence which, if it signified nothing else, at least indicated that there was indeed a good deal from which gay Christians might feel a need to be liberated (Macourt, 1977).

The precise extent to which, by the late 1980s and early 1990s, the GCM and LGCM had succeeded in their efforts and aims is difficult to assess. On the one hand it is quite clear that they were very far from having secured the recognition and acceptance of their sexuality and its expression which they sought, and which they urged upon the churches as an authentically Christian response. Thus, from the Protestant churches, a whole series of official church reports, statements and debates on the subject between the late 1970s and the early 1990s failed to reach even a reasonably clear consensus on the issue. The characteristic and ambiguous balance was one between cautious recognition of the diversity of possible Christian positions on the issue and the fact that Christians differed in their conclusions on the subject; calls for the acceptance of gay Christians as individuals, though often in terms that encouraged, even if they did not actually demand, abstention from sexual activity itself; and reaffirmation of traditional Christian ideals in relation to sexuality – usually including the more or less explicit rejection of the moral legitimacy of homosexual acts (Banner, 1993; Coleman, 1989, pp.148–81; Stuart, 1992, pp.xi–xvii).

In the British context, there was also a significant ambiguity in the position of the Roman Catholic Church. Officially there was little scope for Roman Catholic leaders to adopt anything but a strictly conservative policy: during the 1980s Pope John Paul II and the Vatican had adopted an increasingly censorious tone and articulated an increasingly severe policy, not only towards homosexual acts, but also towards homosexuals themselves. In practice, however, it was noted that the Roman Catholic Church in Britain was far from unanimous, let alone enthusiastic, in its application of the official line from Rome. Thus, although the British Catholic leadership did not openly challenge the official line or offer explicit support to gay and lesbian Catholics (largely in order to avoid outright confrontation with Rome), yet the bishops were, at least until the early 1990s, notably reticent in their application of the Vatican's hard line and offered and allowed pastoral support of gay and lesbian Catholics in private (Stuart, 1992, p.xiii; 1993, pp.6–22). There were also British Catholic moral theologians prepared – despite the genuine possibility of official censure – to challenge the coherence and theological rationality of the Vatican's intensely conservative stance on homosexuality, and indeed on sexuality in general (Moore, 1992). On balance, however, in the early 1990s there remained less scope and more tension, less freedom and more fear, within and in relation to their church, for gay and lesbian Catholics in Britain than for gay and lesbian Protestants (Saunders and Stanford, 1992, pp.74–84).[4]

Even in those churches that extended at least the possibility of a positive evaluation of homosexuality and lesbianism, particular difficulties were experienced in relation to the question of homosexual or lesbian clergy. Thus, if it were to be accepted (in churches without a tradition of clerical celibacy) that the laity might express their homosexuality or lesbianism physically, was this also acceptable in the clergy? And if it was not, then why exactly was heterosexual sex among the clergy acceptable, but homosexual sex not? Such questions were apt rapidly to expose the extent of the pragmatic compromises and calculated ambiguities in official reports and resolutions. They also posed potentially acute pastoral dilemmas, since it was not only known that a significant minority of clergy were indeed homosexual, but in addition surveys revealed that homosexual clergy frequently suffered high and damaging levels of stress as a result of having to suppress or hide their sexuality (Fletcher, 1990; James, 1990; Stuart, 1993; Thatcher, 1993, pp.148–52).

Other indications of the continuing limits to the acceptance of gay Christians included particularly militant opposition to their position and claims by some evangelical Christians – an especially fierce campaign being led by an evangelical Anglican clergyman, Tony Higton, and an organization which he had founded, Action for Biblical Witness to Our

---

[4] There also remained the question of the long-term impact of the Pope's extremely conservative encyclical letter, *Veritatis Splendor* (Catholic Truth Society, 1993), and the possibility of the future appointment of a new generation of more conservative Catholic bishops. The potential conflicts involved here, however, extended to heterosexual as well as homosexual Catholics. For a lively popular account of the ongoing tensions and contradictions between official Catholic teaching, the diversity of the pastoral advice actually available, and the practical responses of a variety of lay Catholics, see Saunders and Stanford, 1992. For a sociological analysis of the *de facto* diversity and independence of lay Catholic opinion on a wide range of moral issues, including contraception, divorce and abortion, see Hornsby-Smith, 1991, pp.80–7 and 164–89.

Nation (ABWON). In a debate in the Church of England General Synod in 1987, Higton sought to secure a reaffirmation of traditional Christian teaching which included the statement that 'fornication, adultery and homosexual acts are sinful in all circumstances' – a most revealing linking of a rejection of homosexuality with rejection of anything other than married heterosexual intercourse. The debate and the lobbying that surrounded it achieved a minor notoriety, principally because of the arguments used and the tactics deployed. The motion proposed by Higton was not passed, but another, less total in its condemnation, but still conservative and traditional in content and direction, was.[5]

By the early 1990s, therefore, the aims of the Lesbian and Gay Christian Movement were far from realized. But they had made progress: thus it was significant that the Higton motion in 1987 was not only rejected in favour of a compromise, but also that such overt attacks on homosexuals – Christian or otherwise – appeared to cause considerable embarrassment to many church leaders.[6] Similarly, although official reports and resolutions remained pragmatic and ambiguous, characteristically calling for acceptance of individuals while simultaneously asserting (or at the very least implying) the less than ideal nature of their sexuality and life style, yet many of them were also far more liberal and far less dogmatic than a generation earlier. Moreover, whatever the official verdict of the churches on the issue, the Lesbian and Gay Christian Movement appeared as strong and self-assured in the early 1990s as it had ever been – a mood symbolized by the publication, in 1992, of a 'Gay and Lesbian Prayer Book' with the title, *Daring to Speak Love's Name*, itself a defiant echo of the *Gay News* prosecution some fifteen years earlier (Stuart, 1992).

Meanwhile, the steady development of Christian feminism brought with it a different but complementary – and cumulatively potentially devastating – critique of traditional Christian thinking about sex, sexuality

---

[5] For the General Synod debate and the events surrounding it, see Coleman, 1989, pp.164–72. For ABWON and its very conservative position on matters of sexuality in general, see the booklet, *Sexuality and the Church*, edited by Higton in advance of the Synod debate and circulated to all Synod members (Higton, 1987).

[6] It should be noted, moreover, that both the intensity and the content of the campaign against homosexuality by Higton, and also that mounted by the CARE organization during 1986–87, caused concern and prompted opposition from other evangelical Christians, who criticized the campaigns for, among other things, their emotionalism, prejudice and selectivity in the use of biblical texts and examples (Vasey, 1991). For a sense of the range and variety of attitudes towards homosexuality within the evangelical tradition alone, one may usefully compare three booklets: *The Homosexual Way – A Christian Option?* (the author's answer is 'no'), *No-Gay Areas? Pastoral care of homosexual Christians*, and *Evangelical Christians and Gay Rights* (Field, 1980; Pierson, 1992; Vasey, 1991).

and sexual morality. On the one hand, historical studies revealed consistently the extent both of the churches' long sexual repression of women and of female sexuality, and also the way in which much biblical and subsequent theological thought were predominantly (and arguably thoroughly) patriarchal, androcentric and sexist (see, for example, Armstrong, 1986; Dowell, 1990; Ranke-Heinemann, 1991). Similarly, theological reflection by Christian feminists explored the extent to which, and the ways in which, the churches' traditional thinking about sex, sexuality and sexual morality often also involved the attempt to dominate and control women, and to define 'the family' in a restrictive and potentially oppressive way. This, in turn, was linked to a more general fear and avoidance of both the body and the bodily, and of the genuine profundity and depth of sexual experience and relationships (see for example, Furlong, 1975, pp.111–6 and 1988, pp.4–15 and chs 4–6; Hurcombe, 1987, chs 10, 12–14, 21 and 23). Such feminist theological reflection also demonstrated the extent to which even biblical passages traditionally associated with a strongly conservative and patriarchal understanding of sexual morality might yield surprisingly challenging insights if read without the constraints of conventional assumptions and preconceptions (West, 1987).

On the other hand, Christian feminists also combined the criticism of traditional Christian sexual ethics with an equally forceful critique of the potentially oppressive consequences for women of an unreflective and uncritical 'permissiveness'. The reduction of the meaning of sexuality and sexual relationships to 'sex as fun', it was protested, was as far from an adequate religious and theological understanding of sex as was the churches' longstanding attempt to constrain and restrict female sexuality (Dowell and Hurcombe, 1987, ch.3, especially pp.41–5). By the early 1990s, the potential significance of a thorough integration into Christian moral theology of a feminist critique of traditional Christian attitudes to sexuality and sexual morality was becoming increasingly clear – not least in the attempt to articulate a comprehensive theology of sex in terms free of patriarchal attitudes and assumptions. The result was a 'sexual theology' which simultaneously affirmed the essential goodness and 'God-givenness' of human sexuality in a variety of forms and expressions, emphasized the moral seriousness and spiritual significance of sexual acts and relationships, and acknowledged the positive insights which might be derived from the Christian tradition – if read both critically and creatively (Thatcher, 1993).

Both the Gay Christian movement and Christian feminism thus provided crucial stimuli to the ongoing debates over Christian attitudes to sexual morality. Similarly, the marked rise in heterosexual co-habitation, in stable relationships but without marriage, prompted increasing – and increasingly searching – Christian reflection upon the pastoral demands and theological implications of such relationships and also, by implication and extension, reassessment of the meaning and significance of marriage itself (see, for example, Dominian, 1989; Forster, 1988; le Tissier, 1993; Nicol, 1989; Oppenheimer, 1990; Thatcher 1993, chs 6–8). And again, the challenge and crisis of AIDS prompted Christians – of all theological persuasions and inclinations – to reflect upon its theological and moral significance. At its worst, such reflection was distressingly shallow and simplistic, implying or asserting a straightforward link between AIDS and the judgement of God. Fortunately, however, there were also more profound Christian responses to the crisis, embodying a variety of theological resources, reflecting critically upon a plurality of ways of interpreting the meaning (or meaninglessness) of AIDS, and exploring the pastoral implications and demands to which it gave rise (see, for example, Crowther, 1991; McLoughry and Bebawi, 1987; Patey, 1988, ch.6; Thatcher, 1993, pp.99–101 and 139).

The complex web of issues to do with Christian discussion of sexuality, sexual relationships and sexual morality thus remained, in the early 1990s, fundamentally *contested* ground within the churches. The scope of debate had broadened steadily from the late 1950s onwards. The *de facto* diversity of Christian positions on a whole variety of issues was manifest. What was most significant for the historian was the sheer lack of a clear consensus, from the Christian churches in Britain as well as from British society as a whole, on most specific issues of sexual morality.

3   Unresolved ambiguities

As the title of this essay suggests, and as the previous two sections have demonstrated, the various debates over personal and sexual morality in Britain between 1945 and the early 1990s were characterized by a continuing tension between 'law and licence'. Thus the laws governing various aspects of sexual practice and behaviour (such as homosexuality, the availability of contraceptive advice, or the censorship of sexually explicit literature, plays and films), together with the laws on related subjects (such as divorce and abortion) had been steadily, though by no means uniformly, liberalized. The location of moral decision making was thus shifted significantly away from the public and into the private sphere: individuals increasingly received the licence to define and determine their own attitudes to matters of sexual morality and practice.

As we have seen, however, these changes did not go unchallenged. From the 1970s onwards attempts were made to reassert the role of the law, and consequently once again reduce the licence granted to individual conscience, in a variety of areas of sexual morality – and morally conservative Christians were notably prominent in these campaigns. At the same time as many conservative Christians supported the attempted reassertion of the priority of law over licence, however, other Christians argued that the shift away from the priority of law and towards the liberty and responsibility of personal decision making in matters of sexual practice and morality was a gain for Christian moral thinking itself. For Christians of the latter persuasion the liberty involved was not a licence to do as they pleased. Rather it was a licence to explore the potential diversity of the Christian tradition in matters of moral theology, and to articulate a responsible Christian morality based neither upon 'law' nor 'licence' alone, but rather upon the ongoing tension between enduring principles and innumerable particular situations. Thus the debate over sexual morality, especially from the 1960s onwards, was as fierce within the Christian churches as it was in British society as a whole.

But why did debates over sexual morality prove *so* intractably unresolvable and excite some of the bitterest controversies and confrontations within the British churches from the 1960s onwards? David Lodge had addressed this question in *How Far Can You Go?* In the novel's crucial central chapter (in which his characters recognize that, by the end of the 1960s, the hell of their childhood has disappeared for ever), Lodge inserted a long authorial passage amounting to an essay on the historical, theological and moral background to the furore among Roman Catholics in 1968 over contraception and the publication of the papal encyclical *Humanae Vitae*. In this, Lodge tried to explain how it came about that the first great test of the unity of the Roman Catholic Church after Vatican II arose not over some major theological issue, such as the nature of Christ or the meaning of his teaching in the light of modern knowledge, but over the precise conditions under which lawfully married Catholic couples might engage in sexual intercourse, a subject on which – Lodge observed drily – 'Jesus Christ himself had left no recorded opinion' (Lodge, 1980, p.115).[7]

That the first great controversy of the post-Vatican II church was over contraception was not in the end, Lodge explained, as absurd as it might at first seem, for the particular issue of contraception within marriage contained a number of profound implications. In particular it raised the

[7] It is worth noting that Lodge's portrayal of the Catholic debates over these issues was warmly commended by Catholic reviewers at the time of its publication, both for its accuracy and for its underlying moral seriousness (see, for example, reviews of *How Far Can You Go?* in *The Tablet*, 26 April 1980, *The Catholic Herald*, 16 May 1980, and *The Month*, July 1980). The novel's significance has also subsequently been acknowledged by a number of Catholic historians and sociologists, for details of which, see Parsons, 1992.

question of whether or not, in the Christian scheme of things, sex was 'a good thing in itself'. Was sex principally and essentially simply the means of procreation, and sexual pleasure and satisfaction therefore only legitimately open and available to married couples who were seeking to have children? Or was sex and the mutual giving and receiving of sensual pleasure in fact 'a good thing in itself'? And if it was, then why shouldn't a whole variety of sexual activities be regarded as morally legitimate – and indeed positively good – provided that those who engaged in them, regardless of their marital status, did so with mutual and genuine love? The traditional Catholic answer, Lodge argued, if applied completely consistently, was that sex was *not* really a good thing in itself, but only in relation to the potential procreation of children: although even here, he noted, conservative Catholic moral theologians had already, in reality, undermined the coherence of their own position by allowing the 'natural' method of contraception. For, by implication, the use of the 'Safe Method' was an attempt to enjoy sex precisely 'as a good thing in itself' while avoiding conception (the fact that the 'Safe Method' was also apt to be spectacularly unreliable in no way diminishing the intention to enjoy sex for its own sake, and for the mutual closeness and love which it might express).

In any case, Lodge argued, the real (though unacknowledged) point of retaining the ban was that it was perceived to be the last barrier between Catholicism and the hedonistic spirit which had already made substantial headway within the Protestant churches and in secular western culture as a whole. The retention of the ban on artificial contraception might at least, therefore, prevent Catholics from the steady exploration of how far they could go in enjoying sex as 'a good thing in itself', outside as well as inside marriage, and in homosexual as well as heterosexual contexts. For, as secular and Protestant examples already suggested, once begun, the exploration of how far you could go rapidly dissolved into the counter-question 'where do you stop?' And that, in its turn, brought into question the whole authority of the Catholic Church: for if traditional teaching was revised here, then what else might follow? How far might the process of change go? As far as a radical rethinking of sexual morality and relationships in general? As far as the end of clerical celibacy? As far as the ordination of women? And if such changes once began, then how were theological and moral *authority* to be re-established? (Lodge, 1980, pp.114–21).

Lodge was writing about a specifically Catholic dilemma at a particular point in the late 1960s. Yet his analysis remained relevant in the late 1980s and the early 1990s, and not only for Catholic debates over sexual morality but also for Protestant ones. By then the agenda of Christian debate over sexual morality had shifted significantly, not least in response to the intense and sustained debates prompted by the issue of homosexuality and the impact of feminist, including specifically Christian-feminist, critiques of conventional Christian attitudes to sex and sexuality. Thus, by the end of the 1980s and the beginning of the 1990s, there was an increasingly common recognition that sex was indeed 'a good thing in itself', at least within the context of marriage. Indeed, a Christian perception of sexuality and sexual morality that did not go at least *that* far was, by the 1990s, both unusual and likely to suffer widespread criticism from Christians of varying theological views.

And yet the question of whether or not sex was 'a good thing in itself' *was* still an issue and, indeed, lay at the heart of the inability of the churches to resolve their internal divisions and reach a common mind on issues of sexual morality. For, if it was 'a good thing in itself', then why, as Lodge had asked, providing certain conditions – such as mutual respect and love, the absence of betrayal of other relationships, and the priority of care for the other over gratification of the self – were met, should not a whole range of sexual acts, practices and relationships be morally acceptable for Christians and Christianity? This, moreover, was a line of questioning which pressed particularly closely upon the question of homosexuality. As Monica Furlong had observed perceptively some years before Lodge's novel was published, 'the acid test of whether Christians *really* believe in the goodness of sex ... lies in their attitude to homosexuality', for 'it poses the question ... in what I am afraid I must call a "naked" form – do we or don't we believe that sexual practice informed by love is a good thing?' (Furlong, 1975, p.121).

By the early 1990s there were many Christians – Catholic and Protestant – who were prepared to answer Furlong's question affirmatively. These included groups such as the Lesbian and Gay Christian Movement, but also extended much further to embrace a variety of Christians seeking to articulate a contemporary Christian moral theology which took account of recent critiques of traditional sexual morality, yet also remained founded upon a critical yet creative reading and interpretation of the Christian tradition, the biblical text, and their legacy of moral insights and principles. By contrast, those Christians – Catholic and Protestant – who affirmed a conservative position on sexual morality, characteristically did so on the basis of a conservative reading of the Christian tradition and the biblical text. As Lodge had argued in his 'essay' in *How Far Can You Go?*, debates over particular aspects of sexual morality did indeed bring with them a whole sequence of further questions about the nature and sources of authority within a given church.

The fundamentally contested nature of Christian attitudes to sexuality and sexual morality thus involved an equally fundamental contest over the nature of the biblical text and the status of the received teaching of the Christian tradition. Contests over specific aspects of sexual morality were therefore always also contests over the nature of the authority of the Bible and of the past teaching of the church (Harvey, 1993). It was emphatically not a confrontation between 'authority' and 'morality' on the 'conservative' side, and 'permissiveness' and 'immorality' on the 'liberal' or 'radical' side. On the contrary, the 'liberals' and 'radicals' within the churches also developed their theologies of sexual morality in dialogue with the Bible and the Christian tradition, but did so in a different manner to the 'conservatives', while also protesting that simple appeals to 'biblical Christianity' were likely to prove selective, illusory and inconsistent (Carroll, 1991, ch.3; Moore, 1992; Thatcher, 1993).[8]

By the late 1980s and early 1990s, therefore, Christian debates over sexual morality remained at once complex in the range and variety of particular positions canvassed, and yet also markedly polarized in that frankly incompatible views – such as those of the Lesbian and Gay Christian Movement on the one hand, and of groups like Action for Biblical Witness to Our Nation on the other – were both presented as authentic expressions of the implications of Christianity for sexual ethics and behaviour. At the same time, as we noted earlier, issues related to the regulation of a variety of aspects of sexual morality had, by the 1990s, once more assumed a significant place in public and political debate – and conservative Christian input to such public and political debate was sufficient to prompt discussion of the emergence of a would-be 'moral majority' or 'new moral right'. Moreover, although the religious input to public and political debate on sexual morality during the mid to late 1980s and early 1990s was predominantly Christian, it should not be overlooked that other religious communities were also exercised by the issues involved.

Thus, for example, in the 1980s the Chief Rabbi, Immanuel Jakobovits, took a notably severe line on 'permissiveness', AIDS and, especially, homosexuality – including the view that not only homosexual activity but

---

[8] This is not to say that *all* conservative appeals to biblical insights and concepts were necessarily selective, illusory or inconsistent, or to imply that there were no 'conservative' voices prepared to challenge over-simple appeals to biblical texts (see, for example, Vasey, 1991). The point is that the predominantly polemical construction of the debates frequently resulted in a rhetorical appeal to an allegedly straightforward 'biblical Christianity', juxtaposed with a liberal Christianity portrayed as essentially permissive and deriving its sexual morality from contemporary values, not the Christian tradition. The intensely polemical nature of many of the debates was also revealed by the use of words such as 'unnatural', 'perverted', 'distorted' or 'disordered', and the concepts of 'healing' or 'deliverance' to characterize the sexual activities or orientations of particular individuals or groups. Such terminology was apt to hinder dispassionate discussion of the complex issues involved.

also adultery should officially be criminal offences. The latter, he recognized, might prove practically unenforceable, but would at least indicate abhorrence and moral disapproval (Bermant, 1990, pp.5–6 and 175). Jakobovits' successor as Chief Rabbi, Jonathan Sacks, was less severe, but he too emphasized the importance of the family and the value of a variety of traditional conventions governing sexual morality, while also questioning the consequences of 'removing the legal and moral sting from cohabitation, divorce, illegitimacy and homosexuality' (Sacks, 1991, ch.3, especially pp.49–50). As in the Christian tradition, however, other sections of the Jewish community sounded a different note, affirming, for example, the acceptability of homosexuality within a liberal interpretation of the Jewish tradition (Greengross, 1982).

The Muslim community in Britain also signalled a growing concern with matters of sexual morality during the late 1980s and early 1990s. Thus, the questions of single-sex schools and of sex education in state schools became significant issues within Muslim campaigns for educational provision in line with Islamic norms and requirements (Sarwar, 1989). These particular concerns were, however, only a part of a much broader Muslim antipathy – amounting to overt hostility and determined opposition – towards the perceived permissiveness and moral laxity of British society (and of western society in general) in matters of sexual morality (Akhtar, 1990, pp.131, 150–1 and 209–10; Sarwar, 1989, pp.5–12). Moreover, sexuality was also central to the controversy over *The Satanic Verses*. The sexually explicit nature of Salman Rushdie's novel, it has been noted, was a key factor in the sheer intensity of the Muslim response – which was itself in turn often expressed in terms of sexual outrage or violation (Easterman, 1992, pp.217–21).[9]

It is likely that in the future the religious input to public and political discussion of sexual morality and its regulation in Britain will include more rather than less comment from Jewish, Muslim and other non-Christian religious sources. How far and in what ways different religious groups – or subgroups – will find it possible to make common cause in campaigning on particular issues of sexual morality remains to be seen, as do the reactions

---

[9] It is worth pondering the significance of the fact that, just as Muslims accused Rushdie of blasphemy because of his literary treatment of the figure of Muhammad in a sexually explicit manner, so also Mary Whitehouse had prosecuted *Gay News* for blasphemy because of its publication of a (homo)sexually explicit poem about Christ, while the considerable evangelical campaign against the showing of Martin Scorsese's film, *The Last Temptation of Christ*, focused similarly upon the film's fictional exploration of Christ's sexuality. At the very least these examples suggest a profound tension between the 'sacred' and the sexual within the groups concerned. For a more detailed exploration of the relationship between artistic creativity, religion, sexuality and the notion of blasphemy, see Maitland, 1990.

of both the political establishment and the public in general to any such *de facto* alliances. However, in the Britain of the early 1990s there remained an intense and often fiercely polemical range of debates over the relative priority of 'law' and 'licence' in matters of sexual practice and morality – debates, moreover, that were fought out not only *within* the Christian churches and other religious groups and communities, but also in the spheres of public morality and political power. Unfortunately, the public, political and polemical dimensions of such debates were apt to obscure a further, different, and in many respects much deeper, more personal and more profound range of ambiguities within the whole area of sexuality, sexual practice and sexual morality. Here, however, we may profitably return to the text of *How Far Can You Go?*, for one of the strengths of Lodge's novel is its acute sense of the intensely personal ambiguities inherent within the expansion of sexual options and horizons which it portrays.

How Far Can You Go? is a deeply compassionate novel precisely because it is so ambiguous. It is unquestionably a novel about 'the permissive moment' and its consequences. Thus at the very centre of the novel are the expansion and liberalization of sexual morality and practice during the 1960s, and, in particular, the liberation of – at least most of – a group of young Roman Catholics from the frustrations of a restrictive and repressive sexual morality and the personal damage that this could cause. In the second and third chapters of the novel, Lodge describes the various ways in which, during the 1950s and early 1960s, the student years, courtships, engagements and early years of marriage of the majority of his characters are marred by a catalogue of doubts, dilemmas, tensions, anxieties and guilts over their sexuality and its expression. As a result, both the individual characters and the relationships in which they are involved are subject to significant and destructive stresses and emotional tensions.

There are also other more specific instances of suffering related to the constraints and demands of the particular sexual morality to which Lodge's characters are committed in the early chapters of the novel. Thus, the fourth child born to one of the couples suffers from Down's Syndrome and – quite apart from the fact that the couple concerned might have chosen not to have a fourth child were it not for their church's ban on artificial contraception – it is suggested that the statistical chances of such affliction were increased by the 'natural' method of contraception which is the only one sanctioned by the Catholic Church (Lodge, 1980, pp.77–8 and 110–12). In two other cases, the tensions created by sexual repression or guilt lead to near or actual breakdown: in the case of Miles, homosexuality leads to serious and seemingly unresolvable depression (Lodge, 1980, pp.137–8); in the case of Violet, her inability to break free from the effects of an acutely negative and repressive education and the fundamental association of sex with sin, guilt and divine judgement leads to a sequence of emotional and psychological breakdowns (Lodge, 1980, pp.15, 32–3, 42–8, 99, 101, 138–9, 154–6, 185–6, 191–2 and 242–3). In the early chapters of the novel, the only characters who apparently escape sexual guilt and anxiety are Polly, who cheerfully sets aside her church's teaching on sexual morality, and Austin Brierley and Ruth, both of whom choose celibacy as a deliberate vocation.

In the latter chapters of the book, most of the characters break with the strict sexual morality of their youth and early adulthood. The married couples choose to defy the official teaching of their church and use artificial contraception. They also become, in various ways and to varying degrees, more adventurous and experimental in their attitude to sex and its significance in their lives. Miles, meanwhile, acknowledges his homosexuality, lives with an ex-monk and defends the legitimacy of his sexuality and its expression.[10] And Austin Brierley gives up his former commitment to celibacy in order to marry (as does another priest in the novel). There is, therefore, genuine liberation for many of the characters in breaking away from the strict and traditional Catholic sexual morality of their earlier years. But there is also ambiguity. Although about the 'permissive moment' and the potentially liberating effects of breaking free from a religiously conservative, repressive and guilt-inducing sexual morality, Lodge's novel is no simple celebration of post-pill permissiveness and the joys of sexual liberation. On the contrary, it is a complex and calculatedly ambiguous text in which the limits, dilemmas and perplexities of 'permissiveness' are also laid bare.

The ambiguity is signalled even as the liberating effect of the passing of belief in hell is first acknowledged. 'On the whole,' Lodge observes, 'the disappearance of Hell was a great relief, *though it brought new problems*' (Lodge, 1980, p.113, emphasis added). In the ensuing chapters, some of the new problems become evident. Significantly, it is Polly, the first to break decisively with the sexual morality of her upbringing, the most sexually adventurous of the group, and 'an early apostle of the sexual revolution', who most explicitly questions the limits of the new permissive ethos, begins to wonder whether things haven't gone too far, and is troubled by the problem of where, once begun, sexual experiment and licence will stop.

---

[10] Although Lodge addresses the issue of homosexuality through Miles, he nevertheless remains one of the less developed and less prominent characters in *How Far Can You Go?* For a much fuller literary exploration of the particular tensions between homosexuality and Roman Catholic belief – including such matters as the influence of belief in hell, the impact of Vatican II, and the deep conflicts which may result from the clash between a homosexual orientation and identity and the guilt induced by a strict Catholic upbringing – see the trilogy of novels by Michael Carson, *Sucking Sherbet Lemons* (1989), *Stripping Penguins Bare* (1992) and *Yanking Up the Yoyo* (1993).

It is also significant that her early enthusiasm for sexual liberation is subsequently tempered by engagement with feminism: 'I always used to say I didn't need Women's Lib because I was liberated already, but now I'm not so sure', she observes in the early 1970s. By the end of the novel she is deeply involved in the Women's Movement and a director of a feminist publishing house (Lodge, 1980, pp.156–7, 162 and 243).

If Polly's questioning of the 'new morality' is the most dramatic instance of the ambiguity of post-sixties permissiveness – because of the sharpness of the contrasts involved – it is by no means the only example of the phenomenon. Thus, among those characters who remain loyal to their church's teaching for longer than Polly, and who seek to explore a more liberated sexuality while remaining within at least the radical wing of the new Catholicism, Michael is the most adventurous. He is a convert to the cultural revolution of the sixties and an enthusiastic advocate of the new sexual freedom and experimentation that it brought with it. Yet it is Michael who, at this point, has two health scares and is thus confronted with his own mortality – experiences that, temporarily at least, deflate both his sexual desire and his enthusiasm for the new permissiveness (Lodge, 1980, pp.152–3 and 213–8). In this, however, Michael is but the most telling example of a general process of ageing and of a consequent irony in the lives of the various characters in the novel. For all of them, the moment of finally, decisively, leaving behind their fear of hell and opting for a fuller expression of their sexuality coincides with the beginning of awareness of ageing, the signals of the approach of middle age, and beyond that the beckoning of mortality. At the very moment of opting for a less restrained sex life, their own sexual desire and performance begin to slow down and the limits of their sexuality become increasingly apparent (Lodge, 1980, pp.150–2).

Nor is it only the physical limitations of a permissive sexual ethic to which Lodge draws attention. He also notes the moral limits and ambiguities involved. Thus, when one of the characters, Dennis, has an affair which at least temporarily causes a breach between him and his wife, Angela, Lodge observes that:

> The breach between Dennis and Angela sent shock waves rippling through their circle of friends. For many, it marked the end of an era, the end of illusion. 'We are not immune', Miriam declared solemnly, and when Michael asked her what she was on about, merely repeated, 'We are not immune.' By 'we' she meant their circle, their peer group of enlightened, educated Christians; and by 'not immune' she meant that there was no magic protection, in their values and beliefs, against failure in personal relationships.
>
> (Lodge, 1980, p.224)

How Far Can You Go? thus points to the continuing perplexity of 'post-permissive' sexual morality and its implications for the delicate fabric of human relationships. Moreover, it is not only continuing perplexity and ambiguity to which the novel draws attention, but also the fundamental plurality of sexual moralities in the aftermath of the 1960s. Thus, as Lodge reviews where his characters have got to in the final chapter of the novel, we find them embracing a wide variety of sexual and moral alternatives. These range from the defence of homosexual relationships and the feminist assertion of the legitimacy of abortion; through the acceptance (by some of them) of pre-marital sex among their children and the 'normal', guilt-free use of contraception; to the affirmation of the continued validity and value of celibacy – and the diversity of responses, including both the 'liberal' and the 'conventional', is mirrored among their children (Lodge, 1980, ch.7).

But what might this imply about the ongoing and polarized debates over the balance between law and licence which continued to dominate discussions of personal and sexual morality in the early 1990s? Perhaps it suggests, in particular, that it is in the complicated and muddled experiences of the ordinary lives of ordinary people that some light might be shed beyond the polarities of the various competing moral interest and pressure groups of the AIDS-conscious era. Certainly, that is what prevents the novel itself from being hopelessly dated.

It would seem unlikely – in the short term at least – that the various competing sides in the still continuing debates over sexuality, morality and religion will find much to agree upon. The basic conflict between 'rules and deeds', between the demands of absolutely conceived moral codes and infinitely varied particular contexts, is likely to run and run. In the British context it is likely, also, as we have seen, to be further complicated by the increasing involvement of new voices from religious groups more newly domiciled in Britain, with their own perspectives and versions of that clash between 'rules and deeds', between 'absolute moral codes' and the newly challenging context of life in the 'permissive' West.

Meanwhile, it is worth ending with a different consideration. All the conflicts over 'traditional moral values' and 'permissiveness', over the legitimate limits of the claims of both 'law' and 'licence', cannot obscure the fact that beyond such debates there remain other more profound questions about human existence. In the same chapter of *How Far Can You Go?* in which Lodge examined the underlying reasons for the sheer scale of the controversy over *Humanae Vitae*, he observed that, although it then seemed clear that the liberal hedonistic spirit had achieved unstoppable momentum in the Roman Catholic church, yet

> There is, however, no cause for progressives to gloat or for conservatives to sulk. Let copulation thrive, by all means; but man cannot live by orgasms alone, and he certainly cannot die by

them, except, very occasionally, in the clinical sense. The good news about sexual satisfaction has little to offer those who are crippled, chronically sick, mad, ugly, impotent – or old, which all of us will be in due course, unless we are dead already. Death, after all, is the overwhelming question to which sex provides no answer, only an occasional brief respite from thinking about it.

(Lodge, 1980, p.121)

By the 1990s, in the AIDS era, there was no longer any cause at all for progressives to gloat – nor yet, it might be hoped, any cause or inclination for conservatives now to begin to do so. Indeed, since the arrival of the HIV virus, sex may itself have ceased – in many instances – to provide even that brief respite from thinking of death which still seemed plausible to Lodge in the late 1970s. On the contrary, by the late 1980s and early 1990s, a responsible sexual morality – whether 'traditional' or 'permissive' – demanded profound reflection upon the all too real potential relationship between sex and death.

Perhaps that was why – as an increasing number of people began to protest that death had become unhealthily taboo in British culture, that it had been over-medicalized and secularized so that even the Christian churches had become notably hesitant in their treatment of its implications (Walter, 1990; 1993, pp.127–30) – it was from within those communities most confronted with the threat of AIDS that some of the most insistent and moving experiments in new and contemporary rituals for death and mourning began to emerge (Stuart, 1992, ch.6; Walter, 1990, pp.115–16, 118, 146–7, 192 and 246; 1991, pp.622–3). If it is true that sexuality and death alike confront human beings with some of the most profound questions as to their true natures, then it is not really surprising that, in confronting AIDS, the urge to create new liturgies should have become so prominent and pressing. In such engagements with the boundaries and finiteness of human existence, and with the implications of both sexuality and mortality within human relationships, there lay, perhaps, the beginning of a route beyond the increasingly shrill and stale sequence of confrontations between the proponents of 'permissiveness' and the upholders of 'morality'.

Bibliography

AKHTAR, S. (1990) *A Faith For All Seasons: Islam and western modernity*, Bellew Publishing, London.

ARMSTRONG, K. (1986) *The Gospel According to Women: Christianity's creation of the sex war in the West*, Elm Tree Books, London.

BANNER, M. (1993) 'Five churches in search of sexual ethics', *Theology*, 96, pp.276–89.

BERMANT, C. (1990) *Lord Jakobovits*, Weidenfeld and Nicolson, London.

BOOKER, C. (1992) *The Neophiliacs: the revolution in English life in the fifties and sixties*, Pimlico, London.

BRADLEY, I. (1992) *Marching to the Promised Land*, John Murray, London.

BRAKE, G. (1984) *Policy and Politics in British Methodism 1932–1982*, Edsall, London.

CAPON, J. (1972) *... and there was light: the story of the Nationwide Festival of Light, 1972*, Lutterworth, London.

CARROLL, R. (1991) *Wolf in the Sheepfold: the Bible as a problem for Christianity*, SPCK, London.

CARSON, M. (1989) *Sucking Sherbet Lemons*, Black Swan, London.

(1992) *Stripping Penguins Bare*, Black Swan, London.

(1993) *Yanking Up the Yoyo*, Black Swan, London.

CATHOLIC TRUTH SOCIETY (1993) *Veritatis Splendor*, Catholic Truth Society, London.

CHADWICK, O. (1990) *Michael Ramsey: a life*, Cambridge University Press, Cambridge.

CHURCH OF ENGLAND (1965) *Abortion: an ethical discussion*, Church Information Office, London.

(1966) *Putting Asunder*, SPCK, London.

(1993) *Abortion and the Churches: what are the issues?*, Church House Publishing, London.

CHURCH OF SCOTLAND BOARD OF SOCIAL RESPONSIBILITY (1987) *Abortion in Debate*, Quorum Press, Edinburgh.

COLEMAN, P. (1989) *Gay Christians: a moral dilemma*, SCM, London.

CROWTHER, C. (1991) *AIDS: a Christian handbook*, Epworth Press, London.

DAVENPORT-HINES, R. (1990) *Sex, Death and Punishment: attitudes to sex and sexuality in Britain since the Reformation*, Collins, London.

DOMINIAN, J. (1989) 'Masturbation and premarital sexual intercourse' in Dominian, J. and Montefiore, H. (eds) *God, Sex and Love: an exercise in ecumenical ethics*, SCM, London.

DOWELL, S. (1990) *They Two Shall be One: monogamy in history and religion*, Collins, London.

DOWELL, S. and HURCOMBE, L. (1987) *Dispossessed Daughters of Eve: faith and feminism*, SPCK, London.

EASTERMAN, D. (1992) *New Jerusalems: reflections on Islam, fundamentalism and the Rushdie affair*, Grafton, London.

FIELD, D. (1980) *The Homosexual Way – A Christian Option?*, Grove Books, Nottingham.

FLETCHER, B. (1990) *Clergy Under Stress: a study of homosexual and heterosexual clergy in the Church of England*, Mowbray, London.

FLETCHER, J. (1966) *Situation Ethics*, SCM, London.

FORSTER, G. (1988) *Marriage before Marriage: the moral validity of 'common law' marriage*, Grove Books, Nottingham.

FURLONG, M. (1975) *Christian Uncertainties*, Hodder and Stoughton, London.

(ed.) (1988) *Mirror to the church: reflections on sexism*, SPCK, London.

GREENGROSS, W. (1982) *Jewish and Homosexual*, The Reform Synagogues of Great Britain, London.

HASTE, C. (1992) *Rules of Desire: sex in Britain from World War I to the present*, Chatto and Windus, London.

HARVEY, A. (1993) 'Marriage, sex and the Bible', parts I and II, *Theology*, 96, pp.364–72 and 461–8.

HIGTON, T. (ed.) (1987) *Sexuality and the Church*, Action for Biblical Witness to Our Nation.

HORNSBY-SMITH, M. (1991) *Roman Catholic Beliefs in England: customary Catholicism and transformations of religious authority*, Cambridge University Press, Cambridge.

HURCOMBE, L. (ed.) (1987) *Sex and God: some varieties of women's religious experience*, Routledge and Kegan Paul, London.

JAMES. E. (ed.) (1990) 'Widening the horizons: towards more Christian action on fear, stress and sex', *Christian Action Journal*.

(1993) 'The flowering of honesty' in Bowden, J. (ed.) *Thirty Years of Honesty: Honest to God then and now*, SCM, London.

LARKIN, P. (1988) *Collected Poems*, Faber, London.

LE TISSIER, L. (1993) 'The church and co-habitees', *Theology*, 96, pp.468–76.

LODGE, D. (1980) *How Far Can You Go?*, Secker and Warburg, London.

McCLOUGHRY, R. and BEBAWI, C. (1987) *AIDS: a Christian response*, Grove Books, Nottingham.

MACOURT, M. (ed.) (1977) *Towards A Theology of Gay Liberation*, SCM, London.

MAITLAND, S. (1990) 'Blasphemy and creativity' in Cohn-Sherbok, D. (ed.) *The Salman Rushdie Controversy in Interreligious Perspective*, Edwin Mellen Press, Lampeter.

(1992) 'Biblicism: a radical rhetoric' in Sahgal, G. and Yuval-Davis, N. (eds) *Refusing Holy Orders: women and fundamentalism in Britain*, Virago, London.

MARWICK, A. (1984) 'Room at the Top, Saturday Night and Sunday Morning and the "Cultural Revolution" in Britain', *Journal of Contemporary History*, 19, pp.127–52.

(1990) *British Society Since 1945*, Penguin, Harmondsworth.

MOORE, G. (1992) *The Body in Context: sex and Catholicism*, SCM, London.

NICOL, C. (1989) 'What do we think we're doing? Marriage and the English churches', *The Modern Churchman*, New Series 31, pp.8–16.

OPPENHEIMER, H. (1990) *Marriage*, Mowbray, London.

(1992) 'Abortion: a sketch for a Christian view', *Studies in Christian Ethics*, 5, pp.46–60.

PARSONS, G. (1992) 'Paradigm or period piece? David Lodge's *How Far Can You Go?* in perspective', *Journal of Literature and Theology*, 6, pp.171–90.

PATEY, E. (1988) *For the Common Good: morals public and private*, Mowbray, London.

PERMAN, D. (1977) *Change and the Churches: an anatomy of religion in Britain*, Bodley Head, London.

PIERSON, L. (1992) *No Gay Areas? Pastoral care of homosexual Christians*, Grove Books, Nottingham.

PRESTON, R. (1988) '*Honest to God*, the new morality and the situation ethics debate' in James, E. (ed.) *God's Truth: essays to celebrate the twenty-fifth anniversary of Honest to God*, SCM, London.

RAMSEY, I. (1966) *Christian Ethics and Contemporary Philosophy*, SCM, London.

(1970) 'Christian ethics in the 1960s and 1970s', *Church Quarterly*, 2, pp.221–7.

RANKE-HEINEMANN, U. (1991) *Eunuchs for the Kingdom of Heaven: women, sexuality and the Catholic Church*, Penguin, Harmondsworth.

ROBINSON, J. (1963) *Honest to God*, SCM, London.

(1970) *Christian Freedom in a Permissive Society*, SCM, London.

ROLPH, C. (1990) *The Trial of Lady Chatterley: Regina v. Penguin Books Limited*, Penguin, London.

SACKS, J. (1991) *The Persistence of Faith: religion, morality and society in a secular age*, Weidenfeld and Nicolson, London.

SARWAR, G. (1989) *Sex Education: the Muslim perspective*, The Muslim Educational Trust, London.

SAUNDERS, K. and STANFORD, P. (1992) *Catholics and Sex: from purity to purgatory*, Heinemann, London.

STANFORD, P. (1993) *Cardinal Hume and the Changing Face of English Catholicism*, Geoffrey Chapman, London.

STUART, E. (ed.) (1992) *Daring to Speak Love's Name: a gay and lesbian prayer book*, Hamish Hamilton, London.

(1993) *Chosen: gay Catholic priests tell their stories*, Geoffrey Chapman, London.

THATCHER, A. (1993) *Liberating Sex: a Christian sexual theology*, SPCK, London.

THOMPSON, W. (1992) 'Britain's moral majority' in Wilson, B. (ed.) *Religion: contemporary issues*, Bellew Publishing, London.

TRACEY, N. and MORRISON, D. (1979) *Whitehouse*, Macmillan, London.

VASEY, M. (1991) *Evangelical Christians and Gay Rights*, Grove Books, Nottingham.

WALLIS, R. (1979) *Salvation and Protest: studies of social and religious movements*, Frances Pinter, London.

WALTER, T. (1990) *Funerals: and how to improve them*, Hodder and Stoughton, London.

(1991) 'The mourning after Hillsborough', *The Sociological Review*, 39, pp.599–625.

(1993) 'Death in the New Age', *Religion*, 23, pp.127–45.

WEEKS, J. (1989) *Sex, Politics and Society: the regulation of sexuality since 1800*, Longman, London.

WEST, A. (1987) 'Sex and salvation: a Christian feminist study of 1 Corinthians 6. 12–7.39', *The Modern Churchman*, New Series 29, pp.17–24.

INDEX

Gow, Ian 115
Graham, Billy 30
Green movement 50
Greene, Hugh 237, 238
Greenham Common Women's Peace Camp 223–4
Guinness, Michele 212
Gummer, John Selwyn 146

Habgood, John, Archbishop of York 93
Hampson, Daphne 210, 216
Hare Krishna 75, 76–7, 206
Harris, Barbara 218
Harrison, George 76
Hastings, Adrian 13
Heath, Edward 128
Heber, Reginald, Bishop of Calcutta 25
Hell, disappearance of 233, 260
Herron, Andrew 104
Hick, John 31–3, 34, 48
Higton, Tony 250–1
Hindus
    and caste 64–5
    and the family 222
    female deities 215
    ISKCON (International Society for Krishna Consciousness) 75, 76–7
    and marriage 65, 66
    and religious pluralism 26–7
    temples 62, 206
    women 202, 204, 205, 206–7, 209–10, 211, 220, 222
Holmes, Ann 60
homosexuality 148, 150, 234, 240, 241
    and Christianity 222, 243, 248–51, 255, 256, 259, 260, 262
    decriminalization of 235, 236, 237, 246
    Jewish views on 257–8
How Far Can You Go? (Lodge) 7–8, 12, 219, 223, 233, 237, 254–6, 259–63
Hubbert, Patricia 207
Huddleston, Bishop Trevor 99
Hume, Cardinal Basil 90
Humphreys, Christmas 71, 73

immigration 98–100
Inter-Faith Network 40
IRA (Irish Republican Army) 103, 110, 114
Ireland 87, 108
    women in Church of 217

see also Northern Ireland
ISKCON (International Society for Krishna Consciousness) 75, 76–7
Islam see Muslims
Iwan, Dafydd 106

Jains 63
Jakobovits, Immanuel, later Lord 94, 141–2, 189, 257–8
Jehovah's Witnesses 81
Jenkins, David, Bishop of Durham 31, 125, 139
Jews
    and animal slaughter 68–70, 153
    and the Church of England 93
    in Parliament 96
    and politics 141–2
    and religious education 80, 81, 189
    and religious pluralism 27, 29
    and sexual morality 222, 257–8
    women 202, 205, 211, 212, 216–17, 222
John Paul II, Pope 111, 249
John XXIII, Pope 29, 111
Johnston, Raymond 38
Jones, Richard Tudur 106
Joseph, Keith 96
Julian of Norwich 201

Kapleau, Philip 74
Keep Sunday Special campaign 94
King, Ursula 224, 225
Kirkup, James 82
Kraemer, Hendrik 27, 28
Kroll, Una 208–9
Küng, Hans 29

Lady Chatterley's Lover (Lawrence) 236, 237, 244
language
    of liturgy 202–3, 214–15
    and minority religious groups 220–1
Larkin, Philip 233
'Lausanne Covenant' 30
Lawson, Nigel 96
Leonard, Graham, Bishop of London 188–9
Lesbian and Gay Christian Movement (LGCM) 249, 251, 256, 257
lesbianism 222, 240, 249–51
Lewis, Philip 102
Lewis, Saunders 106
Liberation Theology 129, 130, 131